OPERATING SYSTEMS

A Systematic View

OPERATING SYSTEMS

A Systematic View

WILLIAM S. DAVIS, *Miami University*

ADDISON-WESLEY PUBLISHING COMPANY

Reading, Massachusetts
Menlo Park, California · London · Amsterdam · Don Mills, Ontario · Sydney

ISBN 0-201-01118-2
ABCDEFGHIJ-HA-7987

TO CATHY

PREFACE

In the summer of 1968, I took my first course in operating systems. The course was taught by an IBM (my employer at the time) programmer. The class was composed of "new hires" and "transfers," all extremely interested in demonstrating their skills to a new employer; in educational parlance, we'd say they were well motivated.

We began by digging into the actual code for the SVC interrupt handler and moved up from there. It didn't work. We were all "lost" right from the start. When intelligent, well-motivated students don't learn, something is wrong. A "bit-level" discussion of actual operating system code is *not* the way to introduce a student to operating systems.

Working as a systems analyst and programmer over the next three years, I gradually, through a process of "osmosis," began to learn about operating systems. As a result of a fortunate series of job assignments, I became deeply involved with two very different operating systems: one, a developing special-purpose production control system based on DOS, and the other, a general-purpose OS/MVT system. A comparison of similarities and differences contributed greatly to my education. Things really began to "click" into place once I had formulated a good, general overview of how all the diverse pieces of a given operating system fit together. To put it another way, I began to understand operating systems only after learning to view them as operating *systems* rather than as groups of diverse, independent functions.

After leaving IBM and resuming my teaching career at Miami University, I was asked to teach a course in Operating Systems, thus beginning a search for a textbook. Most good Operating System texts are aimed at the advanced undergraduate or graduate computer science major. Their approach tends to be quite mathematical; they assume *substantial* prior expo-sure to both computer concepts and higher mathematics. I was to teach sophomores.

Are sophomore-level operating system courses unusual? I think not. Our approach, in Miami's Department of Systems Analysis, is to give our students a solid introduction to the *use* of computers during their first two years, branching into such topics as: mathematical modeling, operations research, systems analysis and design, and courses in related disciplines during the junior and senior years. In addition to our core of majors, we have a large number of actual and "de facto" minors interested (for employment-related reasons) in our freshman and sophomore sequence; most majors *and* minors take Operating Systems. In addition, we have two Associate Degree programs, both incorporating the Operating System course. Other schools offer similar programs; a knowledge of computer programming and the use of computers is viewed as a valuable "marketable skill" in today's job market.

One quarter of trying to teach operating system theory was enough to convince me that a mathematical approach does not work at the sophomore or minor level; the comments and input of my colleagues merely reinforced my view. My own experience told me that a "code it" approach doesn't work either. What was needed, I felt, was a functional-level approach, showing the student the major components of an operating system and illustrating how these pieces fit together to form an operating *system*. I've tried it, and it works! Given the results of my classroom experiments and my view of the potential market, I decided to write this book.

My approach is most definitely *not* theoretical; my intent is to show *why* operating systems are needed and *what*, at a functional, "macro" level, they do. This book does not get into a bit-level discussion of the actual implemen-tation of operating system modules on a given machine. I've assumed that students using this book have completed at least one full year of computer-related studies, usually including an introductory course and one or more programming courses; assembler language exposure would be an ideal, but it's not essential. A professional programmer working with almost any language should have very little trouble with this material. Almost no back-ground in theoretical mathematics has been assumed.

The book has been divided into five sections. Any operating system, at its core, is a resource manager; thus Part I discusses the basic resources of any computer system: hardware, software, and data. My intent in this section is to present basic concepts as they relate to operating system development and to fill in any gaps in the prior preparation of a given student (thus the few pages on number systems for the benefit of the compiler level programmer). To most students, part (perhaps even all) of this material will be review in nature.

In Part II, we begin to move into the development of operating systems, stressing why they are needed and, at a very general level, what functions are performed. Such topics as: compilers, libraries, access methods, multiprogramming, spooling, and others are introduced in this section.

Job Control Language is introduced in Part III, with Chapter 7 covering the basics of IBM's DOS job control and Chapters 8 and 9 getting into S job control. My intent is to show the need for a formal means of job control on a modern, multiprogrammed system; any job control language would do equally well, so instructors should feel free to substitute the job control language of an "on-site" non-IBM computer. This material is inserted near the beginning of the book to allow adequate time for the completion of student exercises. Part III can be skipped, totally or in part, without losing text continuity.

In Part IV we begin to dig more deeply into actual operating systems, describing the operating environment of the IBM System/360 and System/370 series of computers (the PSW, interrupts, and channel communications) and showing how, at a macro level, two different operating systems, DOS and OS/MFT, are implemented in this environment. IBM products were chosen as examples simply because IBM is the dominant supplier of computers, meaning that more students will have access to IBM equipment than to the equipment of any other manufacturer. After covering these two systems in some depth, we move on to the general question of memory management, covering such topics as: variable length regions, dynamic memory relocation, program segmentation and paging, virtual memory, and memory hierarchies.

In the final section, we leave general-purpose operating systems and move into a discussion of a number of special-purpose systems. The primary objective of this section is to illustrate that an operating system, to be considered effective, must meet the objectives of a given application. In this section, we also spend some time on the "hardware vs. software" question, indicating that many operating system functions can be implemented through either hardware or software, or a combination of both.

The book is designed for second year students in a program oriented toward the *use* of computers rather than toward the design of computers. In addition to the traditional four-year school preparing majors or minors, community colleges should find this book useful. In a theoretical "computer science" program, this book might support a first course in operating systems, giving the student a framework against which to measure later, more advanced studies.

Hamilton, Ohio   W. S. D.
October 1976

ABRIDGED CONTENTS

ix

CONTENTS

PART III JOB CONTROL LANGUAGE FOR THE IBM SYSTEM/360 AND SYSTEM/370

Chapter 7 Job Control Under IBM's Disk Operating System

Chapter 8 Job Control Language for the IBM Operating System/360 and System/370 — JOB and EXEC Cards

Chapter 9 The DD Card

PART IV OPERATING SYSTEM CONCEPTS

Chapter 10 The Functions and Objectives of an Operating System

Chapter 13 IBM System/360 Operating System Multiprogramming with a Fixed Number of Tasks

Chapter 14 Multiprogramming with Dynamic Core Allocation

CHAPTER 1

Introduction and Overview

The purpose of any data-processing system is to convert data into more useful information; i.e., to process data. An electronic data-processing system combines hardware, software, and data resources toward meeting this objective. These resources are expensive. Many firms spend millions of dollars each year on hardware—often even more on programming and data management. Because of this high cost, it is essential that these resources be used as efficiently as possible. Operating systems have been developed with this idea in mind—to improve the efficiency of a data-processing system.

Note carefully the use of the word "system." A well-designed operating system is *not* concerned with just hardware or just software or just data management, but with optimizing the way in which *all* of these resources work together in achieving some desired objective. Not all data-processing systems have the same objective—a manufacturing process-control system may stress speed of response while an educational system at a university may stress flexibility. Thus not all installations will want the same operating system; "best" is a relative term. In this text, we'll be discussing operating systems not as an end in themselves but as solutions to a number of data-processing problems, always keeping system objectives in mind.

The purpose of this book is to give the reader a basic understanding of what an operating system is and how it works. Specific examples of operating system design and implementation will be used to illustrate a number of points; we'll try to avoid the bit-level discussion of the intimate working details of the products of any one manufacturer or the theory of operating system design. Our objective is to illustrate the *problems* handled by operating systems and not any single set of solutions to these problems. The text is designed to support a first

1

course in operating systems. The concentration is on the application of this specialized software to a real-world environment; this is *not* a theoretical text.

The book is divided into five parts. Part I, Chapters 2 through 4, covers the basic concepts of software, hardware, and data—the system resources which are managed by an operating system. For many students, much of this material will be review in nature; it's included because subsequent chapters assume a knowledge of this information.

Part II, Chapters 5 and 6, follows the rapidly developing technology of the past two decades and the parallel evolution of operating systems. The concepts of multiprogramming and time sharing are introduced in this section. Emphasis is placed on the importance of economic factors in these developments.

In Part III, we study modern programmer/system communications by analyzing two common job control languages. In Chapter 7, job control for IBM's Disk Operating System (DOS) will be studied; Chapters 8 and 9 concentrate on the job control language for IBM's full operating system (OS/JCL), with the JOB and EXEC cards being covered in Chapter 8 and the DD card in Chapter 9. The products of IBM have been chosen for a very obvious reason— IBM is the dominant force in the computer market. Not all features of the job control languages are covered in this section, only those more commonly used. The intent is to illustrate modern programmer/system communications and not to present an exhaustive course in JCL; the beginning programmer should, however, find the application orientation of this material useful in handling many everyday programming problems.

Part IV, Chapters 10 through 15, covers a number of general-purpose operating systems. Chapter 10 summarizes the basic functions of any operating system, concentrating on various measures of system effectiveness. The next three chapters, 11 through 13, are related; their purpose is to describe a hardware environment and two different operating systems designed to work under this environment. Operating principles of the IBM System/360 (Chapter 11) and two of IBM's operating systems, DOS and OS/MFT, have been chosen to illustrate these ideas. Actually, the products of almost any computer manufacturer would have done as well; however, the products of IBM are known to more potential readers than are those of any other firm. Chapter 14 generalizes the material presented in the preceding three chapters, relating it to other manufacturers' products. The final chapter in this section, Chapter 15, introduces the key concepts of virtual memory and paging.

Finally, in Part V, Chapters 16 through 19, a number of special-purpose systems and their associated support software will be discussed. Chapter 16 will concentrate on production-control applications where the high cost of manufacturing downtime creates a need for rapid response and high reliability. In Chapter 17, data base management and data communications are discussed in the context of a management information application. Applications involving more than one computer, primarily minicomputer and full-sized computer combinations, are discussed. In each of these chapters, we'll be considering the application in its environmental context, with emphasis on how the operating system and other support software help to maximize the utilization of system resources given the measures of effectiveness most crucial to the application.

The text has been written to support a four-credit semester course; by skipping either Part III or Part V, it could support a four-credit quarter course. For most students, much of Part I will be a review. Exposure to at least one programming language has been assumed; readers with no assembly-language background should read the chapter on software carefully, as a basic understanding of binary numbers will be important in Part IV when we get into the operating principles of the IBM System/360. The chapter on hardware relates equipment to a number of concepts we'll be discussing later in the book; channels, control units, and teleprocessing hardware may be unfamiliar. The material on data and file organizations may be new to many readers.

Part II is written in a very nontechnical manner and should provide the student, business manager, engineer, or computer professional with a good, basic understanding of what operating systems are all about. The chapters on job control might be used to introduce this topic at any level. Parts IV and V concentrate on operating systems functions, at a "macro" level, avoiding the bit-level details of operating-system design; given an understanding of the introductory material in Part I, a programmer with a background in any language should find the material quite readable.

PART I

The Basic System Resources

CHAPTER 2

Bits, Numbers, Codes, and Software

Overview

In this chapter, the basic concepts of the binary number system, computer coding, and programming languages will be discussed.

The Binary Number System

Modern digital computers are designed to work with binary data; thus, a basic appreciation of the binary number system is essential if one is to gain an understanding of how a computer really works. Since the decimal numbering system is far more familiar to most of us, let's start our discussion of binary numbers by taking a close look at a few decimal numbers.

Consider the two numbers 3 and 30; both contain the same character, a three, but we all know that we are looking at two different numbers. What's the difference between the three in the number 3 and the three in the number 30? The answer, as any schoolchild knows, is position; the first three is in the "units" column and the second three is in the "tens" column. Closer analysis reveals the fact that the number thirty (30) is really another way of saying three tens and no ones.

Let's put it another way. *Any* decimal number consists of a series of digits—0, 1, 2, 3, 4, 5, 6, 7, 8, 9 in some order—written in very precise positions; the number twenty-three is written as 23 while another combination of the same two digits, 32, represents a different number. The value of a given sequence of digits is found by multiplying each digit by its place or positional value and summing these products.

Consider, for example, the number 3582; what is really represented by this combination of digits is:

$$
\begin{array}{rll}
2 \text{ times} & 1 = & 2 \\
+8 \text{ times} & 10 = & 80 \\
+5 \text{ times} & 100 = & 500 \\
+3 \text{ times} & 1000 = & \underline{3000} \\
& & 3582
\end{array}
$$

In general terms, *any* number is simply the sum of the products of its digit and place values; in the language of mathematics,

$$\text{Number} = \sum (\text{digit value times place value}).$$

Take a closer look at the sequence of place values: 1, 10, 100, 1000, 10000, 100000, 1000000, 10000000, and so on. The pattern is pretty obvious. Using scientific notation and taking advantage of the fact that any number raised to the zero power is one, the place values in the decimal number system can be represented as a series of powers of ten (the base) raised to sequential integer powers—see Fig. 2.1. Decimal fractions, 0.25 for example, have as their place values negative powers of ten:

$$
\begin{array}{rll}
2 \text{ times } 10^{-1} = & 2 \text{ times } 1/10 & = 0.2 \\
+5 \text{ times } 10^{-2} = & 5 \text{ times } 1/100 & = \underline{0.05} \\
& & 0.25
\end{array}
$$

A few concepts stand out in our discussion of the decimal number system. First is the idea of place or positional value represented by the base (10) raised to sequential integer powers. The use of the digit zero to represent *nothing* in a given position is a second key concept. Third, a total of *ten* digits, 0 through 9, are needed to write decimal numbers. Finally, only values less than the base, in this case ten, can be represented in a single position.

$$
\begin{array}{|c|c|c|c|c|c|c|c|c|c|}
\hline
10^6 & 10^5 & 10^4 & 10^3 & 10^2 & 10^1 & 10^0 & 10^{-1} & 10^{-2} & 10^{-3} \\
\hline
\end{array}
$$

Fig. 2.1 Decimal place values

There is nothing to restrict the application of these rules to a base-ten number system. If the positional values are represented by powers of two instead of ten, we have the framework of a base-two or binary number system. Such a framework is pictured in Fig. 2.2.

2^8	2^7	2^6	2^5	2^4	2^3	2^2	2^1	2^0	2^{-1}	2^{-2}	2^{-3}	2^{-4}
Decimal		64	32	16	8	4	2	1				

Fig. 2.2 Binary place values

As in the decimal system, the digit zero is needed to represent *no value* in a given column. In addition to the zero digit, the binary number system uses only one other digit, a 1, to form numbers. Why only two digits? As in the decimal system, only values less than the base, in this case 2, can be represented in a single column; thus, only the digits zero and one are needed. The binary number 1100101 is, using the digit-times-place-value rule, equal to the following decimal number:

$$
\begin{aligned}
1 \text{ times } 2^6 &= 1 \text{ times } 64 = & 64 \\
+1 \text{ times } 2^5 &= 1 \text{ times } 32 = & 32 \\
+0 \text{ times } 2^4 &= 0 \text{ times } 16 = & 0 \\
+0 \text{ times } 2^3 &= 0 \text{ times } 8 = & 0 \\
+1 \text{ times } 2^2 &= 1 \text{ times } 4 = & 4 \\
+0 \text{ times } 2^1 &= 0 \text{ times } 2 = & 0 \\
+1 \text{ times } 2^0 &= 1 \text{ times } 1 = & \underline{1} \\
& & 101
\end{aligned}
$$

The number 2 is written as a 10 in binary; the number 4 is 100; $\frac{1}{2}$ is written as 0.1 which is

$$1 \text{ times } 2^{-1} = 1 \text{ times } \tfrac{1}{2} = \tfrac{1}{2}.$$

Any whole number can be written in binary. Not all fractions can be written exactly in binary, but that's no surprise when you remember that not all fractions can be written exactly in decimal—one third, for example.

We humans, at least in this part of the world, use the base-ten system because that's the number system we are used to. There is nothing inherently "better" about base ten.

For a computer, an electronic device, there is a tremendous advantage to using the binary number system; since data can be represented by only the two digits, 0 and 1, the computer can work with the simple on/off logic of electrical circuits. Binary is truly an electronic number system.

Other number systems, notably octal (base eight) and hexadecimal (base sixteen), have gained popularity in the computer field. The octal system uses powers of eight to represent positional values (Fig. 2.3) and denotes values of numbers by using the digits 0, 1, 2, 3, 4, 5, 6, and 7 within this framework. The

8^8	8^7	8^6	8^5	8^4	8^3	8^2	8^1	8^0	8^{-1}	8^{-2}	8^{-3}	8^{-4}

Fig. 2.3 Octal or base-eight place values

16^5	16^4	16^3	16^2	16^1	16^0	16^{-1}	16^{-2}	16^{-3}

Fig. 2.4 Hexadecimal or base-sixteen place values

hexadecimal system (Fig. 2.4) uses powers of sixteen and the digits 0, 1, 2, 3, 4, 5, 6, 7, 8, 9, A, B, C, D, E, and F. The hexadecimal number $(FF)_{16}$ is:

$$15 \text{ times } 16^1 = 240$$
$$+15 \text{ times } 16^0 = \underline{\quad 15}$$
$$(255)_{10}$$

The reason why these two number systems are so important in the world of computers is the ease of conversion between octal and binary or hex and binary. Each octal digit is equivalent to exactly three binary digits (Fig. 2.5); each hexadecimal digit converts directly to four binary digits (Fig. 2.6). Thus octal

OCTAL	BINARY	OCTAL	BINARY
0	000	4	100
1	001	5	101
2	010	6	110
3	011	7	111

Fig. 2.5 Octal-to-binary conversion table

HEX	BINARY	HEX	BINARY
0	0000	8	1000
1	0001	9	1001
2	0010	A	1010
3	0011	B	1011
4	0100	C	1100
5	0101	D	1101
6	0110	E	1110
7	0111	F	1111

Fig. 2.6 Hexadecimal-to-binary conversion table

BINARY

```
110010101011 000101001000 101100001111
011001100001 100000100011 011101010100
000100000010 011111110000 000010000101
100100100100 100001011111 100000011001
```

OCTAL			*HEXADECIMAL*		
6253	0510	5417	CAB	148	B0F
3141	4043	3524	661	823	754
0402	3760	0205	102	7F0	085
4444	4137	4031	924	85F	819

Note how much more readable and compact octal and hexadecimal are.

Fig. 2.7 Octal and hexadecimal as binary shorthand

or hexadecimal can be used as a sort of shorthand for viewing binary data, and this fact has a tremendous impact on the printed volume and readability of such data (Fig. 2.7).

Numerical Data   Since binary numbers are so well suited to electronic devices, it is not surprising that many computers are most efficient when working on binary numbers. Many machines have been designed around a basic unit of binary data called a word—usually 16, 24, or 32 bits (binary digits), although almost any word length can be (and probably has been) used. One bit, usually the high-order bit, is set aside to hold the sign— 0 for +, 1 for negative numbers—with the binary number occupying the remaining bit positions. There is no provision for a decimal point in such numbers, decimal alignment being the responsibility of the programmer. Word size sets an absolute limit on a given computer's range. A machine with a 32-bit word, for example, can handle a number consisting of a sign followed by thirty-one binary 1's (a number equal to the decimal number 2, 147, 483, 647), while a sixteen-bit machine's limits are $(0111111111111111)_2$ or 32, 767 in decimal.

Negative numbers are normally stored in complement form. The idea of a numerical complement seems a bit strange at first, but it's really quite simple to grasp. One key to complementary arithmetic is that all numbers must be the same size; let's assume for illustrative purposes that we are restricted to three decimal digits. Using three-digit numbers, the complement of 001 is 999; the complement of 002 is 998; the complement of 020 is 980; the complement of 500 is 500; the complement of 997 is 003, and so on. The rule is simple—subtract the original number from 1000 (the first value *outside* our three-digit limit). If we were working with four-digit numbers, we'd subtract from 10,000; we'd use 1,000,000 if all our numbers were six digits in length.

So what? What benefit do we gain from using complements? Complements are used because they allow us to subtract by adding. Consider the following problem:

$$
\begin{array}{r} 852 \\ -137 \\ \hline 715 \end{array} \quad \text{complement} \quad \longrightarrow \quad \begin{array}{r} 852 \\ +863 \\ \hline \underline{1}715 \end{array}
$$

By taking the complement of the number we are subtracting and *adding* it to the first number, we get the same answer as that produced by traditional subtraction, except for the extra high-order digit. But, if we can only hold three digits, that extra high order digit disappears, yielding the correct answer. Is it reasonable to assume that the high-order digit will disappear? On a fixed-length machine, restricted to, let's say, sixteen bits, there's no place for the seventeenth bit to go.

What if the answer is negative? Let's consider the following problem:

$$
\begin{array}{r} 356 \\ -432 \\ \hline -076 \end{array} \quad \text{complement} \quad \longrightarrow \quad \begin{array}{r} 356 \\ +568 \\ \hline 0924 \end{array}
$$

It looks like the approach doesn't work here, but what is the *complement* of 924? The answer is 076, and since the *extra* high-order digit is a 0 instead of a 1, the answer is negative. It does work! The rule is simple, really—find the complement of the number on the bottom and add. If the high-order extra digit is a 1, drop it but if the high order is a 0, the answer is a negative number stored in complementary form.

You may have noticed one little problem—in order to find the complement of a fixed-length, three-digit number, we subtracted from the smallest possible *four*-digit number; if we are really restricted to three digits, where does the extra digit come from? The answer is we don't need it; instead of subtracting from 1000, we subtract from 999 and add 1 to the result. Another advantage of this approach is that it eliminates the need for borrowing during the subtraction process.

Now we get to the real reason for using complements on a computer. Let's use a series of four-digit binary numbers to illustrate what's going on. A real machine with a fixed word length of four bits is unlikely, but four bits allows us to illustrate the principle.

The rule for finding the complement of a three-digit number in decimal was, as you may remember, subtract the number from the largest possible three-digit number (999) and add 1 to the answer. If we were working with four-digit numbers, 9999 would have been our key value. The rule is exactly the same in binary, except that we subtract from the largest possible (given our word size) *binary* number and add 1 to the result. Consider the following complements:

$$
\begin{array}{ccccc}
 & 1111 & 1111 & 1111 & 1111 & 1111 \\
\text{Number} \quad \left.\begin{array}{r} -\,1001 \\ \hline 0110 \end{array}\right\} & \left.\begin{array}{r} -\,0011 \\ \hline 1100 \end{array}\right\} & \left.\begin{array}{r} -\,1110 \\ \hline 0001 \end{array}\right\} & \left.\begin{array}{r} -\,0101 \\ \hline 1010 \end{array}\right\} & \left.\begin{array}{r} -\,0100 \\ \hline 1011 \end{array}\right\} \\
+\,0001 & +\,0001 & +\,0001 & +\,0001 & +\,0001 \\
\hline
\text{Complement} \quad 0111 & 1101 & 0010 & 1011 & 1100
\end{array}
$$

Look carefully at the results of the initial subtraction step; in each case, the partial answer, prior to the addition of a binary 1, is the initial number with *every bit changed*—1's have been changed to 0's and 0's have been changed to 1's. This is *very* easy to do electronically. Since the use of complements allows us to subtract by adding, two arithmetic operations can be performed by the same electronic circuitry, saving the manufacturer (and, subsequently, the customer) the expense of including a separate set of electronics to handle subtraction.

Simple binary integers are fine for many computer applications, but, at times, numbers larger than the fixed word limit and fractional quantities are needed. In the world of science, extremely large numbers (astronomical distances) and very small numbers (subatomic measurements) are written using scientific notation, a decimal fraction followed by a power of ten; the speed of light, 186,000 miles per second, might, for example, be written as 0.186×10^6.

Large numbers, small numbers, and fractions can be stored on a computer by using an approximation of scientific notation. Since computers do not normally work in decimal, powers of ten cannot be used, but a system based on the number "2" gives reasonable results. On the IBM System/360 and System/370, for example, a fullword of 32 bits is set aside for each "floating point" number. The high order bit (Fig. 2.8) holds the sign of the fractional

S	Characteristic	Fraction

Long form

S	Characteristic	Fraction - High-order part
Fraction - Low-order part		

Fig. 2.8 IBM floating-point-data formats

portion. The next seven bits hold a binary power of *sixteen* having the same meaning as the power of ten in normal scientific notation. The remaining twenty-four bits hold the fractional portion of the number.

To simplify the handling of the decimal point, numbers are normally represented as binary values multiplied by a power of sixteen, with the first significant bit following the binary point (as opposed to decimal point); thus, the function of decimal point manipulation is completely handled by the characteristic.

To improve accuracy, IBM has created an extended precision form for its floating-point numbers; an extra thirty-two-bit word is added to the normal floating-point field, increasing the fractional portion of the number from twenty-four to fifty-six bits.

Computer Coding

Binary Coded Decimal (BCD)   For economic reasons, card readers, printers, and other input/output devices are designed to send data to and from the computer as a string of independent characters. The number 12 is treated, for example, as a 1 and a 2, *not* as a twelve. Since each character is treated as a separate entity, each character can be represented by a unique code. Looking first at numeric data, each decimal digit can be represented by its binary equivalent (see Fig. 2.9); four bits are used for each digit even when some are nonsignificant largely because it's simpler to design an electronic device to handle the same number of bits at all times. The number twelve, using this coding scheme on the individual digits, would be: 00010010. If this number were treated as a pure binary number and converted to decimal, its value would be $2^1 + 2^4$, which is 18 and *not* 12. Fortunately, most computers contain special circuitry for converting binary coded decimal numbers into pure binary. Some machines can perform arithmetic on binary coded data; IBM, for example, refers to such data as packed decimal.

Many computer applications require alphabetic as well as numeric data; thus, something more than the simple numeric code shown above is needed.

DECIMAL	CODE	DECIMAL	CODE
0	0000	5	0101
1	0001	6	0110
2	0010	7	0111
3	0011	8	1000
4	0100	9	1001

Fig. 2.9 Binary-coded decimal numbers

CHARACTER	CODE	CHARACTER	CODE
A	11 0001	S	01 0010
B	11 0010	T	01 0011
C	11 0011	U	01 0100
D	11 0100	V	01 0101
E	11 0101	W	01 0110
F	11 0110	X	01 0111
G	11 0111	Y	01 1000
H	11 1000	Z	01 1001
I	11 1001		
		0	00 1010
J	10 0001	1	00 0001
K	10 0010	2	00 0010
L	10 0011	3	00 0011
M	10 0100	4	00 0100
N	10 0101	5	00 0101
O	10 0110	6	00 0110
P	10 0111	7	00 0111
Q	10 1000	8	00 1000
R	10 1001	9	00 1001

Certain unused combinations of bits are used to represent punctuation marks and other special symbols.

Fig. 2.10 The six-bit BCD code

An early solution to this problem was the six-bit BCD code shown in Fig. 2.10. In this code, individual characters are represented by a series of six bits—two "zone" bits and four "numeric" bits. The letters A through I are assigned zone bits 11; since A is the first letter in this group, its BCD numeric part is 0001. The second letter, B, is 11 0010. J through R are assigned zone bits 10 and S through Z zone bits 01; again, the numeric bits show the character's relative position within the group. All things considered, the BCD code makes a great deal more sense than the code developed by Mr. Morse for his telegraph.

The code, to restate a point made previously, allows input and output devices to treat each character as an independent entity; the computer, under program control, puts these individual characters together to produce meaningful data. Any code will do, as long as it is consistently applied. Two codes enjoying great popularity on modern computers are IBM's Expanded Binary Coded Decimal Interchange Code or EBCDIC (pronounced ebb-see-dic) and the ASCII–8 code of the American National Standards Institute (Fig. 2.11). Both are eight-bit codes.

One final note before we move on to programming languages. Data enters the computer from a card reader in a coded form—let's use EBCDIC for

CHARACTER	EBCDIC BINARY	EBCDIC HEX	ASCII–8 BINARY	ASCII–8 HEX
A	1100 0001	C1	1010 0001	A1
B	1100 0010	C2	1010 0010	A2
C	1100 0011	C3	1010 0011	A3
D	1100 0100	C4	1010 0100	A4
E	1100 0101	C5	1010 0101	A5
F	1100 0110	C6	1010 0110	A6
G	1100 0111	C7	1010 0111	A7
H	1100 1000	C8	1010 1000	A8
I	1100 1001	C9	1010 1001	A9
J	1101 0001	D1	1010 1010	AA
K	1101 0010	D2	1010 1011	AB
L	1101 0011	D3	1010 1100	AC
M	1101 0100	D4	1010 1101	AD
N	1101 0101	D5	1010 1110	AE
O	1101 0110	D6	1010 1111	AF
P	1101 0111	D7	1011 0000	B0
Q	1101 1000	D8	1011 0001	B1
R	1101 1001	D9	1011 0010	B2
S	1110 0010	E2	1011 0011	B3
T	1110 0011	E3	1011 0100	B4
U	1110 0100	E4	1011 0101	B5
V	1110 0101	E5	1011 0110	B6
W	1110 0110	E6	1011 0111	B7
X	1110 0111	E7	1011 1000	B8
Y	1110 1000	E8	1011 1001	B9
Z	1110 1001	E9	1011 1010	BA
0	1111 0000	F0	0101 0000	50
1	1111 0001	F1	0101 0001	51
2	1111 0010	F2	0101 0010	52
3	1111 0011	F3	0101 0011	53
4	1111 0100	F4	0101 0100	54
5	1111 0101	F5	0101 0101	55
6	1111 0110	F6	0101 0110	56
7	1111 0111	F7	0101 0111	57
8	1111 1000	F8	0101 1000	58
9	1111 1001	F9	0101 1001	59

Once again, unused bit combinations are used to represent punctuation marks and other special symbols; these symbols are not shown since the pattern of the code is not as obvious. A full listing of these codes can be found in almost any reference manual.

Fig. 2.11 The eight-bit EBCDIC and ASCII codes

our example. Data in this form represents a string of independent, binary-coded characters; such "display" or "external" or simply "coded" data is *not* suitable for computations.

A printer expects to receive data in coded form. For data (an individual's name or social security number) which is simply read, perhaps copied, and then sent to the printer, it makes a great deal of sense to simply store the data in its external or display or coded form. However, for other data (hours worked or hourly pay rate) which is to be used in computations, the form of the data must be changed. On an IBM computer, incoming EBCDIC data is first converted to packed decimal form by stripping the four zone bits, leaving only the numeric portion of each character. Arithmetic can be performed at this level, but for many applications, one additional transformation is necessary to convert the data from packed decimal to binary or floating point. Before the results of a computation can be printed, the data must move back down this chain, going from binary to packed decimal and then back to EBCDIC. Other manufac-turer's computers differ in specific details, but all follow this basic idea.

Programming Languages

Programming at the Machine-Language Level   A computer program is a series of instructions written to guide the computer through some logical function. These instructions are coded in binary, at least at the machine level. Individual instructions consist of operation codes—ADD, SUBTRACT, MOVE, COM-PARE—and operands showing the length and location of the fields to be operated upon.

As an example of machine-language programming, consider the following program segment designed for simply adding two numbers together. Before performing an arithmetic computation, at least in binary, most computers re-quire that data first be moved into a register; in both IBM System/360 and System/370, the instruction for loading a value into a register has the operation code "01011000." Without going into details about each field, the operands of this first instruction will tell the computer where to find the data and which register to put it in; this single instruction looks something like:

$$0101100000110000110000000000000000,$$

which you must admit isn't the clearest thing you've ever tried to read.

Since we plan to add two numbers together, the second value must also be placed in a register; this is done by a second, quite similar instruction:

$$01011000010000001100000000000100.$$

Note that the operation code (the first eight bits) is identical, while the address (the last sixteen) is different.

The addition instruction has "00011010" as its operation code; thus

0001101000110100

achieves the objective of adding together the contents of registers three and four. If the result is to be used in future computations, the answer can be stored by

0101000000110000110000000000001000,

a store instruction with operation code "01010000".

Programming, initially, was done in exactly this way; imagine trying to keep track of all those ones and zeros! A single misplaced bit meant a program error. To help lessen the confusion, many programmers began writing programs in octal or hexadecimal, taking advantage of the ease of conversion to binary and generating the bit strings after writing the entire program (Fig. 2.12).

```
     HEX                          BINARY

58  30  C000        0101  1000  0011  0000  1100  0000  0000  0000
58  40  C004 ——→ 0101  1000  0100  0000  1100  0000  0000  0100
1A  34 ——————→ 0001  1010  0011  0100
50  30  C008 ——→ 0101  0000  0011  0000  1100  0000  0000  1000
```

Fig. 2.12 Programming with manual hexadecimal-to-binary conversion

Since this is essentially a table look-up operation, and since computers are good at table look-up operations, it wasn't long before some enterprising programmer hit on the idea of writing a program, in binary, to do this conversion electronically (Fig. 2.13); thus was born the essential concept of an assembler or compiler program.

The next step in software evolution is not quite as obvious, so be careful. If a program can be written to substitute a binary "01011000" for a hexadecimal "58" by table look-up, why not a program to substitute the same binary operation code for the letter "L"? Certainly, "L" is more like the word "LOAD",

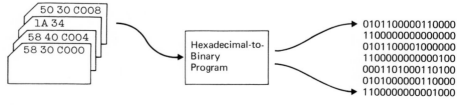

Fig. 2.13 Electronic hexadecimal-to-binary conversion

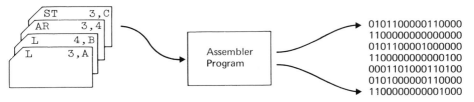

Fig. 2.14 An assembler program

the operation in question, than is $(58)_{16}$. And why not use "A" for "ADD" or "S" for "SUBTRACT" or "M" for "MULTIPLY" or "ST" for "STORE"? Such mnemonic codes are incorporated into assembly-level languages as illustrated in Fig. 2.14; the assembler program performs the function of converting the mnemonic instructions into the binary codes required by the computer.

Higher-Level Languages   Even at the assembler level, programming is a tedious and error-prone activity. A first breakthrough from the "code-each-instruction-the-machine-executes" approach came with the use of macros. A macro is an instruction which, when encountered by the assembler program, generates a number of binary instructions instead of just one. The first application of macros was probably in the area of input and output, where a number of machine-status bits must be tested and retested to ascertain successful completion of the operation; with macro capability, this set of instructions needed to be coded only once and was then simply incorporated into everyone else's program.

The first true higher-level language was FORTRAN. The basic idea behind a language like FORTRAN is pretty obvious once someone points it out to you. Since the addition of two numbers involves two load instructions, plus an add, and a store, why not write a special program to read something like:

$$C = A + B$$

and produce the necessary four instructions (Fig. 2.15)? Humans think in terms of addition; the load and store functions are strictly for the computer's benefit. With such a scheme, load and store are made transparent, thus simplifying programming. There is of course a cost—a good assembler language programmer can invariably turn out a more efficient program than even the best FORTRAN compiler—but FORTRAN makes the power of the computer available to scientists, engineers, mathematicians and others who might never have considered using the machine given the limitations of assembler language programming.

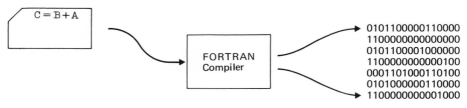

Fig. 2.15 A FORTRAN compiler

Other compilers are designed to produce the same output, a binary machine-level program, from a different form of input. COBOL, for example, is a business-oriented language allowing programs to be written in something like the language of the businessman (Fig. 2.16). PL/I combines many of the features of FORTRAN and COBOL. BASIC is an excellent language for the student just learning to program. Many compiler languages are designed to work with the specialized terminology of a given group—the Civil Engineer's COGO is a good example. There are literally thousands of compiler programs in existence today; each one applies a certain set of rules to the interpretation of a programmer's code with the objective of producing a machine-language program.

Each compiler, generally speaking, is designed to be most efficient (i.e., produce efficient machine-language programs) for a particular type of application; the differences between FORTRAN and COBOL provide an excellent example of this. Data, you may remember, enters the computer in a coded form and must be converted into a computational form such as pure binary or

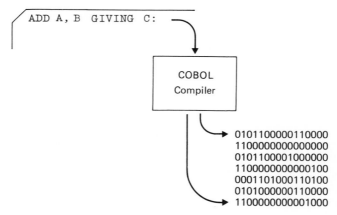

Fig. 2.16 A COBOL compiler

floating point before arithmetic can be performed. In FORTRAN, this conversion takes place as soon as the data is read or just before it is written; thus, in FORTRAN, data is stored in a computational form. The FORTRAN language, as you might expect, is designed to handle mathematical problems. COBOL, on the other hand, was developed to handle business problems with, typically, a great deal of input and output and relatively little computation; thus data is normally stored in coded form, with the conversion to computational form taking place only at the time the computation is performed. FORTRAN is weak in the areas where COBOL shines, and vice versa.

Object and Load Modules A program written in programmer code—FORTRAN, COBOL, Assembler—is called a *source* module; source modules cannot be directly executed by any computer. The source module is read and translated by a compiler or assembler program (Fig. 2.17), and the result, a machine

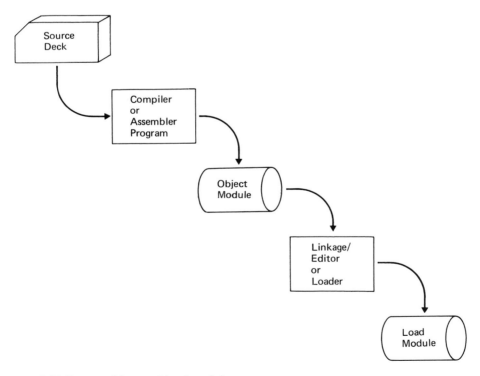

Fig. 2.17 Source, object, and load modules

language version of the program, is called an *object* module. On many computers, the object module must pass through an additional step before it is ready for execution. Another program, a linkage editor or loader (discussed in detail later), performs a number of functions needed to prepare the program for execution on the computer and produces a *load* module (Fig. 2.17 again).

Summary

In this chapter, we reviewed some of the basic concepts of computer software. Key topics included the binary number system, computational data formats like pure binary and floating point, binary codes including BCD, EBCDIC, and ASCII–8, hexadecimal-to-binary and octal-to-binary conversions, assembler languages, compilers, source modules, object modules, and load modules.

Exercises

1. Convert the following binary numbers to decimal.
   a) 1101111   b) 1000010
   c) 11111111   d) 10101001
   e) 1111000011   f) 11.01
   g) 1.1001   h) 1000.0001

2. Convert the binary numbers in Exercise 1 to hexadecimal.

3. Convert the binary numbers in Exercise 1 to octal.

4. Convert the following hexadecimal numbers to binary.
   a) F0   b) 1C
   c) 1111   d) 777
   e) 15   f) FACE

5. Convert the following octal numbers to binary.
   a) 70   b) 33
   c) 1111   d) 777
   e) 15   f) 6543

6. Write your name using the six-bit BCD code. Write it in EBCDIC; in ASCII–8.

7. Write the two digits of your age in EBCDIC—the result will consist of sixteen bits. Treat the resulting string of binary digits as though it were a pure binary number and convert it to decimal. Explain the (obviously) incorrect answer. What would you have to do to get the correct age in pure binary?

8. As a follow-up to Exercise 7, explain the difference between coded (or display) and numeric data within a computer. Why are both types necessary?

9. Explain the difference between a source module, an object module, and a load module. How is each module produced?

10. What is a word? What does the term "fixed-word-length computer" mean? How do the ideas of a fixed-word-length computer and the use of complements to perform subtraction tie together?

CHAPTER 3

Hardware

Overview

In this chapter, we will cover the basic hardware components of a computer system—the computer's central processing unit, memory, and registers, unit record equipment, control units, channels and various input and output devices. We'll also consider, in brief, some key teleprocessing concepts.

The Central Processing Unit

The central processing unit, often called simply the CPU, is the heart of a computer system—although, brain might be a somewhat better analogy. It is here that the computer's arithmetic, logical, and control functions are actually implemented and here that the computer "earns its keep." The CPU is subdivided into two parts, one for arithmetic and logic functions and one for control.

The central processing unit is a mass of highly complex (and very expensive) electrical circuits, a detailed analysis of which is well beyond the scope of this book. At a basic level, the circuitry of the CPU is composed of gates and switches which perform the binary logic functions of Boolean algebra. There are three basic building blocks to this system of logic: an AND gate (Fig. 3.1), an OR gate (Fig. 3.2) and a NOT gate (Fig. 3.3).

By combining these logic gates, it is possible to electronically perform addition, subtraction, multiplication, and division as well as a number of logical functions. Remember, for example, the discussion concerning the use of complements in subtraction from the last chapter? In binary, a complement can be found by changing every bit in the initial number—all 1's become 0's and

Inputs		Output
A	B	C
0	0	0
0	1	0
1	0	0
1	1	1

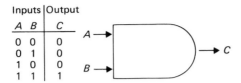

Fig. 3.1 AND logic

Inputs		Output
A	B	C
0	0	0
0	1	1
1	0	1
1	1	1

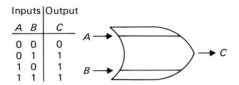

Fig. 3.2 OR logic

Input	Output
A	C
0	1
1	0

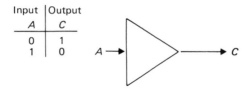

Fig. 3.3 NOT logic

all 0's become 1's—and adding 1. The simplest way to change each bit in a number to the opposite value is to pass the number through a NOT gate. Imagine the sixteen bits of a binary number marching single file through a NOT gate and coming out as a sort of negative, and you have an idea of what really happens.

Timing is crucial to this operation. How, for example, can a NOT gate be expected to recognize the occurrence of a 0 bit when, almost by definition, a 0 bit represents *no* current? If individual bits are sent along the electrical line with absolutely perfect timing—say one bit per nanosecond—the NOT gate "knows" that since nothing arrived "this" nanosecond, it must have been a zero bit. Planning electrical circuits with this kind of timing is what makes computer design the highly technical discipline that it is.

More complex combinations of these basic logic blocks allow the computer to perform more complex functions. Figure 3.4 is an example of a two bit adder.

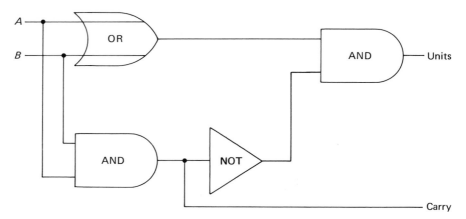

Fig. 3.4 A two-bit adder circuit

Storage or Memory

Since the computer is a binary device, it makes sense to store data and instructions in binary; the best known medium for achieving this objective is core storage which is composed of tiny rings of a ferrite material which can be magnetized in either of two directions—clockwise (which might be a one) and counterclockwise (which, we'll assume, is a zero). (See Fig. 3.5.) Because of the use of such cores, the computer's main memory is often called core storage, a name which continues to be applied to main memory in spite of modern trends toward faster solid-state and monolithic circuits, films, and even laser technologies.

On most computers, individual bits are not directly addressable; instead, the basic addressable unit is a collection of bits. (On an IBM computer, for example, the eight bit "byte" holds one EBCDIC character.) These bits are wired as a single entity and must be treated as such; the CPU can move and manipulate no less than one such entity at a time. Even the assembler programmer's AND and OR functions must work on a full byte to affect even one bit.

On many machines, computational data can be (often must be) spread over a number of these addressable units. The IBM System/360 and System/370 machines offer good examples. On an IBM machine, binary data might occupy a halfword consisting of two bytes (16 bits), a fullword of four bytes, or a doubleword, eight bytes. Bytes zero and one, the first two bytes in main memory, are wired together in such a way (Fig. 3.6) as to facilitate their movement as a single entity. Bytes 2 and 3, 4 and 5, and each group of two bytes beginning

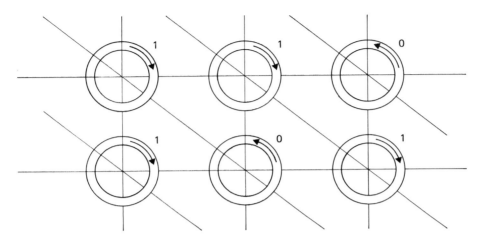

Fig. 3.5 Core Storage

Byte 0	Byte 1	Byte 2	Byte 3	Byte 4	Byte 5	Byte 6	Byte 7
Halfword 0		Halfword 1		Halfword 2		Halfword 3	
Fullword 0				Fullword 1			
Doubleword 0							

Fig. 3.6 The electronic hard-wire relationship between bytes, halfwords, fullwords, and doublewords

with even addresses are similarly wired together, forming halfwords; bytes 1 and 2, and other groups starting with odd addresses are not so wired and cannot be so treated. Bytes 0, 1, 2, and 3, and any group of four bytes beginning with an address evenly divisible by four make up fullwords, and can be manipulated by certain instructions and CPU circuitry as a single entity; bytes 1, 2, 3, and 4 do not enjoy this relationship. Similarly, groupings of eight bytes starting with addresses evenly divisible by eight make up doublewords which, because of their physical, electronic relationship, can, under certain conditions, be manipulated as a single entity. This simple wiring relationship between individual bytes explains the need for boundary alignment on most computational data in an IBM machine.

Registers

Data is stored in the computer's memory; data is manipulated or processed in the central processing unit; thus a mechanism for transfering data between the CPU and memory is essential. On most computers, this function is performed by registers. On the IBM equipment described above, the programmer, through his program which resides in memory, has access to sixteen general-purpose registers each with a capacity of 32 bits or one fullword and four floating-point registers. Data is moved into these registers using any of a number of LOAD instructions and operated upon by the CPU under control of arithmetic instructions. The result is dropped into a register by the CPU, with the programmer moving it into storage by means of a STORE instruction. The registers clearly act as gates or conduits connecting these two major components of the computer.

Notice the relationship between the size of a register and the size of a "word"; a word is that amount of data which will fit into a single register. This statement is true for the computers of most manufacturers, not just IBM. The physical location of the registers might be in main memory, in the CPU, or in a sort of never-never land between these two components—location varies both with the manufacturer and computer size—but the basic function does not vary. In addition to this register relationship, the word is the basic, addressable unit of main memory on many computers.

Unit Record Equipment

Almost everyone is familiar with data-processing cards. The, by now, standard eighty-column card is the best known of computer input media and is used in a variety of applications. The basic card consists of eighty columns, each of which can contain a single character of data; the individual characters are represented by combinations of one or more (in the case of the blank character, no) holes in the column (Fig. 3.7). Individual columns can be grouped together to form fields; a field is nothing more than a group of characters containing a single item of information. A single card will normally contain all the data needed to complete one iteration of a program; each card is termed a record. (The fact that one card contains one record is the source of the term "unit record.") A collection of records—a complete set of labor cards about to be read by a payroll program, for example—is a file.

A card is read by sensing the pattern of punched holes. There are many ways of achieving this objective. In one frequently used technique, the card is wrapped around a metal cylinder and a series of metal brushes is allowed to pass over the card; where no hole is present, the card acts as an insulator, preventing the flow of electrical current; where holes are present, the metal

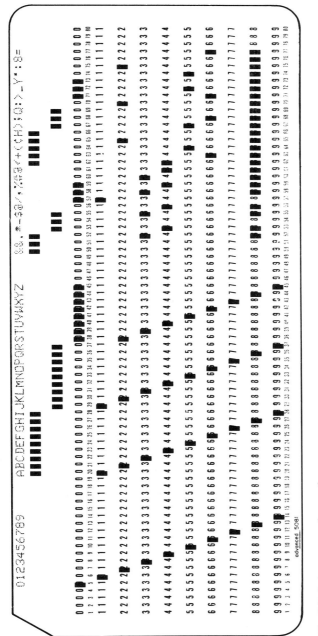

Fig. 3.7 A data processing card

brush drops through, contacts the metal cylinder, and completes a circuit. In a more modern approach, the card is placed on a bank of photoelectric cells and exposed to light; the light shines through the holes only, falling on those photoelectric cells associated with the hole positions.

Cards are not only *read* by electronic equipment, the use of punched card output has been common for years.

In terms of popular exposure, the printer runs a close second to the card reader. Printers work by translating the pattern of electrical pulses coming from the computer into the physical striking of a particular print hammer. Many mechanisms exist for doing this, including chain and bar print units and, lately, a number of nonimpact technologies, but the objective remains the same—to display computer output in human-readable form.

Other commonly used unit record equipment (MICR, OCR, Mark Sense, for example) meets a number of more specialized needs. MICR, which stands for Magnetic Ink Character Recognition, is a banking medium. Checks are imprinted with a magnetic ink indicating the bank's identification number and the account number, with the amount of the check being added after cashing. These magnetic characters are recognized electronically by their different patterns of magnetic intensity. OCR or Optical Character Recognition is an excellent medium for any number of applications in which a limited amount of hand written or typed information must be read into a computer; the basic mechanism for reading such data takes advantage of the difference in reflectivity of white (paper) and black (the lines) surfaces. Mark sense is a simpler version of this same idea, with the location of a mark on a sheet of paper determining its meaning—test answer sheets are a good example.

Control Units

One major problem with the unit record equipment described above is speed; it's quite slow when compared with the internal processing speeds of a computer. Another problem lies in the form of the data itself; this problem is not quite as obvious, but think about it for a minute. The computer expects to send and receive data in some coded form—EBCDIC or ASCII—but card readers read a pattern of holes which, although essentially binary in nature (hole or no-hole), is a completely different code. The printer's print chain is *not* an EBCDIC device. The magnetic peaks and valleys interpreted by the MICR reader are not in the computer's internal code, nor are the degrees of reflected light available to OCR and mark sense equipment.

Both problems are solved through the use of a control unit, an electronic device placed between the input or output equipment and the computer. The control unit performs two important functions: buffering and standard interface. Control unit buffering works this way: as the slow input device reads a record, the control unit places each character in a buffer until a complete record is collected, only then sending the record into the computer; similarly, an output record can be accepted from the computer at a high rate of speed and placed in the buffer to be passed along, at a much slower rate, to the output device. In this way, the computer is insulated, at least in part, from the extreme (relative) slowness of card readers, printers, and other I/O devices.

The words "standard interface" describe another function of control units—the electronic translation to and from EBCDIC, ASCII, or some other binary code. The control unit for a card reader electronically converts the punched card code into the computer's internal code; the printer's control unit transcribes computer code into the signals needed to activate proper print hammers; thus, the computer always sees the same code. All translation from one code to another takes place in the control unit.

Channels

The control unit by itself cannot completely solve the problem of speed discrepancy between input and output devices and the computer; another device, the channel further contributes to at least a partial solution to this problem. Intermediate between the control unit and the computer itself, the channel performs the functions of counting and moving individual characters from one to the other. The function of counting characters seems, at least on the surface, to be rather trivial, but it is a *logical* function and, on computers without such channels, must be performed by the central processing unit. The actual movement of data involves incrementing a core address and checking on the limit of a set of addresses to make sure that protected areas of core storage are not accidently destroyed. In effect, the channel is a small computer, performing a number of logical functions and, thus, freeing the central processing unit to do other work during the input or output cycle.

There are two basic types of channels in use today. The first, a multiplexer, is designed for use with the very slow, unit record equipment described above. The multiplexer overlaps or multiplexes the operation of a number of physical input and output devices, accepting a character from the control unit of a card reader and then sending a character to a printer's control unit while waiting for the card reader to finish reading one more character.

A selector channel, on the other hand, is designed for use with the faster input/output equipment—tape, disk, and drum—described below. Selector channels operate in burst mode, sending a continuous stream of data from (or to) a single device. A sketch of a typical computer center showing the relative location of channels and control units is shown in Fig. 3.8.

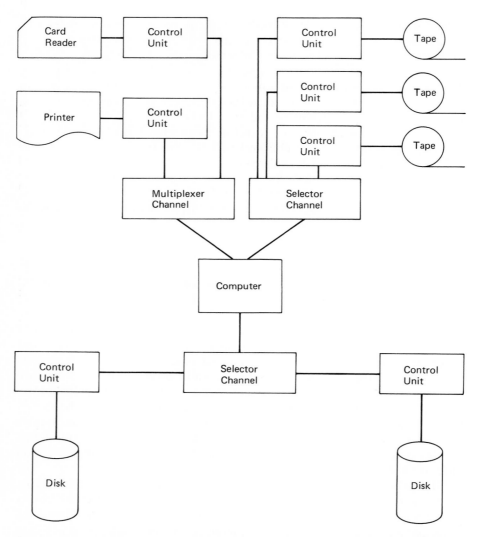

Fig. 3.8 A typical computer installation showing the relative location of channels and control units

Magnetic Tape

Magnetic tape is a high-speed input/output medium, with transfer rates of 60,000 characters per second and more. This is quite fast when compared to a card reader but still slow when compared to the modern computer's million or so instructions per second. Tape is a sequential medium; i.e., to read record number 1000, it is necessary to at least move the tape past the first 999 records. Combined with its speed, compactness, and reusability, tape is an excellent choice for the file-update applications so often encountered in the data-processing field.

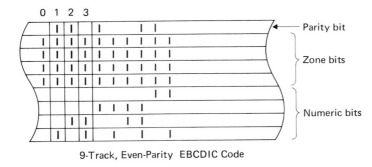

9-Track, Even-Parity EBCDIC Code

Fig. 3.9 Data storage on tape

Data on tape is stored in binary form across the width of the tape (Fig. 3.9). Seven-track tape generally uses a BCD code of six bits to represent each character while nine-track tape uses either the eight-bit EBCDIC code or the eight-bit ASCII code. You may have noticed that nine-track tape uses an *eight*-bit code and seven-track tape uses a *six*-bit code; what about that extra bit? The extra bit is used as a parity bit to help improve the accuracy of the tape drive. *Even* parity says that each character must contain an *even* number of one bits (Fig. 3.9). Thus the parity bit for the number one, $(11110001)_2$ in EBCDIC, is a 1, giving a total of six one-bits, while the parity bit for a three, $(11110011)_2$ in EBCDIC, is a zero. The parity bit is checked by the tape drive's control unit prior to writing or just after reading. If incorrect, corrective action—rereading or termination of the operation with appropriate notification of both computer and operator—is taken. Odd parity (each character must contain an *odd* number of one bits) is an alternative to even parity.

Unlike cards, there is no natural limit to the size of a record on tape. To allow for the separation of individual tape records, an inter-record gap, a length

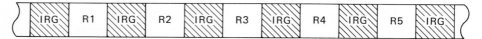

Fig. 3.10 The Inter-record gap

of essentially unused tape, is placed between each record (Fig. 3.10). The tape drive simply reads from inter-record gap to inter-record gap.

The size of this gap is determined by a number of physical factors. Tape data is packed 800, 1600, or more characters per inch, with very precise and consistent spacing between characters. The reading mechanism assumes that tape will be moved past the read/write head at a constant speed, with timing being a crucial factor. It is impossible to bring any mass directly from rest to a constant speed; the inter-record gap provides enough space to bring the tape from an at-rest position up to speed. At the other end of the record, the inter-record gap gives the tape drive the room it needs to slow to a stop between records.

The inter-record gap causes as well as solves problems. Consider, for example, a gap of 0.6 inch, a fairly common length. One card image, stored at 800 characters per inch, would take up 0.1 inch of space on tape. Each 0.1-inch record would be followed by 0.6 inch of unused space. This is equivalent to including six blank cards for each good card in a deck, not exactly efficient utilization of the tape. To improve the physical efficiency of tape, data can be blocked (Fig. 3.11), placing several *logical* records in a single *physical* record. Since the tape drive is designed to read from inter-record gap (or inter-block gap) to inter-record gap, several logical records will be sent to or from the computer at one time. However, the added efficiency of the tape and the improved speed of input or output (fewer starts and stops) more than offset the added cost of blocking and deblocking the data within the computer.

| IBG | R1 | R2 | R3 | R4 | R5 | IBG | R6 | R7 | R8 | R9 | R10 |

Fig. 3.11 Blocking

Disk

One major disadvantage of tape for many applications is its sequential nature; in order to read record number 1000, it is first necessary to read, or at least move past, the first 999. Imagine a tape cut into a series of strips each containing one hundred records. If record number 1000, and *only* record number 1000, were required, only the strip of tape containing this record would have to be searched.

This is the essential concept behind a disk storage unit (Fig. 3.12). Instead of using strips of tape, data is stored in concentric circles on the surface of a disk coated with a magnetic material. To select the proper track, the word used to describe these concentric circles, a movable read/write head is positioned over the desired location. Often, several disk surfaces are stacked together (as in Fig. 3.12) to give added capacity; one position of the read/write heads, covering, in this case, ten tracks, is called a cylinder. (The top and bottom surfaces are not normally used to store data because of the danger of dirt and dust causing read errors.)

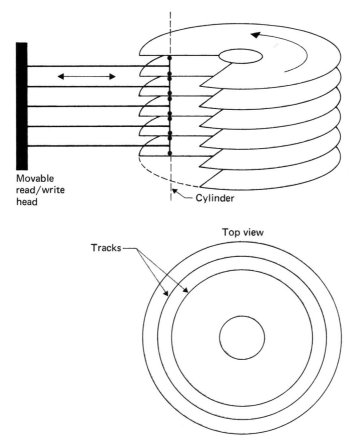

Movable read/write head

Cylinder

Tracks

Top view

Fig. 3.12 A disk

Reading or writing data on disk is a three step operation. First, the read/ write head must be positioned over the proper track; this is called seek time and may involve a movement of anywhere from zero to a few hundred tracks. Once the head is properly positioned, some additional time may expire while the required record rotates beneath the read/write head; this is called rotational delay and may involve as much as one complete rotation. The final component is data transfer time, and represents the time needed to accomplish the actual transfer of data between the disk and the computer, a time which, when compared to seek time and rotational delay, is of minor significance.

Other Direct Access Storage Devices

On a magnetic drum, data is stored, again in concentric circles called tracks, around the outer surface of a unit shaped like an oil drum. Unlike a disk drive, a drum normally has one read/write head for each track, thus eliminating the need to move the head and, hence, seek time. Drum is faster than disk; disk's big advantage lies in its storage capacity. Because of the speed of drum, this device is enjoying increased popularity on modern virtual-storage computer systems, a use we'll analyze in greater detail in Chapter 15.

Another direct-access device, the data cell, is essentially an attempt to implement the concept of storing data on separate strips of magnetic tape, a concept used in introducing direct-access devices in this chapter. Data cells are not in common use; thus, a detailed description is not included.

Traditionally, disk and drum have dominated the direct access market. Lately, however, competition has begun to appear. The "floppy" disk, a slower, less dense, but considerably less expensive alternative to a standard disk drive, is growing in popularity for certain applications—particularly on minicomputers. Another new approach stores data on a series of "honeycomblike" cells, with individual cells being retrieved, mounted on a read/write mechanism, and accessed directly; it's a relatively slow but very high-density medium analogous to the old data cell. As the cost of solid-state main memory continues to drop, some of these technologies will actually become candidates for bulk storage; perhaps we'll see the day when direct-access data storage will in fact be a simple extension of the computer's main memory and thus directly addressable by the CPU itself.

Teleprocessing Hardware

No discussion of computer hardware would be complete without mentioning teleprocessing equipment, perhaps the fastest growing submarket in the data-processing field. The most popular input/output device for teleprocessing, the keyboard terminal, is essentially an electric typewriter. Such terminals normally contain their own buffer—typically, one print line—which is transmitted when the user depresses the "RETURN" button. Since telephones and computers work on different types of electric current, a conversion between these two forms is necessary. This function is performed by a data set or modem, one of which must be located at each end of the telephone line. The major components of a teleprocessing installation are summarized in Fig. 3.13. Data passes from the terminal into the data set and through the telephone system; at the other end, the data comes from the telephone line into a data set, through a control unit and a channel, and, finally into the computer. Going back to the terminal, an exact reverse path is followed.

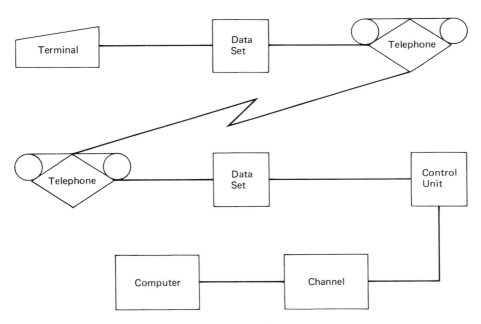

Fig. 3.13 The major components of a teleprocessing system

Many different kinds of control units exist. Some of the more popular varieties take full responsibility for coordinating communications through a number of telephone lines, with the computer dealing with the control unit and ignoring the details of actual, physical terminal location. At times, another control unit is located at the terminal end of the line, concentrating the activities of a number of terminals through the same communication line. The remote control unit is especially important in systems using cathode ray tube (CRT) terminals where, as with a television set, the image must be constantly refreshed.

Teleprocessing applications are not restricted to keyboard terminals; card readers, printers, tape drives, disks, and even other computers can transmit data over communication lines. One popular application is remote job entry; a special terminal with a card reader and a printer is located at the remote end of the line, transmitting programs and data to the computer and accepting and listing the results. Some terminals, often called intelligent terminals, have limited logical capabilities, formatting raw data and producing card listings without going into the computer; some even perform edits on input data, rejecting obvious keypunch errors under program control before sending the data along to the central computer. As these "terminals" gain more and more computational functions, they begin to look very much like minicomputers.

The most popular communications medium is the standard telephone line. Telephone transmission of data, particularly over great distances, is expensive—a cost made even higher by the connect times of an hour or more so common on data transmissions. Many firms attempt to place a limit on these costs by leasing private lines. Such lines come in a variety of transmission capacities. Voice grade can handle roughly 2400 bits per second. Combinations of 2, 3, or 4 voice grade lines yield, respectively, 4800 Baud, 7200 Baud, and 9600 Baud. Special "broadband" cables support even higher transmission rates. The term "Baud," incidently, is derived from the name of Jean Baudot who developed a five-bit data transmission code; it means bits per second. A growing submarket within the data-processing field is made up of firms which have leased a nationwide or regional network of broadband telephone lines and subsequently sublet the use of these lines to a number of different customers, effectively splitting the cost of data transmission among several users. Microwave data transmission, perhaps even utilizing communications satellites, is another possibility.

Just to clear up a possible misunderstanding, not all terminal applications need be remote; it is possible to connect a terminal to a control unit which, in turn, is connected to the channel and, ultimately, to the computer. Such local networks are quite popular.

Summary

In this chapter, we have covered a number of hardware concepts including: the central processing unit, core storage, registers, unit record equipment, control units, channels, tape, disk, drum, teleprocessing hardware such as terminals and data sets, and telecommunications media.

Exercises

1. Relate core storage, or its modern equivalent, to the binary codes and computational data formats described in Chapter 2.

2. Refer back to Fig. 3.4 and show how all possible binary additions (0 + 0, 0 + 1, 1 + 0, 1 + 1) can be performed by this simple circuit. Let "A" represent the first bit to be added and "B," be the second bit; follow these bits through the logic gates of the circuit.

3. Relate core storage, or its modern equivalent, to the AND/OR/NOT logic of the CPU.

4. Discuss the functions of a control unit.

5. Discuss the functions of a channel.

6. The ideal data storage should be extremely fast, able to store an infinite amount of data, compact, and inexpensive. Since no one medium meets all these objectives, the systems planner is often faced with a need to make trade-offs, sacrificing speed for capacity or lower cost. Rank main memory, disk, drum, magnetic tape, and cards with respect to these four criteria. If possible, get actual figures on the speed, capacity, physical size, and cost of each.

7. Relate the speed of a teleprocessing line capable of transmitting data at 2400 Baud to the speed of a card reader and a printer. Assume an 8-bit code is being used. How fast can a card reader or a printer (assume a 120-character line) be driven at 2400 Baud? At 9600 Baud?

CHAPTER 4

Data Management and
File Structures

Overview

A number of essential concepts and definitions pertaining to data, data management, and data file organization are discussed in this chapter, completing our coverage of the three key resources of any data processing system: software, hardware, and data.

Elementary Definitions—Field, Record, and File

In Chapter 3, the idea of grouping characters into fields, fields into records, and records into files was introduced—let's review these concepts once again.

A field is nothing more than a piece of data—a name, an address, hours worked, in short, a single, complete piece of data. A field may be any length, from a one-character job classification to a twenty-character name field and beyond. A field may be composed of a number of EBCDIC or ASCII coded characters, or it may be a binary fullword or halfword, or it may be a floating-point number, or a packed-decimal number. A field is a complete, single element of data.

A record is a collection of fields—normally all the data needed to complete a single iteration or cycle of a program. The logic of a program is usually based on the idea of reading one record, processing that data, and writing one record. On a medium such as cards, there is a physical limit to the length of a record; no such limit exists on tape or disk.

A file is a collection of relevant, like records. If a name is an example of a *field* in a payroll card *record*, the *file* would consist of all the payroll cards, one for each employee. An inventory record would not, obviously, be relevant to the payroll-processing program and, hence, would not be part of the file.

Record Formats

Our discussion of record formats begins with the punched card. Although a multiple card record is a possibility, such groupings are the exception rather than the rule—one record per card is pretty standard. These records are all the same length, normally eighty (or ninety-six on the newer, smaller card) characters. The words "fixed length" are used to describe such records.

Tape and direct-access devices do not restrict the length of records, but fixed-length records, each containing the same number of characters, can still be stored. In fact, it's probably reasonable to assert that most records are fixed length. This is partly due to programming considerations—fixed-length data is easier to work with. Individual fixed-length records on tape are separated by inter-record gaps (Fig. 4.1). Records on a disk, or any direct-access device for that matter, are separated by similar gaps; in addition, count fields and, sometimes, keys are associated with each record (Fig. 4.2) to facilitate direct access.

| Gap | Data | Gap | Data | Gap | Data | Gap | Data | Gap |

Fig. 4.1 Fixed-length data on tape

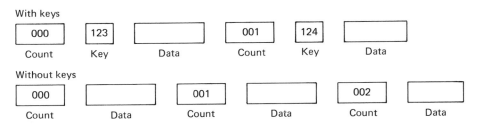

With keys

| 000 | 123 | | 001 | 124 | |
| Count | Key | Data | Count | Key | Data |

Without keys

| 000 | | 001 | | 002 | |
| Count | Data | Count | Data | Count | Data |

Fig. 4.2 Fixed-length data on disk

To conserve space on disk or tape, data is often blocked; blocking also improves the efficiency of a program by reducing the number of *physical* reads and writes (seeks on a disk, starts and stops on tape), thus reducing the time spent reading and writing data. Blocking involves grouping several logical records into a single, large physical record (Fig. 4.3). Note carefully the distinction between logical and physical records; a physical record is the entire

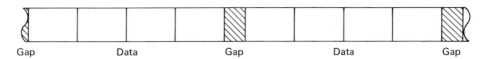

Fig. 4.3 Fixed-length blocked data on tape

block, while a logical record is composed of the data needed to complete a single iteration of a program. Most input/output devices are designed to handle all the data between two gaps; thus *physical* records move between the device and the computer. Prior to output, blocks are built in core by putting a series of logical records together. Following input, the physical block must be de-blocked into logical records.

Not all data is fixed in length; variable-length data is useful for many applications (Fig. 4.4). To allow for processing of variable-length data, the record length is normally a part of the record (the RL field in Fig. 4.4). Variable-length data can be blocked (Fig. 4.5) or unblocked. A good example of a variable-length record is a student's academic record—almost empty as a freshman but quite long following the senior year. Incidently, the BL field in Fig. 4.5 is a block length—information for the access method.

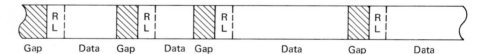

Fig. 4.4 Variable-length unblocked data

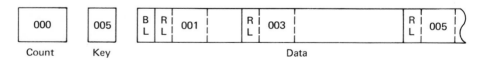

Fig. 4.5 Variable length blocked data on disk

Blocking creates some problems with direct access keys. Consider, for example, the block pictured in Fig. 4.6; should the block key be the key of the first, last, or one of the middle records? Usually, the key of the last record is used. With the last record key as the block key, we know that we've found the block containing the record we seek as soon as our search key is less than

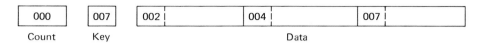

Fig. 4.6 Fixed-length blocked data with keys

the block key. A little analysis should show that it doesn't work as well with any other record key.

There is one other record format available on most computers—undefined. As the name implies, undefined records do not follow any consistent format. A major reason for undefined record formats is the occasional unknown tape or disk pack which shows up in every computer center sooner or later. Since the content of the tape or disk is unknown, the programmer can't define the record format to the system; by using an undefined format, however, he can at least read and dump the tape in hopes of identifying it by its content.

Sequential Files

Cards are read in sequence. A card file is thus a sequential file; data is read in a fixed sequence and there can be no deviation from this fixed sequence.

On tape, individual records are stored in a continuous, unbroken string, determining the order in which data must be processed. Like cards, tape, by its very nature, is a sequential medium, with data being read (or written) in a fixed sequence.

One of the most common applications of the computer is record keeping. A good example of this class of applications is the checking-account master-file-update program run daily by most banks. Checks and deposits are first sorted (account number sequence) to tape, with this "current activity" tape being subsequently merged with the old master file which is also in account number sequence (Fig. 4.7). In this merging process, deposits are added to the old balance from the old master file and checks are subtracted, yielding a new balance. The output consists of a written report (perhaps, statements for mailing) and a new master file. This new master file becomes input to the program the next time the file update is run. It is very important, obviously, that checks and deposits are charged or credited to the proper account; any bank which consistently gets even a small percentage of their accounts confused will soon be on the brink of financial difficulties. The key to the program logic in such file update applications is the sequence of the data; i.e., this is a sequential application.

Direct-access storage devices were not designed with sequential access in mind, but sequential files can be stored and retrieved quite efficiently on both

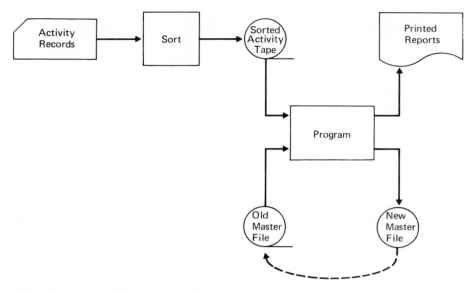

Fig. 4.7 The master file update application

disk and drum. The key concept for understanding sequential access on a direct access device is the relative track address. Consider the single surface disk pictured in Fig. 4.8. This disk surface has been broken into ten tracks (an oversimplification to aid understanding) and these tracks have been numbered 0 through 9. Let's say that we have a file of exactly ten records, two to a track, starting with track number five. Our individual records are stored on tracks described by the following table:

RECORD	RELATIVE RECORD	RELATIVE TRACK	ABSOLUTE TRACK
0001	0	0	5
0002	1	0	5
0003	2	1	6
0004	3	1	6
0005	4	2	7
0006	5	2	7
0007	6	3	8
0008	7	3	8
0009	8	4	9
0010	9	4	9

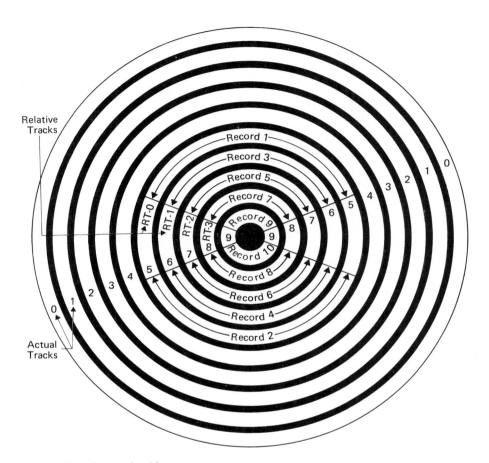

Fig. 4.8 Relative track addresses

The relative record number is the record's position *relative* to the beginning of the file. In this example, there are exactly two records on each track; thus the relative *track* address can be computed by simply dividing the relative record number by 2. Since this file starts on track number 5, the *absolute* track address can be computed by adding the relative track address to the file-start address. This type of addressing is similar to base/displacement addressing in main memory, with the file's start address representing the base and the relative record number representing the displacement. Such files can be processed sequentially by simply incrementing the relative record address. Track numbering on a multisurface disk may be a bit more complex, but the concept of the relative record number is the same.

Why not just take the actual or absolute track address and increment it? As a program is being written, the programmer rarely knows exactly where his data will be stored; using the relative track address approach, data can be located relative to the beginning of the file, "wherever that may be," with the absolute address of the beginning being supplied later.

Direct Access

In contrast to the type of file-update applications described above, some computer uses require the processing of single records in random rather than sequential order. Imagine that you are trying to make an airline reservation to fly from New York to Los Angeles. Airline ABC says to check back at six o'clock after their reservation files have been updated, while airline XYZ, right across the terminal, gives fifteen second confirmation. Which airline would you choose? The probable answer to this question is, to an airline executive, an excellent economic justification for a direct-access reservation system.

Tape is not well suited to such applications because of its sequential nature. If information concerning flight 526 of Treetop Airways for December 26, 1977 is the first record on the tape, retrieval is pretty quick, but that information might be the ten thousandth record on the tape. Direct-access storage devices, primarily disk and drum, were designed to handle this type of application, allowing a program to *directly* access the desired record. Direct-access files can be organized in a number of different ways, several of which are described below.

Simple Direct Access

Imagine a file consisting of exactly one hundred records numbered 00 through 99. To simplify this first example, assume that each record occupies exactly one full track. Create this file sequentially. The record number is now the relative track address. To retrieve record number 55, simply find the absolute address of the first record in the file, add 55, and move the read/write head to the computed track. If, more realistically, records are numbered 001 through 100, the formula for computing the record's absolute disk address becomes just a bit more complex—subtract 1 before adding the relative address to the absolute address of the first record in the file.

One record per track is a bit of an oversimplification, let's assume twenty records per track for a file consisting of exactly one thousand records numbered 0001 through 1000. In this file, records 0001 through 0020 are stored on relative track 0, records 0021 through 0040 are on relative track 1, records 0041 through 0060 are on relative track 2, and so on. To find the relative track address of any single record, simply subtract 1 from the record number and divide by 20, the number of records per track. Record number 0030, which we know must be on relative track 1 computes as follows:

0030 minus 1 = 0029 divided by 20 = 1, remainder 9. The record we are searching for is record count 9[†] on relative track 1—both numbers were derived from the division operation. But, you say, record number 0030 is the tenth record on that track. The first record on a track is assigned a count of zero, making the tenth record number 09. Using the same rule, record number 0020, the last record on the first track (relative track zero) computes to a quotient of zero, the relative track number, and a remainder of 19, the record number. Similarly, the record with a key of 121 is record count 0 on relative track 6.

Indirect Addressing

There is one major problem with the simple direct accessing described above— space must be set aside for each and every record over the entire range of keys. As long as most of the records are active this is no problem, but what happens, for example, on an employee file using social-security numbers as a key? A large firm employing one-hundred-thousand people would use only a fraction of the 999,999,999 possible social-security numbers; even a small firm could expect the range of employee social security numbers to cover several million values. For simple direct access to work, space must be allocated to hold all possible records, because only when all possible records are present will the key translate directly to the proper relative address.

A number of techniques exist for indirectly addressing data on a direct-access device. A few of the more popular techniques are:

1. *The division/remainder method.*   Divide the key by a large prime number, usually a prime close to the total number of records in the file. The remainder, a kind of random number, is the relative record number.

2. *Digit analysis.*   A frequency distribution of the occurrence of the digits 0 through 9 by their position in the key is developed. The three or four most evenly distributed key positions are simply used as the relative record number.

3. *Folding.*   Break the key into two or more parts and add the parts together, producing a relative record number. A 6-digit key might, for example, be broken into two 3-digit numbers—the first three and the last three—and the sum of these two numbers computed.

[†] The count field of the direct-access record described in Fig. 4.2.

4. *Radix transformation.*   The key is converted to a number in a different, nondecimal base, and the result is used as a relative record number.

The objective of all these techniques is to produce a series of relative track addresses evenly distributed over the entire available space. Some "randomizing" techniques yield both a relative track address and a record number, while others result in a relative track address only; the "RTA only" techniques are designed to get the read/write heads to the proper track which can then be searched until the record with the correct key is found.

The major problem with indirect addressing is *synonyms*. A synonym occurs when too many records randomize to the same relative track address, or two or more records randomize to the same relative record number. No randomizing technique will produce a perfect uniform distribution over an entire file. Once a given track is full or once a given record position is occupied, the next key randomizing to that relative address won't fit and must be placed on an overflow track; at retrieval time, the data will not be found in the computed position, necessitating an extra seek and read of the overflow track. A well-designed randomizing technique, custom-made for the data of a specific application, can minimize synonyms (twenty percent is a common target); but none, unfortunately, eliminate the problem.

The Cross-Reference List

A cross-reference list is essentially a table of contents. With this technique, as a file is created, a list of keys and the record number address of the record associated with each key is also built. At retrieval time, this table is searched at computer speeds until the proper key is found, thus yielding the relative address of the record in question. Data can be stored in any order; as along as the cross-reference list is maintained in proper sequence, retrieval is straightforward. There is no need for overflow when using such a system. Sequential access is even a possibility—simply follow the cross-reference list from top to bottom. An example of a partial cross-reference list and its associated data on a single surface disk is shown in Fig. 4.9.

The storage and maintenance of this cross-reference list are the major problems of the table-look-up approach to direct access. On a large file, the table can get quite long. For the fastest possible access, the table might be stored in core, but core is relatively expensive; the table might, alternatively be stored on disk and read into the computer only as needed, but this means two seeks and two reads are required to obtain each record. In some installations, careful programming makes the table core resident at peak-use times and disk resident at other times. Table maintenance is also a problem—since most table look-up techniques depend on the sequence of the table, the table must be sorted to

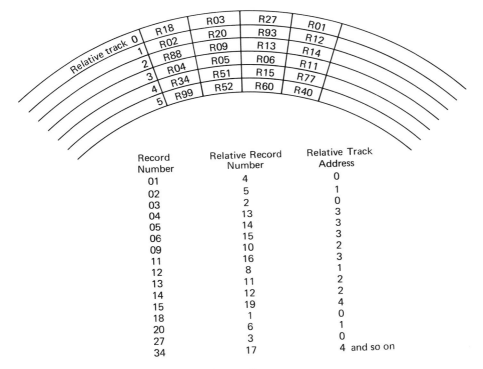

Record Number	Relative Record Number	Relative Track Address
01	4	0
02	5	1
03	2	0
04	13	3
05	14	3
06	15	3
09	10	2
11	16	3
12	8	1
13	11	2
14	12	2
15	19	4
18	1	0
20	6	1
27	3	0
34	17	4 and so on

Fig. 4.9 Direct access using a cross-reference list

maintain sequence as records are added to the file. Even given this long list of negatives, the use of a cross-reference list is an excellent approach to direct access for many applications.

Indexed Sequential Files

A number of computer manufacturers and software houses provide the computer user with the programming needed to build and maintain the kind of cross-reference table described above. Indexed sequential files are a good example of this type of support. The indexed sequential file organization was developed to facilitate both direct and sequential access of the same file. These files are usually created sequentially, making sequential access fairly straightforward. The only problem encountered in sequential access is the overflow records added to the file after initial creation. They're not in sequence, and a surprisingly big chunk of indexed sequential processing software has been written to deal with this problem.

A hierarchy of indexes is used to permit direct access of data. For a disk file, a *cylinder index* lists the value of the largest key stored on each cylinder in the file. Each cylinder has its own *track index*, listing the largest key stored on the track. To locate a record, the cylinder index must first be searched—one seek and one read. This gets us to the track index, which must also be read before we can seek and read data from the proper track. That's a total of three seeks and three reads for each record of data! Overflow data means an extra set of I/O operations. Although it is possible, using software, to make at least the cylinder index core resident during processing, other organizations tend to be a bit more efficient for direct access.

Record Chaining

A well maintained indexed sequential file is most efficient when processing data sequentially, suffering some inherent inefficiencies when working in the direct mode. A very good organization for a file which is usually accessed directly but must be processed sequentially on occasion involves the use of a chaining technique. A part of each record in the file contains the key and (perhaps) relative address of the next record in sequence (Fig. 4.10); in other words, each record points to the next one. Sequential processing may involve frequent movement of the read/write access arm and, hence, inefficiency, but if such processing is relatively rare, who cares? The file can be organized using the most efficient direct-access technique, thus optimizing its primary use.

Another application of pointers is the linking of logically related records. Assume, for example, that a company maintains a personnel file on all employees. Some of the data in this file—name, social-security number, hourly wage—is

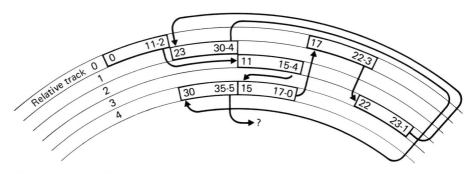

Fig. 4.10 Chaining

used every pay period, while other information is needed only infrequently. Rather than insist that the payroll program provide space for an employee's history of education and training, a separate education and training file is created, with the main personnel record containing a pointer to the associated entry in this new file. Thus a trail to a complete set of data is maintained without creating extremely long, inefficient records. The use of pointers to connect logically related records is common in modern data base management systems, a topic we'll be discussing in Chapter 17.

Virtual Storage Files

When IBM announced their System/370 series of computers, a series which implements a memory management technique known as virtual memory, a new access method—the Virtual Storage Access Method or VSAM—was also introduced. Based on the assumption that most readers of this book are not, at this time, familiar with the intimate details of virtual memory, we won't go deeply into VSAM here, but VSAM does support a different approach to file organization and should, at least, be mentioned. We'll come back to this topic in Chapter 15, after the virtual memory concept has been covered.

Under VSAM, data is stored in fixed-length blocks. Within a block, individual logical records can be stored in sequence by some key—employee number, social security number, part number—or in entry sequence (the order in which the records are received). Assuming key sequence, probably the most common approach, an index is maintained indicating the key of the last record in each block. So far, VSAM looks very much like ISAM.

At this point, however, VSAM departs from the ISAM mode, offering some significant improvements. ISAM, with its cylinder and track indexes, is specifically designed for disk files; VSAM uses a "relative byte" address, analogous to a main memory address, to access data, thus making this access method device independent. Let's repeat that statement: *VSAM is, at least in theory, device independent!* When disk was the only "DASD" game in town, device independence was no big thing, but technology is changing and VSAM provides the flexibility needed to change with it.

Another major weakness of ISAM is the way file additions and deletions are handled. VSAM spreads "free space" throughout the physical file and VSAM software includes the code needed to rearrange records and pointers, making file updates and data retrieval much more efficient.

Perhaps the biggest potential benefit of the virtual access methods, however, is derived from the relationship of these access methods to virtual memory itself. As we'll see in Chapter 15, the virtual memory concept allows the programmer to address program instructions and data areas which actually reside on some secondary storage device (like disk or drum) as though they were in real core memory. The virtual memory control program takes care of converting these addresses into real addresses; it's like base/displacement addressing one more step removed. Since program instructions are handled in this way, the computer manufacturer is very strongly motivated to make the "disk-to-core" or "drum-to-core" transfer operation as efficient as possible by using special software and, probably, special hardware. VSAM allows data to be treated in much the same way. If computers are going to be designed to make this special kind of I/O as efficient as possible, it makes sense to utilize these extra efficiencies in handling data.

Virtual access methods are in fairly common use today. Their use will grow.

Which Organization is Best?

The answer to the question, "What's the best file organization?" depends on the detailed requirements of a particular application. It is, for example, ridiculous to even consider a direct organization for a file of five or six records. By the time the relative track address is computed, the entire file could have been searched sequentially; *size*, the number of records in the file, is an important consideration. Another key factor is the *volatility* of the data; an indexed sequential organization would, for example, *not* be a good choice when a significant rate of record additions and deletions is expected.

File *activity* is another critical factor. On a real-time system, where each transaction must be processed independently as it is received, some form of direct access is essential; on a master-file update, involving the modification of a substantial percentage of the records in the file, sequential is the obvious choice. In between these two extremes is a large, grey area. Indexed sequential is fine for a "mostly sequential with some direct" application. If direct access is the primary requirement with sequential needs running a distant second, record chaining or the use of a "programmer created and maintained" cross-reference list might be the best choice. "Best" is a relative term.

Volumes, Labels, and Other Things

In data-processing terminology, a *volume* is a single, physical unit of some input/output medium—one tape or one disk or one drum. A volume might contain a single file, several files, part of a single file, or parts of several files.

On tape, "one volume/one file" is the usual condition, but other approaches are possible. A multifile volume of tape is illustrated in Fig. 4.11. Each file, even when there is only one file on a given volume, is preceded by a header which can be electronically checked by the computer, thus avoiding an attempt to read

Fig. 4.11 Multiple files on a tape volume

the wrong file. Multivolume files—a single file spread over several tape volumes—are also possible.

The problem of multiple files on a direct-access volume, the usual condition on disk or drum, is solved through the use of a volume table of contents (VTOC) which simply lists all the files or data sets stored on the volume with the absolute (cylinder/track) address of the first and last records in the file (Fig. 4.12). The VTOC is the source of the absolute "file start" address which is added to the relative track address to compute the actual address of any single record, a concept discussed several paragraphs back.

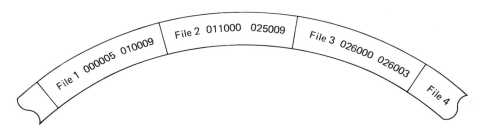

Fig. 4.12 The volume table of contents

Summary

In this chapter, we have covered several key data concepts, including: fields, records, files, fixed- and variable-length records, blocking, sequential file organization, a number of direct organizations—simple, indirect, and via cross-reference table—indexed sequential organization, record chaining, labels, volumes, the VTOC, and factors influencing the choice of a file organization.

Exercises

1. Define and relate the terms: field, record, and file.
2. Describe or sketch: fixed unblocked data, fixed blocked data, variable unblocked data, variable blocked data, and undefined data.

3. Differentiate between sequential and direct access.

4. Discuss the relative address concept on disk. How can a relative track address be converted to an absolute disk address?

5. One method for supporting direct access is to create and maintain a cross-reference list of actual keys and their relative record numbers. Relate this approach to an indexed sequential organization.

6. Discuss record chaining. How does it work? Of what value is it?

7. What is the difference between a file and a volume?

8. Relate the VTOC of a direct access file to the relative track address concept.

9. A personnel file is used weekly by the payroll program. At regular intervals, the personnel department makes changes—new hires, changes of address, terminations—to a small number of the records on the file. How would you organize the file? Explain your logic.

10. A company has an on-line inventory system. Each time material enters or leaves a warehouse, the inventory file is changed to reflect this "latest" inventory status. Once a year, the file must be dumped in part-number sequence for physical inventory purposes. How would you organize this file? Once again, explain your logic.

PART II

Operating System Development

CHAPTER 5

Single Program Systems:
the Second Generation

Overview

Many important operating system concepts were developed during the so-called second generation of data processing—that period covering the 1950s and the early 60s when computers came into fairly common use. Computers were small and, relative to a modern machine, quite slow. Most systems were operated in what might be called a serial batch mode, i.e., programs executed in sequence, with the program in control of the computer having complete command over all system resources from start to the moment of completion.

A key factor during this time period was the movement of electronic data processing into the business environment. Early computers were largely scientific and military machines, computing ballistic tables and mathematical relationships of interest to the scientist; these applications involve very little input and output, and, since the computations are very difficult, even impossible, without the aid of the computer, the efficiency of the machine itself was not an issue. The businessman, on the other hand, tended to view the computer as another piece of capital equipment to be used as efficiently as possible; how to get the maximum amount of work from the least amount of equipment became an important consideration. Hardware, being the most obvious component of cost in a data-processing system, became the focus of cost consciousness; *throughput*, a measure of the amount of work moving through a computer over a given period of time, became an accepted measure of effectiveness. The cost of software and programming was also recognized, but largely in hardware terms— a good program was one which achieved a given data processing objective using minimum core for a minimum period of time.

Although largely hardware oriented, a number of software concepts intended to shorten program-debug time and simplify the job of the programmer were developed during the second generation, an indication that the cost of the software itself was recognized. In the area of data management, many of the concepts and file organizations discussed in Chapter 4 were products of this period of computer evolution.

In this chapter, we will discuss several of the more important second generation developments, showing how control and support functions evolved to meet specific needs, leading to ideas and techniques crucial to the development of operating systems. Don't forget the primary measure of efficiency being assumed throughout this chapter—throughput; almost invariably, the operating system concepts we'll be discussing were designed to improve the efficiency of the system.

Setup Minimization

Before any program can be run, it must first be set up (cards loaded in the card reader, the printer loaded with either regular single-part paper or special forms, tapes and disk packs mounted, and so on). This takes time (Fig. 5.1). On a slow machine—say one thousand instructions per second or so—this is no big problem; five minutes of setup might be followed by a few hours of computation. As computers became faster, however, setup became a problem. Setup time is not affected by machine speed—if it took five minutes before, it still takes five minutes now—but run time drops by a significant amount as the computer becomes faster. Suddenly, instead of wasting an insignificant five minutes setting up a two-hour job, that five minute setup is good for only a fifteen minute job (Fig. 5.2); a substantial percentage of available computer time is blown on a nonproductive activity. Such excessive idle time on an expensive piece of capital equipment is intolerable to a good businessman.

Fig. 5.1 Setup vs. run time—a slow machine

Fig. 5.2 Setup vs. run time as computer speed increases

Simple elimination of setup is impossible; tape mounts, printer loading, and the other setup activities must be performed. One partial solution, long used in industry for minimizing idle time on production equipment, is scheduling. Consider, for example, the following four jobs with varying printer-paper requirements:

JOB	PAPER
A	1-part
B	4-part
C	1-part
D	4-part

Running these jobs in the given sequence (Fig. 5.3) necessitates three printer-forms changes; changing the sequence to group similar jobs (Fig. 5.4) allows the same work to be done with only a single forms change, yielding a significant reduction in total setup time. Not all job combinations are so obvious, but the idea of grouping similar jobs to take advantage of common setups is a good one.

Setup	A	Setup	B	Setup	C	Setup	D

Fig. 5.3 Job setups, no scheduling

Setup	A	C	Setup	B	D

Fig. 5.4 Job setup with scheduling

Scheduling is often implemented through the use of job classifications. Tests, compilations, and assemblies might, for example, be assigned a classification of "A"; jobs running under this classification might be restricted to the use of the card reader and printer—single-part paper only. As class "A" jobs arrive at the computer center, they are simply held until some scheduled time when the entire "batch" is run through the computer with no need for intermediate setups. Other classes—"B" for tape, "C" for multiple tapes, "D" for multipart paper—allow for the grouping of other types of jobs.

How can the operator identify the class of a program deck? One common way is through the use of a job identification card. This card, placed on top of the deck, shows the job class and, perhaps, other information like the programmer's name and accounting data. Many different card formats have been tried, including different colored cards for each class; the important point is the ability to group like jobs, thus facilitating scheduling to minimize setup.

Input/output device availability is another basis for scheduling. A job requiring a number of tape drives might, for example, be set up while a job using no tapes is running, thus avoiding the expected idle time for tape mounting. This kind of scheduling is difficult to plan and implement, but a little work and foresight can achieve significant reductions in setup. During the second generation, this planning was facilitated by the programmer's run book, a formal document describing all the operator activity required on a given job.

The opportunity for priority overrides is an important part of any scheduling system—unplanned "hot" jobs do occur in spite of the best planning. Often the job card described above has provision for a priority parameter, aiding the recognition of such jobs.

Before leaving the topic of scheduling, consider for a moment the basic measurement of a computer system—throughput. While a computer is being set up, it is idle; this has a negative impact on system efficiency. The objective of scheduling is to decrease setup time, thus making more time per hour available for processing. The difference between good scheduling and poor scheduling might be an hour per day; ask any businessman about the economic value of one hour per day. Good planning, by reducing setup time, improves system efficiency.

Compilation Time and Object Modules

Setup is not the only source of wasted time on a computer; a number of possibilities for substantial waste in run time exist as well. Consider, for example, compilation.

A programmer might prepare the job deck pictured in Fig. 5.5. This is a fairly typical multistep job, with data editing followed by a sort followed by a master file update. All three programs are written in COBOL; thus, all three modules must be preceded by a copy of the COBOL compiler program. Just reading all those cards at relatively slow card reader speeds is time consuming.

Why not store the compiler object module on disk instead of cards? In Fig. 5.6, the COBOL compiler object decks have been replaced by EXEC cards, indicating that a copy of the COBOL compiler is to be loaded from disk. Note also the new version of the sort program—it too has been replaced by an EXEC card followed by a single data card describing the sort fields. Sorting is such a common data processing activity that most firms long ago either purchased, or assigned a programmer to write, a general sort routine and placed this routine, in object module form, on disk, thus making it available to all the programmers

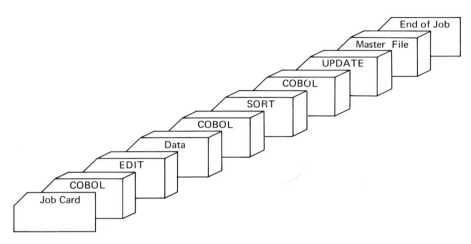

Fig. 5.5 Job deck with compilers in object module form

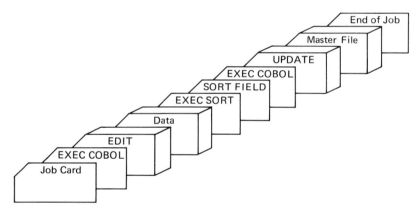

Fig. 5.6 The same job with compilers and the sort routine stored on disk

in the data-processing department. The elimination of so many cards, by itself, leads to a significant reduction in total job runtime.

The compiler and sort object modules are stored on a library. A number of special programs are needed to support the library, programs for adding and deleting members and for loading programs from the library into core storage. Programs of the latter variety are called loaders. A flowchart illustrating the flow of programs for our edit/sort/update job is shown in Fig. 5.7.

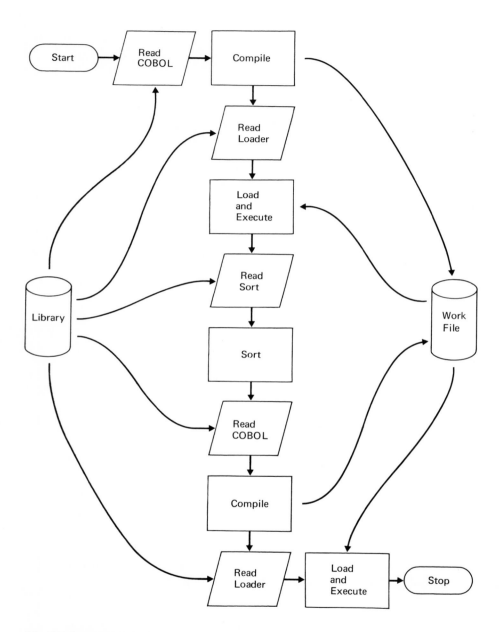

Fig. 5.7 Program flow for an edit/sort/update job using a loader program and object modules stored on a library

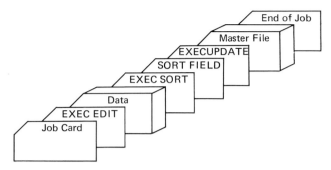

Fig. 5.8 Job deck with all programs stored on a library

What about the compilation process itself? Once a program is completely debugged, compilation, the conversion from programmer language to machine language, is a waste of time, simply producing the same output over and over again. Why not store the program's object module (or load module) on a library? It can be done. A job deck using library modules is illustrated in Fig. 5.8. In addition to cutting the number of cards to be read and replacing slow card input with faster disk input, the compilation operation itself has been eliminated. The use of libraries can significantly reduce program runtime, thus increasing the time available for executing other jobs. This increases throughput, subsequently improving system efficiency.

The I/O and Computer Speed Disparity

A card reader pushing through six-hundred cards per minute handles one card in about one tenth of a second; in this same one tenth of a second, a microsecond computer is capable of executing something like one-hundred-thousand instructions. Most programs are not nearly that large. Put simply, the computer is capable of working at speeds significantly in excess of the ability of its I/O devices to provide data.

This concept is best illustrated by an example. The precise program used in this example is not important; it consists of a read followed by the execution of one-hundred instructions, followed by a write (Fig. 5.9). The program then repeats. Each cycle involves one read, one hundred instructions, and one write, and anything we say about the timing of a single cycle can, by a simple process of multiplication, be applied to any number of cycles.

Our computer is a slow millisecond machine, capable of executing a mere one-thousand instructions per second. With card input and printer output, the time needed to complete a single cycle is illustrated in Fig. 5.10. To read one

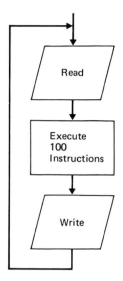

Fig. 5.9 A sample program

card, our 600-card-per-minute card reader takes 0.1 seconds. At 1200 lines per minute, a single line of output can be written in 0.05 seconds—twenty lines per second. On a millisecond machine, one hundred instructions consume 0.1 seconds of machine time. Total cycle time is 0.250 seconds. Of this total cycle time, fully 60 percent—0.150 seconds—is spent on input and output. While input and output are being performed, the CPU, the most expensive component of the data processing system, does nothing. In effect, the CPU is actually used only forty percent of the time the system is "running"; sixty percent of the time is spent waiting for input and output devices to complete the transfer of data.

Hardware provides a good solution to this problem, especially on such a slow machine. Magnetic tape can be read at rates in excess of sixty-thousand

Read one card .... 0.100 seconds
Execute 100 instructions .... 0.100 seconds
Print one line .... 0.050 seconds
    Total cycle .... 0.250 seconds

Run time = 0.100 of each 0.250 seconds = 40%.
CPU idle time = 0.150 of each 0.250 seconds = 60%.

Fig. 5.10 Program cycle time

characters per second. At this speed, an eighty-character card image can be read in slightly more than 0.001 seconds instead of the 0.1 seconds needed by the card reader, while a single one-hundred-twenty-character output line could be sent to tape in 0.002 seconds. The speed of the computer is not affected by the fact that faster I/O devices are in use, remaining at 0.100 seconds for the execution of the one hundred instructions of this program. Total cycle time works out to 0.103 seconds, with the CPU being active for 0.100 seconds each cycle—roughly 97 percent of the time (Fig. 5.11). Disk or drum could be used as well, with equally dramatic results. These numbers are not intended to be a precise picture of reality but are intended to illustrate orders of magnitude only. The improvement from using fast input and output is not as dramatic on a faster computer, but this example does show the advantages to be gained by using tape and disk.

Read one card image .... 0.001 seconds
Execute 100 instructions .... 0.100 seconds
Write one record .... 0.002 seconds

   Total cycle .... 0.103 seconds

Run time = 0.100 of each 0.103 seconds = 97%.

Fig. 5.11 Program cycle time with tape I/O

Blocking, Buffering, and Access Methods

The use of tape and disk generally means that data will be blocked to improve the utilization of these media; thus blocks of data must be built in core prior to physical output and logical records must be deblocked following input. Although not really difficult, blocking and deblocking do represent one more problem for the programmer. To relieve the programmer of much of this burden, access methods were developed. An access method is similar to a subprogram; a key component of an access method is the code needed to block and deblock data.

A software technique which can lead to significant improvements in system efficiency involves the use of *multiple* buffers. As an example, let's work with data blocked in groups of ten eighty-character records. We'll set up two buffers, each eight hundred characters, the size of a physical record or block, in length. As the program begins, these two buffers are filled and the first logical record is moved from the first buffer into the programmer's work area (Fig. 5.12). As the program completes a cycle and issues a second read instruction, the second logical record is simply moved from the buffer—no physical I/O operation is needed yet. The program continues (see Fig. 5.13 for a flowchart of program

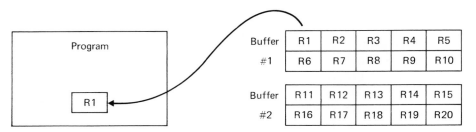

Fig. 5.12 Multiple buffers in a program

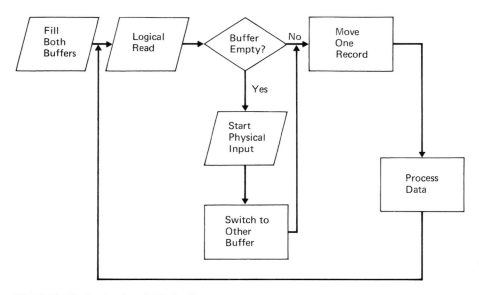

Fig. 5.13 The logic of multiple buffering

logic) moving data from the first buffer into the work area until the first buffer is emptied; at this point in time—the eleventh read—the program logic switches to buffer number two and, simultaneously, issues a physical read instruction. While the tape or disk drive is doing its (relatively) slow thing, the computer is processing data from the second buffer, in parallel, thus significantly reducing wasted time. When buffer two is exhausted, data is moved from the by now (hopefully) full first buffer while the second buffer is replenished.

The software to support multiple buffering is generally part of the access method. The use of more than two buffers is possible—four and even more are

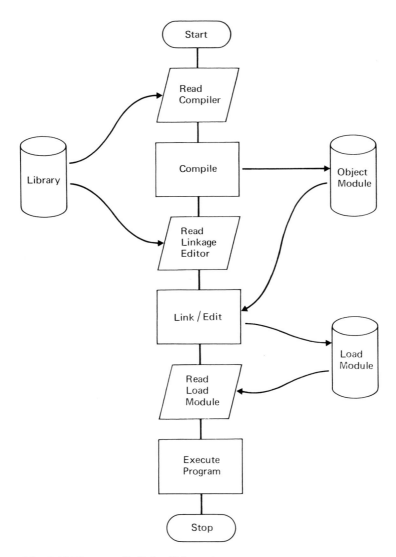

Fig. 5.14 The compile/link edit/execute sequence

sometimes used. With a well-written access method, the programmer is totally oblivious to the problems of blocking, deblocking, and buffering, writing his program as though he were working with simple, unblocked records. Some access methods allow the programmer to process data within the buffer rather than moving records into a work area; this is done by maintaining a pointer for the current record and using relative addressing, all invisible to the programmer.

If blocking and buffering are to be transparent to the programmer, how are the access method and buffers to be added to a program? This is frequently a function of the loader program discussed in an earlier paragraph. Look at the compilation process described in Fig. 5.14. The output of the compiler program is, as before, an object module; this object module is written to disk in preparation for the second step in this cycle. The loader program, sometimes known as a linkage editor, adds the access method software and space for buffers to the object module, creating a load module. As its last official act, the linkage editor causes the load module to be loaded and executed.

Spooling

The use of cards and printers cannot be totally eliminated from data processing. One technique for minimizing the impact of these slow devices is spooling. In a simple version of spooling, cards are read, off-line, directly to tape (Fig. 5.15).

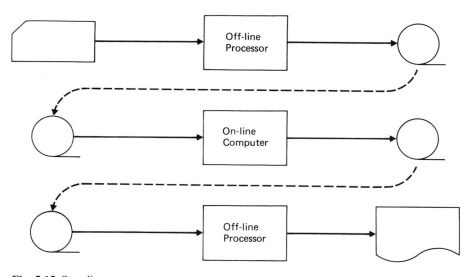

Fig. 5.15 Spooling

The tape is then mounted on an on-line drive, allowing the computer to get all its data from the higher speed device. Printer output, rather than going directly to the printer, is spooled to tape for later, off-line printing. Ideally, the programmer should not have to worry about the intermediate storage of his data—spooling should be transparent. Special software is needed to support spooling.

Checkpoint/Restart

Every programmer has heard horror stories in which the entire set of results from an expected three-hour run is destroyed because of a computer failure or a program or data error occurring two hours and fifty minutes into the run. Such errors are an obvious waste of computer time. The use of checkpoints and restarts can minimize the impact of these errors. In using this technique, the intermediate results of a program are dumped to tape or disk at regular intervals—perhaps every ten minutes to cite an example; sometimes, a copy of the entire program is included in this dump. Should an error occur, the program is simply restarted at the last checkpoint, a loss of at most ten minutes of processing in our example. The software for checkpoint/restart logic is usually stored on a library and might be added to the load module at link-edit time along with access methods and buffers.

Timers

Another problem most programmers have at least heard about is the endless loop, a set of code which simply repeats and repeats without end. An endless loop eats computer time to no good purpose. In the early days of the computer, the programmer was usually present when his program was run; if expected results were not forthcoming in what he knew to be a reasonable period of time, he could cancel the program.

 With the programmer not present, this responsibility fell to the operator, who could not be expected to possess an intimate knowledge of each programmer's product. The use of a timer is one solution. With timer control, the programmer is expected to estimate the total run time of his program, adding this estimate to the other parameters on his job card. If this time estimate is exceeded, the program is terminated.

Minimizing Run Time—a Summary

We have, to this point, discussed a number of techniques for minimizing the actual run time of a given program. Among the topics we've discussed are: libraries, loader programs and linkage editors, blocking and buffering, access methods, spooling, checkpoint/restart, and timer logic. All these techniques are implemented by software. This collection of software, along with compilers and assemblers, constitutes an early operating system.

Core Utilization—Overlay Structures

In the serial batch world of the second generation, a program used as much core as was available and that was it; attempts to minimize the utilization of core just didn't make sense. The real problem was getting *enough* core, not minimizing the amount used.

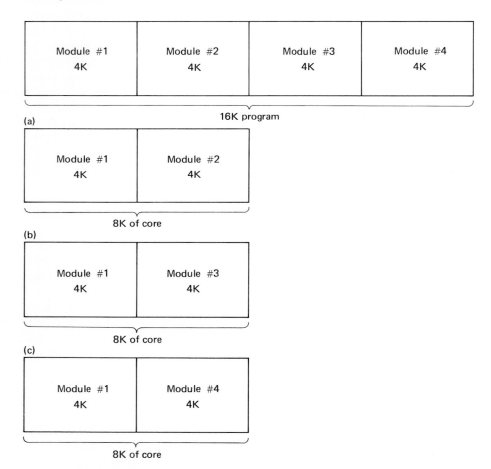

Fig. 5.16 Programming with overlays

A few outstanding programmers got around the problem of fitting a 16K program into an 8K machine by using overlays; the basic logic of overlay structures is illustrated in Fig. 5.16. The program is broken into a number of modules; let's assume four 4K modules for this example. One module, the main or control module, contains a number of work and data storage areas common to the entire program; frequently, the input and output routines are part of this section. The other three sections are pretty much self contained in that module number two is designed to access addresses and fields in modules one and two but not in three or four, while number three is restricted to itself and the control section (module one) and number four does not access anything in two or three. It takes an outstanding programmer to design and implement such a structure.

Once the structure is set up, it works something like this. The main module (number one) and module number two start in core—that's a total of 8K, filling the entire available storage space. The program progresses through the logic of these two modules until eventually module number two is no longer needed. At this point in time, module number three is read into core right over module number two (Fig. 5.16b), in effect, overlaying the transient module. Next, the final module replaces the third; later, the cycle may start over again. Note that the main control segment remains in core at all times.

This is an example of inventive programming and is not the kind of activity easily implemented with generalized software on a second-generation machine. The concept of overlays is introduced here mainly because it was the ancestor of modern paging and virtual storage software to be discussed in more detail in Chapter 15.

Data Management

Many of the techniques and file organizations discussed in Chapter 4 were developed during the computer's second generation. Among the new software for supporting these data management techniques were modules for creating and updating files, routines for maintaining indexes and labels, routines for checking labels, data and library protection programs, randomizing algorithms, and others.

Two macros, OPEN and CLOSE, allowed the programmer to bridge the gap between the old, "everybody is responsible for his own data" methods and newer data management. The OPEN macro is coded by the programmer just prior to the first input or output operation against a given file. The functions of this macro include issuing operator mount messages where appropriate, checking the label on an input file, writing a label to an output file, and in some cases filling a set of input buffers. The CLOSE macro is coded at the end of a job; it writes end-of-file markers and frees any temporary work space on direct-access devices. Through these macros, data management and protection features are implemented. Label checking insures that the proper file is being used. By routing all initial file access through logic not under the application programmer's control, a number of checks and tests can be performed to prevent the intentional or accidental destruction of data or a library.

Summary

During the computer's second generation, a number of software techniques were developed to improve the efficiency of a computer system. Most of these were intended to improve throughput, the amount of work passing through the computer in a given period of time. These software techniques composed an early operating system and remain an integral part of a modern operating system. Other problems and solutions discussed in this chapter—setup and scheduling, core-use minimization, and data management—made some use of software, but weren't the problems they were to become in a third-generation multiprogramming system, the subject of the next chapter.

Exercises

1. Define throughput.
2. Define turnaround. It's not defined in this chapter; find the definition in some other source. Compare turnaround to throughput.
3. Relate the use of a JOB card to scheduling. How does scheduling help to improve throughput?
4. What are some of the advantages arising from loading and executing load modules from a library rather than going through the compile/link-edit sequence starting with a source module?
5. What is an access method? What functions are performed by an access method?
6. How does multiple buffering work? How can a channel make multiple buffering even more valuable?
7. What is spooling?

CHAPTER 6

Multiprogramming and Time-Sharing

Overview

In the mid-1960s, computers incorporating Solid Logic Technique (SLT) circuits hit the market. Although a detailed discussion of the intricacies of SLT is beyond the scope of this book, the increased speed made possible by this technology was largely responsible for the development of modern operating systems. The old millisecond speeds of the second generation had been replaced by the microsecond (one million instructions per second) and even the nano-second; the old solutions—spooling, blocking, multiple buffering—were, by themselves, no longer able to guarantee anything approaching an economically acceptable level of machine utilization. Input and output continued to be as important as ever, but the time needed to complete an I/O operation had become interminable when compared with the almost incomprehensible pro-cessing speeds of these newer machines.

One solution was to place more than one program in core at a time, with the CPU turning its attention first to one, then to another, much as a chess master plays twenty-five or more concurrent chess matches. Multiprogramming and time-sharing, two techniques for achieving this objective, will be discussed in this chapter; essentially, these are software concepts, and the programs needed to support multiprogramming or time-sharing make up a significant part of what has come to be termed an operating system.

Throughout this chapter, two terms will be used in referring to the efficiency of a data processing system—throughput and turnaround time. Throughput, as before, is a measure of the amount of work passing through a computer. Turnaround time is a measure of the elapsed time between job submission and job completion. System objectives might be stated as: "maximize throughput

73

while maintaining a reasonable turnaround" or just "maximize throughput" or "minimize turnaround" or some other combination. It is important to note that these two objectives are often in conflict. In a supermarket, to cite an example, throughput of checkout clerks could be maximized by staffing only one checkout lane, forcing customers to wait in line in order to keep that clerk busy, while the turnaround of customers could be minimized by providing one clerk for each and every customer yielding zero (or almost) customer wait time. Obviously, neither solution is acceptable and some compromise is essential; the attitudes and objectives of management play an important part in determining the weight given to throughput and turnaround. The same need to weigh and balance these two objectives is faced in the area of operating system design, a topic we'll be alluding to throughout this chapter.

Input/Output vs. Processing Speed in the Third Generation

Consider the one-hundred-instruction program used to introduce the idea of wait time back in Chapter 5. The program in that example ran on a millisecond machine, and we found that by using high-speed I/O devices like tape and disk coupled with such essentially software techniques as blocking, multiple buffering, and spooling, extremely high levels of CPU utilization could be achieved. Let's take a technological leap and upgrade our computer to a microsecond machine capable of executing one-million (as opposed to one thousand) instructions per second. With the card reader and the printer as our input and output devices (Fig. 6.1) input still takes 0.1 seconds and output takes 0.05 seconds as before, but the time needed to execute one hundred instructions drops from 0.1 (100 times 1/1000) to 0.0001 (100 times 1/1,000,000). The total time for a complete program cycle drops to 0.1501 seconds of which, and this is the important part, only 0.0001 seconds, less than 0.07 percent of a cycle, belongs to the CPU. The computer, renting for perhaps one-hundred-thousand dollars per month, spends over 99.9% of its time waiting for I/O devices to finish transferring data! To put these figures in a slightly different perspective,

```
Read one card .........................................  0.1000 seconds
Execute 100 instructions .............................  0.0001 seconds
Print one line  ........................................  0.0500 seconds
   Total cycle  ........................................  0.1501 seconds
```

$$\text{Percent "run" time} = \frac{0.0001}{0.1501} = 0.00066 = 0.066\%$$

Fig. 6.1 Computer utilization on a microsecond machine

the computer, if actually used in this manner, would be performing useful work for about one minute of each twenty-four hour day. Total cycle time on the old millisecond machine was, if you remember, some 0.2500 seconds; this has been cut to 0.1501 seconds—not quite in half—on the faster machine. But the microsecond machine is one-thousand times as fast as its predecessor. And probably ten times as expensive. Why bother with the faster machine?

Faster I/O devices provided an answer before; let's consider them again. A processing time of 0.0001 seconds between a tape read of 0.001 seconds and a 0.002-second tape write (Fig. 6.2) yields a total cycle time of 0.0031 seconds of which only 0.0001, or 3.2%, is utilized by the CPU. A scientist or engineer working on a complicated mathematical problem like a moon shot might be willing to pay for the pure speed of a third-generation machine, but the businessman, given an expectation of only four or five percent utilization and, at best, a marginal cost justification over the older, slower computers, would probably not buy. Why, to use an analogy, should we invest in two-hundred-mile-per-hour trains when track conditions restrict us to fifteen or twenty miles per hour in many places? Speed is great, but only if we can utilize it.

Read one card image	0.0010 seconds
Execute 100 instructions	0.0001 seconds
Write one record	0.0020 seconds
Total cycle	0.0031 seconds

$$\text{Percent "run" time} = \frac{0.0001}{0.0031} = 0.032 = 3.2\%$$

Fig. 6.2 Utilization using tape

Multiprogramming—One Solution

Let's, just for a moment, drop computers and imagine ourselves running a telephone-answering service. We have one subscriber and, based on past experience, expect only three or four calls each night. Our job, in other words, consists of occasional periods of brief work followed by lengthy waits. What do we do with all our spare time? We might read or write or work puzzles. If we were really industrious, we might take on a few more clients, figuring that calls for another would not interfere with our ability to handle those of our first customer. There is, of course, a limit to the number of new clients we can take on. At some point, our phone would become so busy as to discourage potential callers from trying, thus defeating the purpose of our service—but the idea of working on some other task during slack periods is a good one.

Chess provides another example of this type of approach. We've all read about some chess master playing twenty or twenty-five opponents concurrently; how does he do it? The answer is really quite simple—he concentrates on one game at a time. Starting with his first opponent, the expert surveys the board, decides upon his move, and makes it. He then continues on to the next game board to repeat the process, completely forgetting, until the next time around, the move he has just made. His skill is one of speed; he has the ability to look at a chess board, quickly identify the situation, make and implement a decision, and move on. The fact that the average chess player needs some time to consider his next move merely adds to the interest generated by these multiple opponent matches.

Back to computers again. The problem of a relatively brief run time followed by an extensive wait for completion of an I/O operation is illustrated in Fig. 6.3. Why not use this wait time, when the central-processing unit is doing nothing anyway, for some other purpose? Why not put another program into core? Then, when program "A" starts an I/O operation and enters a wait state, control of the CPU can be turned over to program "B" (Fig. 6.4). This same logic might be applied to three programs (Fig. 6.5) or four or even more. This basic concept of loading a number of programs into core and allowing them to share the CPU is known as multiprogramming. One important note of caution—the programs do not execute "simultaneously"; they execute in an overlapped fashion, with the CPU (much like the chess expert) concentrating on only one at a time. The word usually used to describe this type of program execution is *concurrent*. The distinction between concurrent and simultaneous is subtle, with the former term implying "over the same time period" while the latter means "at the same time." Multiprogramming means the concurrent execution of more than one program on a single computer. All the programs are in memory at the same time (simultaneous core residency), but they share the facilities of the central processing unit in an overlapped manner.

The benefits arising from multiprogramming should be obvious. Quite simply, time spent waiting for completion of an input or output operation is applied to the solution of some other problem rather then wasted; using multiprogramming techniques, it is theoretically possible to complete four or five or more programs in the same amount of elapsed time that would have been needed to complete just one program in the serial-batch mode. Some program interference is inevitable, so this theoretical limit is rarely achieved, but multiprogramming does lead to a significant increase in the amount of work going through a computer (throughput). The economic implications of getting five or six times the work done in the same amount of time were not lost on the business community. Multiprogramming was instrumental in selling modern high-speed computers to business.

Fig. 6.3 The wait time/run time cycle

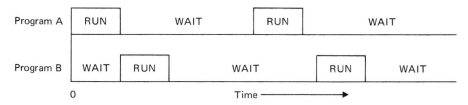

Fig. 6.4 Multiprogramming with two programs

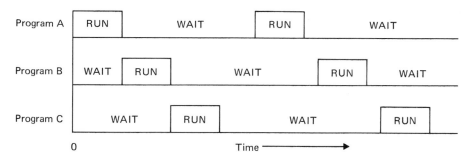

Fig. 6.5 Multiprogramming with three programs

Time-Sharing

In addition to its highly positive impact on system throughput, multiprogramming does tend to improve turnaround time as well. If more programs are completed during the same time interval, "my program" will probably come back sooner. There is, however, one problem, at least from a turnaround-time point of view, that multiprogramming does not deal with—the compute-bound job. From the standpoint of throughput, compute-bound jobs are great; they simply sit in core and use the CPU without interruption, adding to the percent utilization statistic. Meanwhile, other jobs wait. As long as throughput is accepted as *the* measure of system effectiveness, this causes no problem, but this is not always the case. In some applications, turnaround predominates, and a slightly different approach is needed.

An interactive time-sharing system with fifty or more users attempting to solve problems and write programs through terminals is an example of such an application. Typically, the time-sharing user makes rather light demands on the resources of a computer, rarely processing large amounts of data or executing lengthy programs; the only thing that makes time-sharing economically feasible is the fact that computer resources can be shared among many such users. Occasionally, a long-running, compute-bound job will sneak into a time-shared system (a regression analysis, for example) forcing the forty-nine or more other users to wait; a well-run time-shared system must be able to deal with this problem.

With multiple users in core, time-sharing is, as you might expect, quite similar to multiprogramming in its basic mode of operation, but there is one major difference (designed to handle the "long job" problem). A multiprogramming system is driven in a rather passive manner by the input and output timings of the individual programs on the system; the decision to release the CPU to another program is made at the whim of the individual programmer. In time-sharing, a program is given a time limit—say one tenth or one one-hundredth of a second. If, during this interval of time, the program encounters a natural break point (I/O), fine; if, however, no such break occurs, the program is interrupted and placed at the end of the line to wait for another shot at the CPU. Time-sharing is an active technique in that the basic driving mechanism is under control of the system itself and not the individual users of the system.

Software for Multiprogramming and Time-Sharing

The presence of multiple programs in core creates a number of problems which are normally handled by software. In the next several pages, we'll take a look at some of these problems and discuss, in general terms, the software solutions which might be applied. To provide a framework for this discussion, let's break the computer system into the following five parts:

1. CPU time,
2. main memory space,
3. registers,
4. I/O devices,
5. data files and libraries.

Multiprogramming and time-sharing create problems in all these areas; an effective operating system must be concerned with optimizing the use of all of them.

One further point before we continue. There are few pure turnaround or pure throughput systems in existence; most often, some form of compromise between these two objectives is sought. We'll be touching on this point throughout much of the rest of this chapter.

Allocating CPU Time

What happens when two programs complete an I/O operation at precisely the same instant in time? Both are ready to resume processing (Fig. 6.6) but the CPU is capable of working on only one at a time. Who goes first? The first program in core? The last one? The biggest one? The smallest one? The one that has been in core the longest? To quote a well-known "law" of data processing and engineering, "if it can happen, it will." Thus any functioning multi-programming system must be capable of handling this situation.

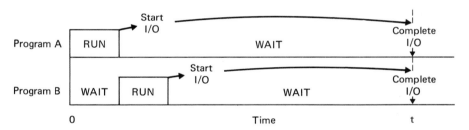

Fig. 6.6 Program Interference—both programs are ready to resume at the same instant

One solution might be to print a message on the operator's console describing the situation and asking for a decision. This might take, at best, a few seconds. During these few seconds, a microsecond computer is capable of, in all likelihood, taking *both* programs to their next I/O point. Human reaction times are much too slow.

The usual approach is to write a program to make this decision. Almost any decision rule (last in, first out; first in, first out; biggest first; and so on) can be and probably has been, built into this program. There are good rules and there are bad rules, but the important point is that the decision is made by a program written especially for this purpose.

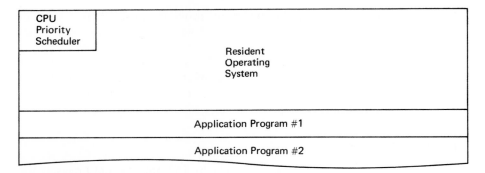

Fig. 6.7 Core layout for multiprogramming, with an operating system

This small program is one part of an operating system. Often, this software is made core resident, with a section of core being set aside to hold the operating system or supervisor programs. Figure 6.7 shows a sketch of the layout of core storage in a typical multiprogramming system; space for an on-line or resident operating system has been set aside in low core, and the possible location of the CPU allocation program described above is shown. Whenever conflicts occur, this program is called and executed, resulting in a decision at computer speeds.

Some form of priority scheme is often used in making this decision. A job's priority might be indicated on the job card and, once in core, the job with the top priority goes first whenever conflicts occur. Almost any conceivable priority rule can be implemented in this operating system module, with the only restriction being programmability. There are, of course, some practical limits—why spend ten seconds determining which three second program should go first? The important point to remember is that the decision is made by a program, a program written using the same instruction set available to any assembly language application programmer.

Time-sharing uses a timer to force a sort of pseudo-I/O operation on a lengthy program, thus forcing the program to surrender the CPU to some other user. Most modern computers have a built-in hardware timer which can be set by an operating system program. Much like an alarm clock, if time runs out on an application program the timer sends a signal, called an interrupt, to the CPU. Since most CPU's cannot act independently, a program must be provided to handle the timer interrupt. This program is another operating-system module (Fig. 6.8).

The timer, in addition to its use in time-sharing, plays an important role in minimizing the impact of the "infinite loop." Consider the following trivial

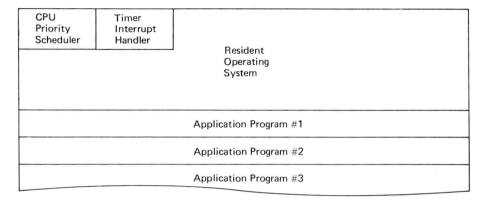

Fig. 6.8 The timer interrupt handler as an operating system module

case in FORTRAN:

```
5      GO TO 5
```

The result of coding this instruction should be obvious (so obvious that very few programmers actually make this particular error); statement number five executes over and over and over again, without end. Unless, of course, the program is given a time limit after which the program is interrupted and cancelled.

Priorities and the timer can be used to improve either throughput or turnaround or, in some cases, both. The exact nature of the operating system modules used to control CPU time allocation will depend on the weight given each of these measures by a particular installation.

Core Allocation

Most programmers are at least familiar with the accidental destruction of data where, often due to a program bug, a constant is destroyed or a counter reset to zero. Program overlay structures, as described in the last chapter, are a good example of the intentional destruction of portions of a program. Very early in his training, the programmer learns that the computer can "forget" just as efficiently as it "remembers."

This is a serious problem on a multiprogramming system. Imagine the effect on your program if some "mad mover" were to sort your instructions into alphabetical order while you were waiting for the completion of an input or output operation. The accidental or intentional destruction of data *within* a program is one thing; the potential for unpredictable *inter*-program effects is something else. If core is to contain more than one program, these programs must be protected from each other. Core protection is another operating system function. No human operator could possibly react rapidly enough to prevent the destruction of one program by another. Core protection must be implemented at computer speeds; thus the core-protect module is an extremely important resident operating system module.

Core Allocation—Job Scheduling

Simply getting programs into core is a problem on a multiprogramming system. On the serial-batch systems described in Chapter 5, this was an operator function; job classes and, perhaps, priorities helped, but the task of scheduling jobs for initial core introduction was essentially a manual process. Is it reasonable, however, to expect a human operator to keep track of ten or fifteen different core-program locations? Could a human being be expected to watch the changing status of all these programs and, at exactly the right moment, introduce a new program into the proper position in core? A really sharp operator might be able to keep track of such a complex problem, but certainly not at microsecond speeds. On most large multiprogramming systems, the scheduling problem is handled by operating system software.

One commonly used technique involves job queueing. Each job is assigned to a job class. Class "A" might be restricted to ten-second jobs using the card reader and printer only; Class "B" might be for jobs needing up to thirty seconds of CPU time and up to two tape drives, and so on. The class of each job is indicated on the job card. The jobs are read by an operating system module and spooled to one of a number of job queues; class "A" jobs go to the "A" queue, "B" jobs to the "B" queue, and so on (Fig. 6.9). In this way, similar jobs can be grouped together.

Later, these jobs can be retrieved from the on-line device (often disk) to which they were spooled and loaded into core for execution by a job-initiation operating system module. Since similar jobs are grouped together, this job initiator program can be designed to load programs in a sequence which maximizes system efficiency. Often, one part of the computer's memory is set aside to hold the simple card-reader/printer jobs which, since input card data was read along with the job deck and is thus also on-line, require little or no additional operator intervention. Tape jobs can be run in parallel in another section of core (Fig. 6.10). Once a job completes, another module, a job terminator, clears all references to the job and returns control to the job initiator which repeats the cycle. All this happens, of course, at computer speeds.

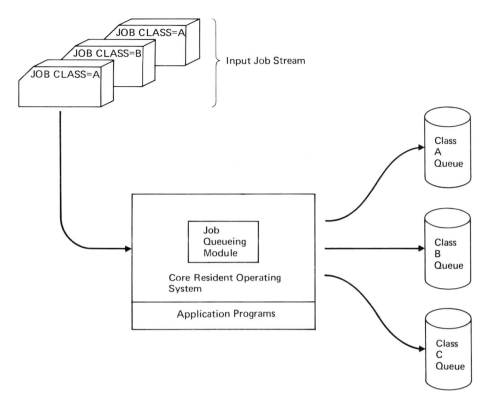

Fig. 6.9 Building job queues

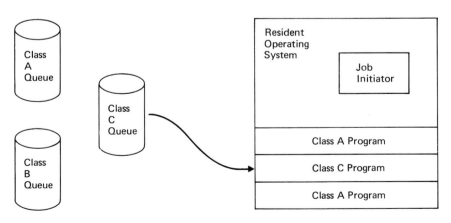

Fig. 6.10 Job initiation

We have already discussed the problems associated with the scheduling of the use of the CPU among jobs already in core; in this section, our discussion centers on the problem of getting those programs into memory in the first place. The problems are not unrelated; a good job initialization routine can minimize the problems of internal scheduling.

Scheduling on a time-shared system is just a bit more complex. Often, a large number of users are attempting to communicate with the computer via (often remote) terminals. The sheer number of programs creates a serious problem—core is a limited resource. The problem is often solved by some form of roll-in/roll-out procedure. In its simplest form, once a program completes a burst of activity, it is copied to disk, making room in core for another program. When the program in question is about ready for another crack at the CPU, it is copied back into core. Human reaction speeds of a few seconds or more make all this input and output activity pretty much transparent to the user. See Fig. 6.11 for an example.

Roll-in/roll-out logic is not restricted to time-sharing applications, being a long-time tool of the professional programmer. The basic concept has evolved into the virtual memory systems described in a later chapter.

Job scheduling has a rather obvious impact on system efficiency. Certain job classes might be taken first, improving the turnaround of programs in these classes. Alternatively, jobs might be scheduled so as to increase throughput at the expense of turnaround—longest running jobs first. Software to queue and initiate jobs must be carefully balanced so as to maximize whatever a given computer installation considers to be its measure or measures of efficiency.

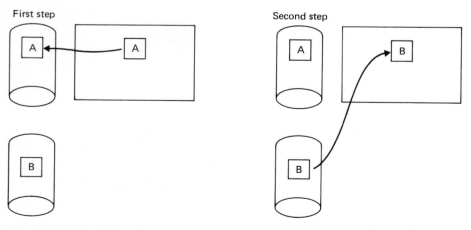

Fig. 6.11 Roll-in/roll-out logic

Registers

Contrary to popular belief, the registers used by a programmer are not his exclusive property; every program must make use of the same set. Since register contents can change as a program executes, this can cause a problem.

Register conventions provide at least a partial answer. Just before a program is placed in a wait state, the contents of all the registers are copied into a save area in core storage. When the program is ready to resume the registers are reloaded from this save area. Assembly language programmers are familiar with register conventions, at least in the form of a macro. Compiler language programmers don't see the conventions, but they are still present. The functions of saving and restoring registers are a part of many operating system modules; to avoid excessive duplication of this code, register conventions are often included in the resident operating system in the form of a common subprogram.

I/O Device Allocation

Consider the outcome of two different programs attempting to use the same tape drive, one for input and one for output. Chaos! What happens when a program needs a tape or disk drive which, for some reason, is not available? The program sits in core until the device is free, wasting resources. These are but two of the many problems multiprogramming creates in the area of I/O device allocation. In a serial-batch system, each program has control of the CPU and *all* the I/O devices while running; in multiprogramming, these devices must be shared with a number of other programs. It is possible for several different programs to seek or write data on the same direct access device, but tape, cards, the printer, and many other devices do not share this flexibility. Some form of I/O control is essential.

The first control involves program loading. Put simply, if all the I/O devices needed to support a given program are not available, why bother to load and initiate the program? Load some other program and try again at a later time. To achieve this objective, a table of all the I/O devices available on the system is normally maintained somewhere in the region of core assigned to the operating system. Before a program is loaded, its I/O device requirements are checked against this table, and any reserved units are noted. When other programs are being similarly prepared for loading at some later time, the fact that all must go through this same table minimizes the danger of multiple programs trying to access the same device or of a program sitting in core because a device is not available. Programs which might suffer these problems are simply kept out of core until the desired device is free. This checking is normally a part of the program-initialization module described above. The actual details of implementation vary from operating system to operating system, but the idea of checking a table for device availability is pretty common.

If I/O device requirements are to be checked by a program, they must be communicated to the system in machine readable form; the old second generation run book just won't do. IBM uses special control cards to achieve this objective. We've already discussed the function of two control cards:

```
//    JOB    CLASS=A
```

and

```
//    EXEC    COBOL
```

which, respectively, separate jobs and identify the program to be executed. The third type of control card is a data definition card; the programmer is required to include one for each data set accessed by a program. A typical DD card, such as:

```
//TAPE    DD    UNIT=2400,...
```

describes, using a series of parameters, the details of a particular (in this case, tape) data set. We'll discuss IBM's Job Control Language in some detail in Part III.

Once a program is in core, we know that all requested I/O devices are available and that all expected input and output operations are, thus, possible. But that's not the end of our problems. How do we prevent the accidental or intentional destruction of existing data? How do we avoid the interference resulting from two or more programs attempting to, legitimately, access the same disk pack? A common solution is to force all input and output operations to go through the resident operating system. The instructions which actually perform input and output are made privileged; i.e., they can be executed *only* by an operating system module. Application programs cannot communicate directly with an I/O device but, after setting up a number of control fields, must transfer control to the operating system to get things started. In this way, all input and output is forced to pass through the same module, where extensive checks and controls are implemented.

I/O Device Allocation—Spooling

Off-line spooling was, as you may recall, a second-generation concept. In the third generation, spooling becomes an on-line operation. The job queueing function described above is essentially a form of spooling, moving card data from a card reader to some faster, on-line device. Program data in card form is, of course, included in the card-deck image and can be read, when needed, directly from the on-line device. Many systems include output spooling as well as input spooling, with printer output going first to disk or tape and later to paper.

On-line spooling takes advantage of the high speeds of a modern computer; essentially, it represents one more level of multiprogramming. When all the programs on a system are in a wait state, a common occurrence even with ten or fifteen programs on a fast computer, the input and output spooling routines take over, starting the operations of physically reading a card and printing a line. These slow operations take place when the system has nothing else to do anyway.

I/O Devices and Time-Sharing

Keeping track of input and output on a time-shared system is even more complex, with perhaps one-hundred or more different terminals capable of being connected to the system. One solution to this device proliferation problem is to essentially ignore it by viewing the I/O operation as though it involves a control unit and nothing more. Consider, for example, the system pictured in Fig. 6.12. Here, the control unit is divided into four distinct regions called ports. Port number 1 might have any one of a hundred or more terminals connected to it via telephone line, but, as far as the computer and its operating system are concerned, communications are with port number 1 only. The logistics of the physical connection are left to the control unit—hardware.

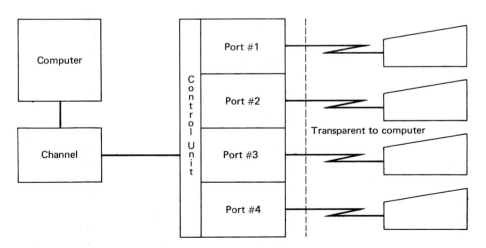

Fig. 6.12 Time-sharing control units

Control of Data Resources

Second-generation data management has been largely carried over into the third generation with a few important improvements and modifications. The old file organization techniques, access methods, label creation and label checking routines, libraries, compilers, and macros are still around. One major advancement is the use of on-line spooling as described above. The major advances of the third generation took place within the computer itself; thus, it is not surprising to find fewer major breakthroughs in the area of data management.

Largely because of the multiple program nature of a modern system, the OPEN and CLOSE macros are more complex than they were in the second generation. In addition to checking labels and issuing mount messages, the OPEN macro is the ideal spot for building the tables needed to support an input or output operation. The CLOSE macro destroys these pointers as soon as the program is finished with them; in this way, a device is tied up only when the program is actually using it. Since these two macros are almost certain to be used by every program in core, they are frequently made a part of the resident operating system (Fig. 6.13), with the individual programs simply linking with these modules.

Libraries

A library is a very special form of file. Third-generation systems normally support the same types of libraries we discussed in the last chapter—one for compilers and utility programs, another for user programs, and a third for macros. A few additional types of libraries are needed to support some of the special requirements of the third generation and multiprogramming. One is a supervisor library, containing operating system modules whose use does not justify core residency. Another stores job control statements for certain common applications; one member of this library might, for example, contain all the JCL statements needed to compile a COBOL program.

A library differs from other data. The old concepts of fields, records, and files are not really relevant; the basic unit on a library is a complete program or a complete macro. The term *data set* has been coined to refer to any logical collection of data—either a standard data file or a library; it's more inclusive than the term "file."

Library members are often stored using something called a *partitioned* organization. Visualize, for a moment, a library of object modules on cards. Each program deck is carefully marked and placed on a table (Fig. 6.14). To run a given program, the operator need only select the proper deck and feed it into a card reader. In a partitioned data set, these object or load modules

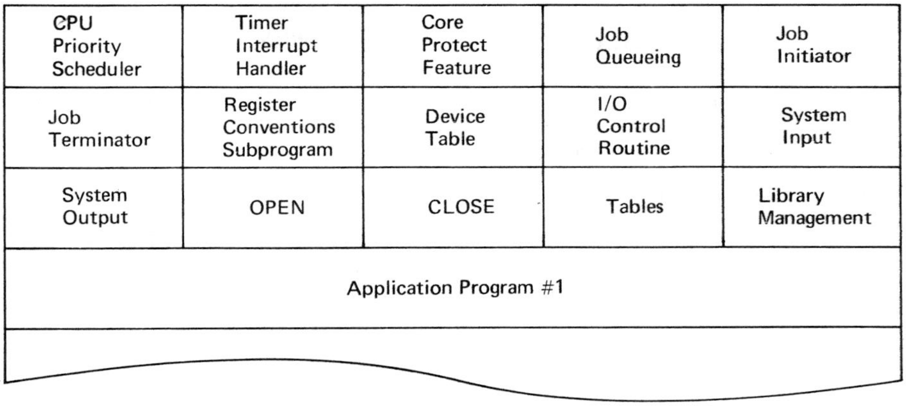

CPU Priority Scheduler
Timer Interrupt Handler
Core Protect Feature
Job Queueing
Job Initiator
Job Terminator
Register Conventions Subprogram
Device Table
I/O Control Routine
System Input
System Output
OPEN
CLOSE
Tables
Library Management
Application Program #1

Fig. 6.13 The resident operating system

Load Module A
Load Module B
Load Module C
Load Module D
Equivalent
Pgm. A
Pgm. B
Pgm. C
Pgm. D
Partitioned Data Set

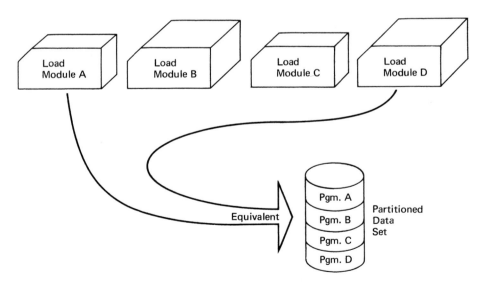

Fig. 6.14 A partitioned data set

are copied to disk, with the start and end address of each member noted in an index. To load a program, the start address is found in the index and the member simply copied into core.

Library management is an operating system function. The programs to support this function are often a part of the resident operating system.

The Operating System

An operating system is a collection of programs. The purpose of these programs is to improve the efficiency of the data processing system. Individual programs are designed to improve the utilization of each of the major system resources—CPU time, core space, registers, input and output devices, and data. Ideally, because of their heavy use, operating system modules are tight, well-written routines. They must be reentrant—capable of supporting a number of concurrent executions—and reusable. Often, they must be recursive—able to be entered over and over again. But they are still programs. With the exception of a few privileged instructions, the instruction set is the same as that used by any assembly language programmer.

Not all operating system modules are core resident. Many computer installations use a disk operating system, with individual routines being moved from disk to core on an as-required basis. This saves core but takes time—even high-speed direct access I/O is slow when compared to internal processing speeds. Disk operating systems are normally used on smaller, slower computers, where core space is at a premium and the disparity between I/O and processing speeds is at a minimum.

At the other extreme is an all-resident operating system. In terms of processing speed this is an optimum configuration, but all those operating system

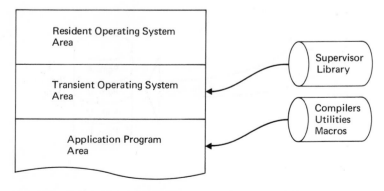

Fig. 6.15 An operating system in core and disk resident parts

modules take up space that might better be used for application programs. Most systems compromise, with the more heavily used modules being core resident while other less critical routines are stored on a direct-access library and read into core as required (Fig. 6.15). Often, one library holds the actual operating system routines while such programmer aids as compilers, utilities, and macros are maintained on another system library.

The programs of an operating system are pure overhead; their purpose is to improve the efficiency of the system but, by themselves, they perform no useful work. Like any program, an operating system module consumes processing time. They take up space. But without the resource management provided by these routines, modern high-speed computers would represent a marginal economic investment.

Summary

In this chapter, we covered the development of software to support multiprogramming and time-sharing. Multiprogramming, the concurrent processing of a number of programs, evolved in response to the extreme disparity between input/output and processing times; essentially, it allows the system to switch its attention to another job during the relatively lengthy input and output wait times. The existence of multiple programs in core creates a number of problems in the allocation and control of central processor time, core space, register utilization, input and output device allocation, and data management. The operating system is a collection of programs designed to deal with these problems.

Exercises

1. Why was something like multiprogramming so necessary when third-generation computers hit the market?
2. In the text, we stated that multiprogramming is essentially passive while the time slicing of a time-shared system exerts more positive control over system operation. Explain.
3. Why is CPU allocation so crucial on a multiprogrammed system? Why can't the operator allocate CPU time?
4. Why is core allocation so crucial on a multiprogrammed system?
5. Why is I/O device allocation so crucial on a multiprogrammed system?
6. Differentiate between a program's internal (within the computer) and external priority.
7. Why is core protection needed on a multiprogrammed system?
8. Explain how job queueing works.

PART III

Job Control Language for the IBM System/360 and System/370

CHAPTER 7

Job Control Under IBM's Disk Operating System

Overview

Back in the computer's second generation, detailed instructions for running a job were communicated to the system operator via the programmer's run book; on a modern multiprogrammed system, many of the functions previously performed by a human operator are handled by operating system modules—programs—instead. Old Bob, the third-shift operator, may have been able to figure out the meaning of "MONT TAP NMBR AB1253," but most programs are not quite so flexible or forgiving. The old handwritten or typed run book is no longer adequate; modern programmer/system communications must be carefully structured.

IBM has developed what is, for all practical purposes, a new language—Job Control Language—to achieve this objective; in the next three chapters, we'll take a look at some of the features of this language. In this chapter we'll be concentrating on job control for IBM's Disk Operating System (DOS). Chapters 8 and 9 will cover the considerably more complex job control language developed in support of Operating System/360 and System/370. It is *not* our objective to cover these job control languages fully or in depth. (Entire books have been written on just that subject.) Rather, we will concentrate on a number of the more commonly used features of job control, those features encountered by the typical programmer as part of his everyday work. All too often, the programmer's first introduction to job control is a confusing "snow job" with statements, parameters, subparameters, and other fields swimming together like an op-art creation. Hopefully, by skipping many of the rarely used features of job control, this problem will be avoided and a sense of the true purpose of these special languages will come through.

95

IBM's Disk Operating System (DOS) is a good example of an operating system written to support application programs on small and medium scale computer systems. DOS supports multiprogramming, with recent releases supporting up to six concurrent programs, including the resident operating system, in core. The Job Control Language for DOS is straightforward and fairly easy to follow; thus, it provides a good starting point for our study of structured programmer/system communication.

A few points must be made before we begin our discussion of job control. First, even though they are called languages, no programs are actually written in pure job control language; job control serves in a support role, describing the real programs to be executed and the input and output devices to be used in the processing of a job. Second, a language designed for such a support function must be literally all things to all people; thus, every possible technique for using an I/O device must be supported, even those more esoteric techniques of interest only to a few professional system programmers. Much of the confusion surrounding job control arises from an attempt to teach every programmer all possible language parameters, even the little known or rarely used ones. Normal, everyday job control is not difficult to understand. It's exacting and it can be frustrating, but it is *not* difficult.

The DOS JOB Card

Two key functions performed by job control are job separation and job identification; under DOS, these functions are performed by the JOB card. The general form of the DOS JOB card is as follows:

```
//    JOB    jobname    accounting-information
```

The two slashes (//) identify this as a control card; they *must* appear in columns 1 and 2. One or more blanks separate the slashes from the key word "JOB," which identifies this as a job card. The "jobname" consists of from one to eight alphanumeric characters chosen by the programmer to identify the job. Accounting information is optional; if a given installation chooses to require this field, the accounting information is separated from the job name by one or more blanks.

Note the use of blanks on the JOB card; blanks are used to separate fields. For this reason, blanks may not be embedded in the middle of a job name.

Any combination of from 1 to 8 alphanumeric characters makes up a valid job name; thus,

```
//    JOB    DAVIS
```

is a perfectly good JOB card. If a programmer wishes to identify individual programs with different names, he might code:

    //   JOB   DAVIS1

for his first job, and:

    //   JOB   DAVIS2

for his second.

A few seconds in almost any telephone book should convince anyone that such a technique for selecting job names can lead to an occasional problem of duplicate job names. To avoid this problem, most firms have developed a standard procedure for naming jobs. In some cases, a job might be assigned a prefix identifying a particular department followed by a sequence number;

    //   JOB   PC0015

might, for example, identify the fifteenth job written for the production-control department. Other job names might identify the function of a program, with

    //   JOB   PAYROLL

identifying one of the more popular programs run in any installation.

The JOB card *must be* the first card in a program deck. It marks the start of a new job.

The DOS EXEC Card

An EXEC or execute card identifies the particular program which is to be loaded into the computer and run or executed. The general form of this card is:

    //   EXEC   program–name

Once again, the two slashes (//) must be punched in columns 1 and 2. One or more blanks serve to separate the slashes from the key word "EXEC" which identifies this as an execute card. One or more additional blanks are needed to separate "EXEC" from the program name; the program name serves to identify a specific module stored in a library. It should be noted that the program name bears absolutely no relationship to the job name; the program name, like the job name, consists of from one to eight alphanumeric characters, but here the similarity ends. A job name serves to identify "this" particular job being run on the computer "right now"; when the job ends, the job name ceases to exist, as far as the computer system is concerned, until the job is rerun. A *program* name, on the other hand, serves to identify a particular program on a system library; when the "current" job terminates, the program still exists on the library ready, perhaps, to be used by another job. The job name, to cite another important difference, might identify a job consisting of several separate programs, *each* having a program name.

Consider, for example, the typical data processing job illustrated in Fig. 7.1. In the first "job step," labor cards are read into an edit program which eliminates

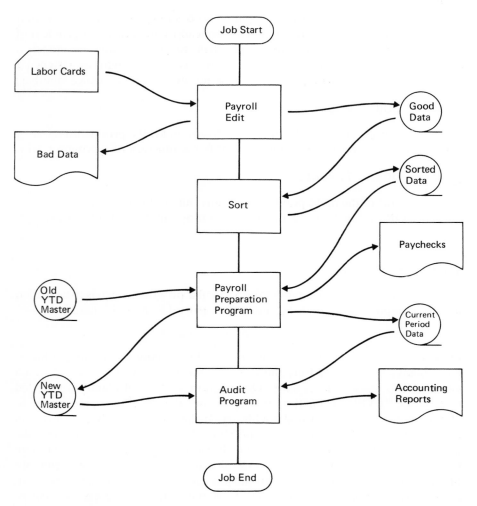

Fig. 7.1 A typical four-step unit

certain keypunching errors. The "good" data is then sorted by a second program or "job step." Sorted data is next read, along with a master year-to-date-
earnings file, into a payroll-preparation program. The final job step (note that
the words "job step" are no longer in quotes, a job step is nothing more than a
single program run as part of a job) is an audit program which prepares reports
for the accounting department.

The job control statements for this job might be as follows:

```
//    JOB    PAYROLL

//    EXEC    PAYEDIT

//    EXEC    SORT

//    EXEC    PAYROLL

//    EXEC    PAYAUDIT

/&
```

Each individual program in this job (in other words, each job step) requires an
EXEC card; each of the four named programs exist, in load module form, on
a system library. When the DOS loader program hits the

```
//    EXEC    PAYEDIT
```

statement, it loads a copy of the program with this name into core and turns
control of the CPU over to the first instruction in the program.

You may have noticed that the job name is PAYROLL and the name of
the third program is also PAYROLL. There is nothing wrong with this, it's
perfectly legal. But it's pure coincidence, the job name and a program name
within that job bear no relationship to each other unless the programmer
chooses to use consistent names. The operating system doesn't care; we could
have called this job "MELVIN" as in

```
//    JOB    MELVIN
```

and still have used the same programs.

Compiling and Link-Editing

Most programmers are interested in getting their programs onto a library and
not simply in using programs already there. The first step in this process is
usually compilation. A compiler is a program written to convert input data in

the form of programmer source statements into an object module. Like any other program, compilers are stored on a library and loaded into core by the operating system when an EXEC card names the compiler. To compile a COBOL program, a programmer might code:

```
//    JOB    TEST1

//    EXEC   COBOL
```

> source deck

```
/*

/&
```

Incidentally, this is the second time we've seen a "/&" card. This card marks the end of a job.

The job shown above will produce a listing, compiler error messages, and an object deck, and that's all. Once a clean assembly or compilation is obtained, the programmer will almost certainly want to test his program; in order to do this, a new job control card, the OPTION card, must be used. The general form of this card is as follows:

```
//    OPTION    option1,option2,option3,...
```

To cite one easy-to-understand OPTION, a programmer might wish, during his first few compilations, to bypass the punching of an object module (no sense punching an object module when a program still has compiler errors). He can do this by coding:

```
//    OPTION    NODECK

//    EXEC    ASSEMBLY
```

There are many options available to the DOS programmer—we won't attempt to cover all of them. The option we are primarily interested in is the "LINK" option:

```
//    OPTION    LINK

//    EXEC    FORTRAN
```

The LINK option causes the object module to be written to a file where it can be accessed by the LINKAGE-EDITOR program and converted to a load module.

The following set of job control statements allows a program to be compiled (COBOL is shown, but it could have been any compiler), link-edited, and run:

```
//    JOB    DAVIS1

//    OPTION    LINK

//    EXEC    COBOL
    ⎫
    ⎬ source deck
    ⎭
/*

//    EXEC    LNKEDT

//    EXEC
    ⎫
    ⎬ data cards
    ⎭
/*

/&
```

The last EXEC card doesn't name a specific program; when the program name field is blank, the system assumes that the load module just created by the linkage-editor is to be loaded and executed.

Another new card, the "/*" card, appears in the above example. This is an end-of-data marker; it follows the last card in the source deck and the last data card (if any) and tells the processing program that the last card has been encountered. Some programmers use "/*" cards to separate job steps.

Cataloging Programs

Under IBM's Disk Operating System, load modules cataloged on the "core image" library are called phases. In order to catalog a new program to this library, the programmer must give the linkage editor a name for the program; under DOS, it's called a phase name and is provided through a PHASE control statement. To assemble a program and have the resulting object module link-edited into a load module which is then cataloged to the core image library, the programmer codes:

```
//    JOB    PGM14
//    OPTION    CATAL
      PHASE    MYPGM,*
//    EXEC    ASSEMBLY
      ⎫
      ⎬ source deck
      ⎭
/*
//    EXEC    LNKEDT
//    EXEC
      ⎫
      ⎬ data cards
      ⎭
/*
/&
```

If, at a later time, the programmer wishes to use this program again, all he need code is:

```
//    JOB    WHATEVER
//    EXEC    MYPGM
      ⎫
      ⎬ data cards
      ⎭
/*
/&
```

The program has been cataloged to the core image library in load module (i.e., executable) form. This library is called the "core image" library because individual load modules or phases are stored in executable form; i.e., all one must do to execute a phase is copy it into core.

The second operand in the PHASE statement shown above is an asterisk (*). This operand indicates the address within the DOS core partition where the phase is to be loaded for execution; the asterisk indicates that the phase is to be loaded at the first available location in the partition. This load address can be specified in a number of different ways which will not be discussed here. Note that column 1 of the PHASE card is blank. This isn't a standard job control card, it's for the benefit of the linkage-editor.

Programmers often find it necessary to include subprograms, standard headers, and other modules written by other programmers as part of their own program. Under DOS, this can be done by using an INCLUDE statement. These subroutines are stored on a "relocatable library" in object module form and can be added to a cataloged phase or load module by the linkage-editor by coding statements such as:

```
//    JOB    NAME

//    OPTION    CATAL

      PHASE    PGMA,*

//    EXEC    ASSEMBLY

      ⎱source deck
      ⎰

/*

         INCLUDE    SUBR1

         INCLUDE    SUBR2

//    EXEC    LNKEDT

//    EXEC

      ⎱data cards
      ⎰

/*

/&
```

The cataloged phase will include the main program and the two indicated subroutines. The INCLUDE is another linkage editor card; thus, column 1 (at least) is blank.

DOS I/O Control

Under DOS, every physical I/O device attached to a system is given a fixed symbolic name. Programmers read their input cards through SYSIPT, send lines to be printed to SYSLST, handle tapes through (perhaps) SYS006, and so on. The exact meaning of a particular symbolic name may vary from installation to installation, but within a particular computer center, symbolic names have a consistent meaning. Unless a programmer wishes to change the meaning of a symbolic name from the standard to some other physical device, no job control is needed.

The key element in DOS I/O control, as far as the programmer is concerned, is the DTF or Define The File macro; the programmer is required to code a DTF (Define The File) for each file accessed by his program (often, the actual DTF's are stored in a relocatable library and added to a load module through the use of INCLUDE statements as described above, but the programmer still has one DTF for each file). The function of the DTF is to define key parameters of a given file and to indicate the access method needed to process the file. Each general type of I/O has its own DTF. The DTFCD defines parameters for a card file; the DTFPR defines a print file; the DTFMT defines a magnetic tape file; the DTFSD defines a sequential disk or other sequential direct access file; the DTFDA defines a direct access file on a direct access device. Other combinations of device and access method are also represented. The DTFCD provides a good example of the type of parameters included in this macro; a sample assembler language program with a DTFCD is shown in Fig. 7.2.

Three parameters are shown in the sample DTF: the DEVADDR is the symbolic name of the physical I/O device, the IOAREA1 is the label of an eighty-character region of core set aside to hold an input record, and EOFADDR is the address (label) of the instruction to be executed when the end of file marker (/*) is sensed. In this example, the device address (DEVADDR) is SYSIPT, which just happens to be the symbolic name of the physical device normally used to provide card input to application programs; this program could be run with no job control reference to the I/O device.

Other parameters which might be coded in a DTF include: blocksize, the name of a second I/O area for dual-buffer overlapped I/O, label types, the file type (input or output), record form on devices where this can be a variable (blocking, fixed length, variable length), logical record length, information identifying a direct access or indexed sequential key, and many others.

```
PGMA       START   0

GO         BALR    12,0        INITIALIZE BASE REGISTER

           USING   *,12

           OPEN    CARDS

RUN        GET     CARDS

            ⎫
            ⎬ other instructions
            ⎭

           B       RUN

QUIT       CLOSE   CARDS

           EOJ

*

*          * * * * * * * * * * * * * * * * * * * * *

*          *   THE DTFCD MACRO DEFINITION.         *

*          * * * * * * * * * * * * * * * * * * * * *

*

CARDS      DTFCD   DEVADDR=SYSIPT,IOAREA1=INPUT,EOFADDR=QUIT

            ⎫
            ⎬ other data definitions
            ⎭

INPUT      DS      CL80         CARD READER INPUT AREA

           END  GO
```

Fig. 7.2 A program segment containing a DTFCD macro

Changing Standard Assignments—the ASSGN Statement

There are times when a programmer may wish to change a standard device assignment. Assume, for example, that a DTFMT (magnetic tape) refers to DEVADDR = SYS010 and that SYS010 is assigned to a particular tape drive. As the programmer enters the computer center, he sees that his tape drive is tied up on a two-hour job, but two other tape drives are free. By using an ASSGN card, he can change SYS010 from its standard device assignment to one of the available devices *for his program only.*

To understand the way the ASSGN card works, it is first useful to have an understanding of how devices are addressed on an IBM computer system. All I/O takes place through a channel; devices are attached to the computer through the channel. Each channel has a number—the multiplexer channel is number 0 while selectors are numbered 1, 2, 3, and so on, up to a maximum of 7.

Each device is given a two-digit hexadecimal number ranging from a minimum of 00 to a maximum of FF (255 in decimal); thus up to 256 devices can be attached to any one channel. The system address or device address of any physical I/O unit attached to the system is simply the device number preceded by the number of the channel to which it is attached. Device 008 is found on channel 0 and has a device number of 8; device 00E is also on channel 0 (the multiplexer) but has a device number of 14 (0E in hex). Device 181 is found on channel 1, while device 281 is found on channel 2. Look around any computer center, and you'll find each and every physical device has a permanent number attached; these numbers look much like the kind of numbers we've been discussing in this paragraph. The first digit identifies the channel; the second and third digits identify the device.

If SYS010 has a standard assignment of device 180 and device 181 is free, the programmer can change the device for his job by coding

```
//   ASSGN   SYS010,X'181'
```

and placing this card in front of the EXEC card for the job step using the device. The change in assignment holds for *this job only*; after the program completes processing, the standard assignment once again takes over. The standard assignment of other core partitions is not changed by an ASSGN card.

Other DOS Job Control Functions

Most DOS programmers use very little job control beyond the few statements we've already discussed. The JOB card is, of course, essential, and EXEC cards are needed to describe the specific programs to be run. On compile and test runs, an OPTION card is required. Once testing is completed, load modules are often cataloged to a core image library, meaning that OPTION, PHASE, and possibly one or more INCLUDE cards must be part of the job deck. Occasionally, an ASSGN card is used to change a standard device assignment. That's about all the average DOS programmer really needs. Other job control functions are usually left to one or more "experts" within the computing center.

Since the purpose of this chapter is to cover some of the more commonly used features of DOS Job Control, we won't spend much time discussing the details of the "lesser used" job control statements; we will, however, briefly describe some of those which the average programmer may occasionally encounter.

Most magnetic tape and direct access files are created with labels. The DLBL statement provides information for writing and/or checking direct access labels; the TLBL statement performs the same functions for magnetic tape labels. The LBLTYP statement tells the linkage-editor how much main storage space is to be set aside for label processing.

A single direct access volume (one disk pack, for example) can hold several different files; to prevent the accidental destruction of data, the physical location of a new file on a disk or other direct access volume must be carefully controlled. This control is implemented through the use of the EXTENT statement which passes such information as: the symbolic unit name (SYSnnn), the file serial number, the file type (index, main data area, overflow area), the number of the track on which the new file is to start, and the number of tracks to be assigned to the file. DASD file creation usually involves the use of both the EXTENT and the DLBL statements. Often, a specialist within the data-processing function is responsible for maintaining a "book" showing the location of each file on each physical volume; new files must be authorized by this individual.

Under DOS, the programmer has access to a set of "user program switch indicators." These are often used to indicate certain key conditions at the start of a program run—they can be tested using standard assembly language statements. These switch indicators can be set to a particular configuration by the UPSI job control statement.

Summary

In this chapter, we've covered some of the basic features of the job control language for IBM's Disk Operating System (DOS). The two key job control statements, at least as far as the average DOS programmer is concerned, are the JOB card which separates and identifies individual jobs and the EXEC card which identifies the specific load module to be run or executed. A single JOB card may be followed by more than one EXEC card; each EXEC card marks a single job step.

On a compile and test run, the programmer must inform the system that the load module produced by the linkage-editor is to be loaded and executed. This is done through the OPTION card. When the programmer codes

```
//    OPTION    LINK
```

the object module is written to a system file (usually a direct access file) and, following an EXEC card with no program name, is loaded into core and started.

In a production environment, programs are usually run by loading and executing a load module directly from a library, bypassing the lengthy assemble (or compile) and link-edit steps. Under DOS, these library load modules are known as phases. To catalog a phase to the core image library, the programmer first codes:

```
//    OPTION    CATAL
```

This OPTION statement performs two distinct functions: first, like the LINK option, it causes the load module to be written to a system file; and, second, the CATAL option informs the linkage editor that the load module (or phase) is to be cataloged to the core image library.

Each cataloged phase must be given a unique name; this is provided through a PHASE statement. Additional subroutines and other precoded modules can be added to the phase with an INCLUDE card. The PHASE and INCLUDE cards provide information to the linkage editor; the first column (at least) of these two cards is blank. The other job control cards we've discussed in this chapter—JOB, EXEC, and OPTION—must begin with two slashes (//) in columns 1 and 2, with column 3 (at least) blank.

Each physical I/O device on a DOS system is assigned a symbolic name. If a programmer wishes to change the physical device indicated by a given symbolic name for the current run of a job, he can make the change by using an ASSGN card. Like the JOB, EXEC, and OPTION cards, the ASSGN card starts with (//) in columns 1 and 2.

The key element in DOS I/O control is the DTF macro which is coded within the problem program. Each combination of a physical device and an access method has its own DTF (define the file); the DTFCD defines a card file, the DTFPR defines a printer file, the DTFMT defines a magnetic tape file, and so on. This macro indicates the specific input or output device, the access method to be used on this device, and detailed data descriptions.

For the average programmer, these few, relatively simple control statements are enough. In most DOS installations, the other, less commonly used features of DOS job control are generally left to a few specialists.

Exercises

1. What are the functions of a JOB card?
2. What are the functions of an EXEC card?
3. Explain the difference between a job name and a program name.
4. What is implied when the program name field on an EXEC card is blank?
5. Explain the process of cataloging a program to the core image library starting with a source module.
6. What functions are performed by the DTF macro?
7. What does the ASSGN card do?

Your instructor may assign additional job control exercises.

CHAPTER 8

Job Control Language for the IBM Operating System / 360 and System / 370—JOB and EXEC Cards

Overview

IBM's Disk Operating System was designed to control operations on smaller computers; DOS can handle, depending of computer size and the release level, from one to five application programs in addition to the operating system itself. On a system of this size, techniques such as assigning each I/O device to a specific symbolic name or requiring a file specialist to keep track of the location of each and every file on each and every DASD (direct access storage device) volume do not cause too great a problem.

IBM's Operating System/360 and Operating System/370, including the virtual memory operating systems designed for more current versions of System/370, allow for the control of many more concurrent application programs. On such large systems, the relatively simple approaches of standard device assignments and single source DASD file control just won't do. Additional software support is essential. If a program is to perform the function of allocating disk space, for example, the job control language for such a system must be capable of communicating considerable information to the responsible operating system module; thus a job control language for this larger system will probably be considerably more complex than that of a DOS level system. The job control language for IBM's larger operating systems *is* considerably more complex than that of DOS.

As with DOS, the average programmer needs only a limited subset of the full job control language in his everyday work. We'll concentrate on those job control statements and parameters which are likely to be used by this "average" programmer. Since the job control language for the full operating system is a bit more complex than that of DOS, we'll divide our analysis into two parts:

110

here in Chapter 8, the JOB and EXEC cards will be discussed; in Chapter 9, the DD or data definition card will be covered. We will not attempt to cover all the features of IBM's System/360 and System/370 Job Control Language (JCL), only the more commonly used features. Hopefully, by using this approach, we'll be able to avoid the "total confusion" so often felt by the beginning programmer encountering JCL for the first time.

The Cards

There are three basic JCL cards:

1. The JOB card serves to separate and identify jobs. Secondary functions include passing accounting and priority information to the system. This JOB card is an expanded version of the DOS JOB card.
2. The EXEC or execute card. This card serves to identify the specific program or load module to be run or executed; again, this is an expanded version of the DOS EXEC card.
3. The DD or data definition card which is used to define, in detail, the characteristics of each and every input and output device used by the job. The need for this card was discussed back in Chapter 6.

In this chapter, we'll concentrate on the first two types of cards and a few general concepts, leaving DD cards for the next chapter.

Jobs and Job Steps

Consider the job diagrammed in Fig. 8.1. This job involves three distinct steps— a compilation, the link-edit step, and the final execution of the programmer's actual load module. To the programmer, all these steps constitute a single job producing a single set of output data. To the system, three distinct programs must be executed. The programmer sees a job; the computer sees a series of job steps. The job consists of all the code needed to complete a given data processing objective; it's an independent entity. A job may consist of a number of separate programs—compilers, linkage editors, sorts, application programs—all sequenced to obtain this objective; each of these programs is a separate job steb.

One JOB card must be provided for each job. It must be the first card in the job deck. One EXEC card must be provided for each job *step*. There may be almost any number of EXEC cards in a single job.

As an example, let's consider the simple compile, link-edit, and execute program of Fig. 8.1. We have already noted the need for three distinct job steps; let's add the input and output device requirements to our discussion and attempt to list the job control language cards needed to support this application.

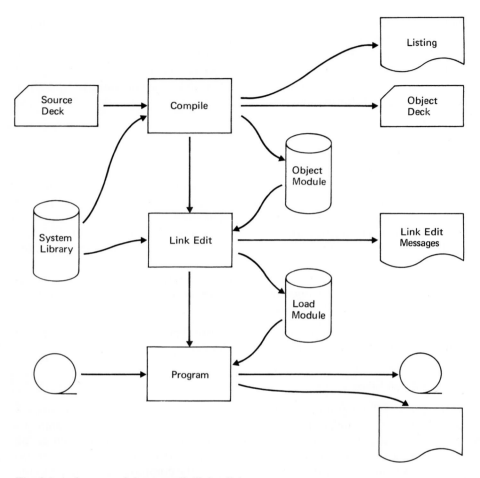

Fig. 8.1 A three-step job—compile/link-edit/execute

In the first job step, compilation, input comes from the card reader and output goes to the printer or the card punch for an (often optional) object deck, and to disk, where a copy of the object module is saved for future job steps. The linkage editor gets its input from the disk file created by the first job step and, perhaps, from a system library. Output goes to the printer and to a disk file where a copy of the load module is stored. Input to the final job step starts with this load module and includes any input and output devices specified by the programmer. In this example, input comes from tape and output goes to the printer and to another tape.

Now, let's consider the job control language needed to support this job. Before listing the cards, we must remember two points: first, the computer treats each job step as a separate entity, and second, one DD card must be provided for each and every input and output device. To support this job, we need the following cards:

1. a JOB card;
2. an EXEC card for the compilation step;
3. a DD card for the disk object module file;
4. a DD card for the printer output;
5. a DD card for card output;
6. a DD card for card input;
7. an EXEC card for the link-edit step;
8. a DD card for the object module input from disk—this is the same object module file described in number three but, since this is a different job step, a separate DD card is needed;
9. a DD card for the load module output to disk;
10. a DD card for printer output;
11. an EXEC card for the load module;
12. a DD card for the input tape;
13. a DD card for the output tape;
14. a DD card for printer output;
15. a DD card for the program load module—this is the same file created in (or by) card number nine, but, once again, this is a new step.

The first card identifies the job; cards 2, 7, and 11, the three EXEC cards, mark the start of each of the three job steps, respectively. Note carefully that, within a given job step, *all* the DD cards actually needed by the job step are listed.

Cataloged Procedures

That's a lot of JCL for a simple compile/link-edit/execute job! And with the exception of a few DD cards describing the actual input and output requirements of the final job step—cards 12, 13, and 14 in our example—the cards are meaningless to the typical programmer. Also, every job involving a compile/link-edit/execute is just about like any other job with the same three steps, and who cares about the exact nature of a temporary file created strictly to hold the results of a compile operation and having little or no direct bearing on the final results? For years, programming languages have handled such repetitious activities with macros. The job control language equivalent of a macro is a cataloged procedure.

A cataloged procedure is a set of precoded JCL statements. This macro-like module is normally stored on a library and added to the programmer's deck as it enters the system; the function of grafting cataloged procedures into a job deck is performed by the job reader or job-queueing operating system module described in Chapter 6. Using cataloged procedures, our JCL deck for the compilation program we've been discussing becomes:

1. a JOB card;
2. An EXEC COBOL or EXEC FORTRAN card describing, in programmer terms, the cataloged procedure desired;
3. a DD card for tape input;
4. a DD card for tape output;
5. a DD card for printer output.

Upon reading the EXEC card, the job reader goes to the cataloged procedure library, obtains a copy of the JCL included in the requested procedure, and adds this JCL to the programmer's deck, which is about to become a series of card images on a class queue anyway. The programmer need be concerned only with the JCL which is unique to his job; all of the repetitious code is contained in the procedure. The programmer need not be concerned with the actual names of the compiler programs or the linkage-editor, and he can ignore the details of the temporary work data sets of these routines.

A bit later, after we've looked at a few actual JCL statements, we'll analyze some typical cataloged procedures.

The Language—Basic Parameters

Let's get down to specifics. A traditional place to begin the discussion of any language is with the basic format of a statement; job control language is no exception. The basic format of an IBM Job Control Language statement is:

```
//NAME    OPERATION    OPERANDS    COMMENTS
```

Verbally, the individual fields can be described as follows.

1. Columns 1 and 2 *must* contain the "slash" character (/). This is the same character used to denote division in FORTRAN.

2. The "NAME" field (essentially a label) begins in column 3. This field serves to identify a particular job, job step, or data set; as we shall see, the NAME field allows the programmer and the operating system to identify or refer to a particular JCL card.

3. The NAME field is followed by at least one blank. If column number three is blank, the system assumes that there is *no* NAME; the blank character serves as a field separator.

4. Following the first set of blank characters is the "OPERATION" field which describes the type of JCL card. The three basic operations are: JOB, EXEC, and DD.

5. The operation field is followed by one or more blanks.

6. Following this second set of blank characters come the "OPERANDS", a series of parameters providing detailed information about the job, job step, or data set.

7. Again, one or more blanks separate the operands from the next field.

8. Optional comments.

9. Except for comments, the JCL code cannot go beyond card column 71.

The programmer may choose almost any name for his name field, the only restrictions being: a maximum of eight characters, the use of letters and digits only, and the use of a letter of the alphabet as the first character. The operation and operands fields must be coded according to some very exacting standards; only the three operations mentioned above are legal, and we'll be discussing some of the rules for coding operands in this and the next chapter. Comments are, of course, up to the programmer.

Note very carefully the use of blanks on a JCL card; *blanks are used to separate fields.* Stray blanks are the most common cause of JCL errors among beginners. Stray blanks *will* be interpreted as field separators. Coding

```
//    STEP1    EXEC    COBOL
```

will result in a very strange error message—there is no such operation as STEP 1; only JOB, EXEC, and DD are valid. You know what you mean, but the computer doesn't. Try

```
//STEP1    EXEC    COBOL
```

with no blanks between the // and the name field.

The JOB Card

The basic function of the JOB card is to mark the beginning of a job and thus separate it from all other jobs coming into the computer. The name field serves to give each job the unique identification required in a multiprogramming system and thus must normally be coded. Any combination of eight or fewer characters, as long as the first is alphabetic and only letters and numbers are used, is a legal job name, although many computer centers place their own restrictions on job names. Often, a computer center will issue job cards with prepunched and prenumbered job name fields; frequently, the cards are numbered in sequence, thus practically eliminating the problem of two or more jobs with identical job names.

In some computer centers, only the job name and operation fields are used:

```
//JOB396    JOB
```

Other centers require additional information, which gets us into the operand field of the JOB card.

The JOB Card—Accounting Information

One important secondary function of the JOB card is passing accounting information to an accounting module in the operating system. This information is coded as the first parameter in the operands field;

```
//JOB396    JOB    1234
```

might, for example, indicate that the cost of running the job named JOB396 is to be charged against account number 1234. Often, multiple accounting subparameters must be provided, as in

```
//JOB435    JOB    (1234,875)
```

which might mean that job JOB435 is to be charged against account number 1234, user number 875. The exact content of the accounting field is up to the individual installation; i.e., each computer center can define its own requirements.

Notice the use of parentheses; when more than one subparameter is coded, parentheses are required. Note also the position of the accounting information—the first set of information in the operands field. Accounting information is a good example of a *positional* parameter; the meaning of the accounting field and the meaning of the individual subparameters within the accounting-information parameter is determined by position.

We've been using the terms "parameter" and "subparameter" throughout our discussion of the accounting-information field; what do these terms mean? A parameter is simply a single, logically related set of information in the operand field of a JCL card—a collection of accounting information is a logical entity.

A subparameter is a single piece of data within a parameter. A subparameter would, for instance, be analogous to an individual's name, with the parameter being his or her complete mailing address.

The JOB Card—Programmer Name

To simplify programmer identification, the programmer's name is often placed on the JOB card. A second positional parameter is provided for this purpose, as in:

```
//JOB098    JOB    (2987,235),DAVIS
```

A slightly different format is sometimes used:

```
//JOB098    JOB    (2987,235),' DAVIS '
```

The use of apostrophes is required only when special characters—a period, blanks, etc.—are desired as a part of the name field.

The JOB Card—The CLASS Parameter

A few chapters back when the concept of a JOB card was first introduced, the use of this card to indicate a job's class (priority) was mentioned. In IBM's Job Control Language, this function is performed by the CLASS parameter. Adding this to our existing parameters, we get:

```
//JOB760    JOB    (3984,444),' W.S. DAVIS ',CLASS=A
```

The JOB Card—The TIME Parameter

Remember the computer's timer and the way the timer routines in the operating system can be used to cancel a program caught in an endless loop? The data for setting the timer must come from somewhere; the source is often a TIME parameter coded on the JOB card. The TIME parameter has two possible subparameters:

$$TIME = (minutes, seconds)$$

The TIME parameter:

$$TIME = (5,30)$$

asks for five minutes and thirty seconds of CPU time, while:

$$TIME = 5 \quad or \quad TIME = (5) \quad or \quad TIME = (5,0)$$

asks for exactly five minutes, and:

$$TIME=(,30)$$

requests thirty seconds. Notice the use of parentheses. When the first sub-parameter *alone* is coded, they can be skipped if desired; when more than one parameter is coded, however, parentheses *must* be used. The values coded for minutes and seconds are positional subparameters; i.e., they are defined by their position in the TIME parameter. In the "seconds only" form, a comma was coded to indicate the *absence* of the "minutes" positional subparameter.

The CLASS and TIME parameters are themselves *keyword* parameters; i.e., the word CLASS and the word TIME give these parameters a meaning *independent* of their position on the JOB card. Once the accounting and programmer-name *positional* parameters have been coded in their proper position, the *keyword* parameters can be coded in any order. Here are a few examples:

```
//XY1    JOB    (345,86),JONES,CLASS=C,TIME=3

//XY2    JOB    (296,25),'A.SMITH',TIME=(,45),CLASS=A

//XY3    JOB    (111,22),DAVIS,CLASS=D,TIME=(3,30)
```

The REGION Parameter

On some systems, a job's priority is determined, in part, by the amount of space it requires. The programmer can indicate the amount of space needed by his program by coding a REGION parameter; this is another keyword parameter, with core being allocated in blocks of 2048 (2K) bytes, as in

```
REGION=34K
```

or

```
REGION=124K.
```

The MSGLEVEL Parameter

Programmer-coded JCL cards, the JCL cards included in a cataloged procedure, and messages indicating what action the system has actually taken with respect to various data sets and devices are valuable to the programmer during program debug, but once this stage is completed this information becomes excess and is usually meaningless to a nonprogramming user of a report. The MSGLEVEL (or message level) parameter allows the programmer to select which JCL and device allocation messages are to be printed. The general form of this parameter is:

$$MSGLEVEL = (JCL\text{-}cards, messages)$$

The two subparameters have the following values and meanings:

JCL-CARDS	MEANING
0	Print only the JOB card.
1	Print all JCL statements, including programmer-coded statements and those added by a cataloged procedure.
2	Print only programmer-coded JCL.

MESSAGES	MEANING
0	Don't print any allocation messages unless the job ends abnormally.
1	Print all messages.

The parameter:

    MSGLEVEL=(1,1)

means to print everything, while the parameter:

    MSGLEVEL=(0,0)

means print only the JOB card unless the job fails. The parameter:

    MSGLEVEL=(1,0)

instructs the system to print all JCL cards but to skip allocation messages.

Default Options

Rather than insisting that each and every JOB card parameter be coded by the programmer, many computer centers use default values. Stated very simply, if the programmer fails, for any reason, to code a particular parameter, the system assumes a value for him. Often, a number of key parameters—accounting information, the programmer's name, and the job class—must be coded; defaults are based on the job class with, for example, all CLASS = A jobs being assigned a REGION of 90K and a TIME limit of thirty seconds while CLASS = B jobs get 120K and a two-minute time limit. If the programmer is not satisfied with the default value, he simply codes the parameter he wishes to change, thus overriding the default.

Other JOB Card Parameters

Other parameters, all keyword in nature, allow the programmer to specify such things as: job priority, run type, condition code limits, roll-in/roll-out options, and restart options. We won't attempt to cover these parameters except to mention the fact of their existence; when a need arises, check these parameters with a system programmer or look them up in a JCL manual.

Some JOB Cards

```
//JOBA     JOB    (2938,24),ADAMS,CLASS=B


//C1234567   JOB    (3998,659),'A.B. JONES',CLASS=A ,

//              TIME=(5,30),REGION=128K
```

Continuing a JCL Statement onto a Second Card

The second sample JOB card shown above won't fit on a single card; thus this is as good a place as any to introduce the rules for continuing a JCL card. The rules are quite simple:

1. Interrupt the field after a complete parameter or subparameter, including the trailing comma, has been coded; i.e., stop after a comma (which you must admit is a natural break point).
2. *Optionally* code any nonblank character in column 72. Column 72 may be left blank; the use of a continuation character is optional.
3. Code slashes (//) in columns 1 and 2 of the continuation card.
4. Continue your coding in any column from 4 through 16—column 3 must be blank and code must be resumed no later than column 16.

In other words, just break after a comma and resume coding on the next card.

The EXEC Card

An EXEC card marks the beginning of each job *step*; its purpose is to provide the system with the identification of the program (or cataloged procedure) to be executed; thus, it is only fitting that the first parameter on an EXEC card be the one which identifies the program or procedure:

```
//    EXEC    PGM=SORT6
```

or:

```
//    EXEC    PROC=COBOL
```

When indicating a cataloged procedure, as in

```
//    EXEC    COBOL
```

the keyword **PROC** may be skipped. When executing a *program*, the keyword **PGM** *must* be used.

A good example of what the EXEC card does can be found in a typical cataloged procedure—let's look at the FORTRAN procedure. Coding

```
//    EXEC    FORTRAN
```

identifies a cataloged procedure, causing the following code to be read from the procedure library and added to the programmer's job stream:

```
//FORT    EXEC    PGM=IEYFORT

//SYSPRINT    DD    parameters    (printed output)

//SYSLIN    DD    parameters    (object module output)

//LKED    EXEC    PGM=IEWL

//SYSLIB    DD    parameters    (system library)

//SYSLMOD    DD    parameters    (load module output)

//SYSPRINT    DD    parameters    (printed output)

//SYSUT1    DD    parameters    (work space)

//SYSLIN    DD    parameters    (object module input)

//GO    EXEC    PGM=*.LKED.SYSLMOD
```

That final card is just a bit confusing. What it says is "execute the program created in the job step named LKED and stored on a data set named SYSLMOD." The name field of a JCL card serves much the same purpose as a label, allowing a given step to be referred to by another statement; the particular format used for the reference in question

```
*.LKED.SYSLMOD
```

is called qualification. To cite another example of qualification, there are two data sets named SYSLIN in this procedure, one in each of the first two job steps; the first one would be referred to as *.FORT.SYSLIN, while the second becomes *.LKED.SYSLIN—the asterisk denotes a reference back to another job step.

The programmer coded a cataloged procedure. The procedure itself contained, in this case, three EXEC cards, each calling for the execution of a specific program. All references to a specific program contained the keyword "PGM =."

Often, the program or cataloged procedure identification is all the programmer need code on his EXEC card. Some applications, however, require more information, and a number of additional parameters do exist.

The COND or Condition Parameter

Most programmers have, at one time or another, submitted a job with one or more compiler errors. The result is usually a compilation with a listing of errors followed by a message indicating that, because of the compiler errors, the link-edit and go steps were not executed. This makes a great deal of sense—why bother with subsequent steps if the first one is wrong? You've probably never thought about it before, but just how does the computer system know enough to skip a job step, particularly when a cataloged procedure tells it to execute the link-edit and go steps?

You may have noticed something called a severity code on your compiler errors—warnings are worth 4, simple errors might be worth 8, severe errors might be worth 12 points; a program containing severe errors will almost certainly not run. The compiler reports the value of the highest encountered severity code to the system by placing a condition code in one of the registers—assembler language programmers are probably familiar with the idea of a condition code as part of normal register conventions. The operating system's job initiator module can check this condition code prior to loading and executing a job step, bypassing the step if the actual condition code returned by a prior job step is not acceptable; the programmer passes along the limits for this comparison via the COND or condition parameter.

The general form of the COND parameter is:

COND=(value,comparison,stepname)

The parameter

COND=(12,LE,FORT)

attached to the EXEC card for the link-edit step tells the initiator program that if 12 is less than or equal to the actual condition code returned by the FORT step (an EXEC card with a step name of "FORT"), the link-edit step is to be skipped. Let's run through that logic again. The COND parameter on the following EXEC card

//LKED   EXEC   PGM=IEWL,COND=(12,LE,FORT)

means that the step named LKED is to be *bypassed* if 12 is less than or equal to the actual condition code returned by the step named FORT. The logic is a bit unusual, so be careful. Most programmers, when comparing a variable and a constant in an IF statement or a logical comparison, will code the variable first—its pretty much a standard programming procedure. On the COND parameter, the *constant* is coded first, making the logic seem to read backwards. The fact that the comparison is made to implement a negative decision, skipping a step, adds to the confusion. The safest way to handle COND logic is to read it as it's coded, from left to right—the step is skipped if some constant meets a certain condition with respect to the actual condition code returned by a prior job step. Incidentally, the third positional subparameter (the step name of the prior job step whose condition code is to participate in the comparison) can be skipped; if the step name is not coded, the most recently completed step in the job is assumed.

A number of comparisons can be coded, including greater than (GT), equal to (EQ), less than (LT), greater than or equal to (GE), less than or equal to (LE), and not equal to (NE). In the FORTRAN cataloged procedure described above, COND parameters are found on the EXEC cards for the link-edit and go steps; they were left off simply because we had not yet covered the parameter. By coding

//LKED   EXEC   PGM=IEWL,COND=(4,LT,FORT)

we are instructing the operating system to skip the LKED step if 4 is less than the actual condition code returned by the FORT job step. The JCL statement

//GO   EXEC   PGM=*.LKED.SYSLMOD,COND=(4,LT,FORT)

places the same restriction on the go step. In some cases, multiple conditions are coded, as in

COND=((4,LT,FORT),(4,LT,LKED))

which causes "this" job step to be skipped if 4 is less than the actual condition code returned by the FORT step *or* if 4 is less than the actual condition code returned by the LKED step. Note the use of parentheses; punctuation can become tedious in coding JCL, and accounts for the bulk of programmer errors and difficulties.

The programmer can code and test his own return or condition codes, allowing him, for example, to skip the printing of a list of data errors if no errors were found in a prior job step. The logic of the COND parameter seems a bit cockeyed to many people, perhaps because the test is performed in order to implement a negative decision—skipping a job step. So be careful when using or interpreting this parameter; read it exactly as coded, and you shouldn't go too far wrong.

Other EXEC Parameters

Other EXEC parameters allow the programmer to pass parameters to a job step, provide *job step* accounting information, set a dispatching priority for the step, set a time limit for the job step, specify the region size, and handle roll-in/ roll-out and restart options. Several of these parameters could have been coded on the JOB card; the programmer has the option of specifying such things as a time limit, core limit, roll-in/roll-out options, restart options, and conditions for the complete job or for each job step independently.

Programmers often encounter the PARM option in the form

// EXEC   FORTRAN,PARM.FORT='NODECK,LIST'

which informs the FORT job step, the compiler, that no object deck is to be punched and that a list is to be printed. Detailed information on the meaning of parameters for any compiler language can be found in the programmer's guide to that language.

Summary

In this chapter, we've studied some general ideas of IBM's Job Control Language and covered specific parameters of the JOB and EXEC cards. A detailed summary of these parameters in reference form is found in Appendix B. These ideas will be carried into Chapter 9.

Exercises

1. Differentiate between a job and a job step. Relate the JOB and EXEC cards to these two concepts.
2. What is a positional parameter? Give some examples.
3. What is a keyword parameter? Give some examples.
4. What does "MSGLEVEL = (1,1)" mean when coded on a JOB card?
5. What is a cataloged procedure? Why are cataloged procedures used?
6. Explain default options.
7. Code a JOB card, using the job name of your choice, your course number as an accounting field, and your own name, requesting 90K of core for one minute and thirty seconds in the Q job class. Don't bother printing allocation messages. Print only the JCL that you code.
8. Code an EXEC card to execute a cataloged procedure named COBOL (compile, link-edit, and go). Skip this step if STEP 1 returned a condition code of 100.

CHAPTER 9

The DD Card

Overview

In this chapter, we continue the discussion of IBM's Job Control Language begun in chapter eight, concentrating on the data definition or DD card. The DD card allows the programmer to pass to the system a detailed description of each data set used by his program. There is one JOB card per job, one EXEC card for each job step, and one DD card for each and every data set accessed by the individual programs in each job step.

There are many different types of input and output devices. Each type has its own characteristics, strengths, and weaknesses. Job control language must be capable of handling even the most esoteric of applications on even the least often used devices; thus the number and complexity of DD statement parameters is mind-boggling. In this chapter, we'll concentrate only on the most common of the DD statement parameters—those used by most programmers in their everyday work. Coverage of the more advanced topics and lesser used parameters is left to a more advanced course in job control. Expert advice—your local systems programmer or a consultant—is a good idea when planning for a data set involving some of the trickier aspects of job control language.

Many JCL texts present the parameters of a DD card as a series of independent entities; this can be confusing. In this text, we'll take a somewhat different approach, concentrating on the input and output devices and describing the JCL needed to define data on a given device type. Essentially, we'll be following a three step approach:

1. Discuss the characteristics of a particular input and/or output device.

2. Identify those characteristics which must be communicated to the operating system.

3. Introduce and discuss the specific DD statement parameters needed to communicate this information.

Unit record equipment, tape, direct access devices, and the system input and system output devices (spooling) will be covered.

One more point before we start. JCL is an independent entity, attached to a program in order to communicate information to an operating system; it is *not* a part of the actual program but serves in a support role. This creates no problem with JOB and EXEC cards, but the DD card defines a data set which must be accessed by the program; the program and its DD cards must therefore be linked in some way. Under the IBM operating systems we are currently studying, this link is achieved by the name field of the DD card and a program macro called a data control block or DCB. This link is the subject of the next several paragraphs.

DD Cards and Data Control Blocks

Back in the second generation, the decision to change from, say, card to tape input on a program was a potentially expensive one, often involving an almost complete rewrite of the old program to allow for blocking, multiple buffering, and a complete new set of input and output macros. Operating system modules, in particular the access methods discussed previously, helped, but did not eliminate the problem. This expense made many firms hesitant to change to a new technology. The continued use of something less than the best technology was wasteful and, from the manufacturer's point of view, often meant the loss of a potential sale; thus the concept of device-independent programs became an important part of IBM's System/360 design philosophy.

Device independence means that a programmer should be able to change one or more input and/or output devices with a minimum of effort and a minimum of program rewrite. The IBM System/360 solution to this problem involves the input and output macros, a new macro called a data control block, and the DD card.

Let's start inside the program. The data control block or DCB macro, coded in assembler language as

```
INPUT    DCB    MACRF=GM,DSORG=PS,DDNAME=CARDS,        C
                other-parameters
```

sets up a series of constants and addresses describing the characteristics of the physical and logical records to be manipulated. Three parameters are coded above. The MACRF or macro-form parameter and the DSORG or data-set organization parameter, taken together, describe the access method to be used. The DDNAME parameter is the link to a DD card; more about this parameter later. Other parameters which might be coded describe the logical record length, blocksize, record form, buffering technique, density (tape), and numerous other physical characteristics of the record. The three parameters coded above represent the minimum which must be coded within the program; other parameters, as we shall see, can be coded on the DD card and incorporated into the data control block at OPEN time.

The actual input or output macro is a pretty simple affair. The basic macro for input from a sequential data set is:

```
label    GET    dcbaddress,areaaddress
```

The output macro for sequential files is:

```
label    PUT    dcbaddress,areaaddress
```

Consider the simple "read a card and print it" program of Fig. 9.1. The DCB macros are coded in among the constants and work spaces; this macro contains no executable code but consists of constants and addresses. The DSORG and MACRF parameters define the access method. The EODAD or end-of-data address parameter is a new one; it gives the program an address to branch to when an end-of-data marker is encountered in the input data.

The EXEC card specifies a cataloged procedure—ASMFCLG; this is a procedure for compile, link-edit, and go, using the assembler program in the first step. The assembler creates an object module, containing the skeleton of a data control block. The access method identified in the DCB is grafted onto the load module by the linkage editor. The GET and PUT macros contain a DCB address and an address for storing input data or finding output data; these macros generate into two constants and a branch to the actual access method. The load module for this program is pictured in Fig. 9.2.

The input operation works in the following manner. A GET macro is encountered as part of the program's normal cycle. This results in a branch to the access method. The access method knows the detailed specifications of the data from the data control block (address of the DCB is part of the GET macro) and also knows, again from the GET macro, where to put the data once it enters core. In short, everything is here except for the identification of the physical input device. This is the function of the DD card. The DCB

```
//JOB33    JOB    (2398,34),DAVIS,CLASS=A
//         EXEC    ASMFCLG
//ASM.SYSIN   DD   *
           STARTUP      macro to handle register conventions
           B     GO        branch around constants and work area
CARDOUT   DC    CL1' '
CARD      DS    CL80
          DC    CL51' '
INPUT     DCB   MACRF=GM,DSORG=PS,DDNAME=CARDS,EODAD=QUIT
OUTPUT    DCB   MACRF=PM,DSORG=PS,DDNAME=LINES

GO        OPEN   (INPUT,INPUT)
          OPEN   (OUTPUT,OUTPUT)

RUN       GET    INPUT,CARD
          PUT    OUTPUT,CARDOUT
          B      RUN
QUIT      CLOSE   (INPUT,OUTPUT)
QUIT2     CLOSEOUT      macro to handle end of job housekeeping
/*
//LINES  DD   parameters
//CARDS  DD   parameters
/*
```

Fig. 9.1 An assembly language program using device independent input and output macros

(a)

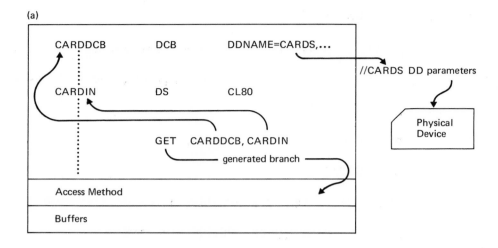

(b)

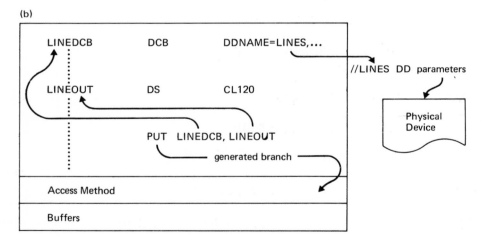

Fig. 9.2 System/360 I/O

contains a parameter—the DDNAME parameter—which points to the DD card associated with the data set in question. The parameters on the DD card identify the physical input device.

Let's review these steps by looking at what happens on output. The data control block, output macro, and access method are all part of the program load module (Fig. 9.2b). The access method to be used has been defined by the programmer through his DCB parameters; the linkage editor has simply grafted the proper one to the load module. The PUT macro causes a branch to the access method. Using the addresses provided by the PUT macro, the access method can locate the DCB and the data address, giving it the detailed record information needed to control output. The DCB contains a pointer to the associated DD card which identifies, via a series of parameters, the physical output device.

A switch from tape to disk can be accomplished by changing a job control language card. Most production programs, once past the compiler debug stage, are stored on a library in load module form and run without additional compilation. Since the JCL statements are not a part of the program load module, the change from tape to disk doesn't even involve recompilation! Even if a recompilation is needed to allow a new blocking factor or a new access method to be used, a modification of a single DCB macro may be all that is needed.

How about a higher level language like COBOL or FORTRAN? The source of the GET or PUT macro is obvious—the READ and WRITE instructions—but where do the data control blocks come from? In COBOL, a data control block is built from a SELECT . . . ASSIGN clause in the ENVIRONMENT DIVISION and a number of DATA DIVISION clauses such as BLOCK CONTAINS, LABELS ARE, and others. In FORTRAN, the DCB is built as soon as a READ or WRITE statement is encountered by the compiler, and is assumed to call for sequential access unless a FILE statement specifies otherwise. In COBOL, the DDNAME parameter is part of the SELECT . . . ASSIGN clause, with

```
SELECT DATAIN ASSIGN TO UT-S-CARDS.
```

pointing to

```
//CARDS    DD    parameters.
```

In FORTRAN, the DDNAME is built from the device number of the input or output instruction, with

```
WRITE (6,15) A,B,C
```

pointing to a data-control block containing

```
label    DCB    DDNAME=FT06F001,...
```

which leads to a JCL statement like

```
//FT06F001   DD    parameters.
```

Let us now turn our attention to the DD cards themselves.

Unit-Record Equipment

Very few programmers read data *directly* from a card reader or send data directly to a printer on a modern, high-speed computer; for reasons of economy, such data is normally spooled to tape or disk by an operating system module. Unit-record equipment is, however, the least complicated class of input and output devices and, thus, gives a convenient starting point for our discussion of the DD card.

What are the characteristics of unit-record data? First, and perhaps obviously, we are discussing "unit" records; there is no blocking to be concerned about. All records are the same length, and the logical and physical record lengths are identical. Labels are not normally present. The cards and paper containing this data are not reusable except as recycled scrap; thus, standard operating procedures—give the stuff back to the programmer and let him dispose of it—are adequate for unit record data. Printers can handle different length lines and not all card readers are restricted to the "standard" eighty-column card. But, aside from this possible need to specify the record length, the only thing the programmer must give to the system is the identity of the specific input or output device. This is done via the UNIT parameter.

The UNIT Parameter—Unit-Record Equipment

The UNIT parameter allows the programmer to specify a particular input or output device. This parameter can be coded in any one of three forms:

1. UNIT = unit-address
2. UNIT = device-type
3. UNIT = group-name.

The first form, UNIT = unit-address, permits the coding of an actual device address. Every piece of equipment attached to an IBM system is assigned a specific, three-digit address; if, for example, a particular printer is device number 8 on channel 0, its unit address is 008, and a DD card to permit a program to access this device and only this device would be coded as:

```
//PRINTR   DD    UNIT=008
```

If the requested device is busy, or for some other reason not available, the program must wait to be loaded. This is a very specific request—*no* other printer will do. As a consequence, this form of the unit parameter is rarely used.

The second form of the UNIT parameter, UNIT=device-type, is a bit more inclusive. If the programmer wants a 1403 printer, and *any* 1403 printer will do, he codes:

```
//OUTS    DD    UNIT=1403
```

Assuming that the system has a number of 1403 printers, the job can be loaded and run as soon as any one of these devices is free; it's a much less restrictive form and thus more heavily used. A 2501 card reader can be requested by coding UNIT=2501; a 2520 card-read punch is requested by coding UNIT= 2520. Any unit of the specified device type can be used by the requesting program.

UNIT=group-name is the final form of the UNIT parameter. The DD card:

```
//XYZ    DD    UNIT=READER
```

might be a request for any available card reader, be it a 2501, a 2520, or a 1442; it's the general form of the UNIT parameter. Each computer installation can define its own group names; there are no universal standards, although UNIT= PUNCH is a *typical* way of defining a request for a card punch and UNIT= PRINTER is an obvious group name for the printers attached to a system. In using this form of the UNIT parameter, the programmer is asking for any card reader or any punch or any printer, regardless of its device type, physical address, manufacturer, or other characteristics.

Note that there are *no* blanks in "UNIT=READER." Blanks, remember, are used as field separators on a JCL card.

The Data Control Block (DCB) Parameter—Unit Record

The programmer must code within his program a Data Control Block macro for each data set accessed by that program; this is the logical place to indicate the logical record length of a unit record. This approach presents one small problem—a decision to switch from eighty-column cards to the newer ninety-six column card, to cite one example, means a recompilation of the program.

There is an alternative; DCB parameters can be coded on the DD card. This is done via the DCB parameter. In the example cited above, the old DD card might have been:

```
//CARDIN    DD    UNIT=READER,DCB=(LRECL=80)
```

Replacing this JCL card with:

```
//CARDIN    DD    UNIT=READER,DCB=(LRECL=96)
```

changes the logical record length without recompilation. The (LRECL) sub-parameter specifies logical record length. DCB subparameters can be specified either within the program data control block or on the DD card. The use of DD card subparameters is a bit more flexible, allowing for changes in record characteristics without a need for recompilation.

Data control block subparameters[†] are moved into the *program DCB* at OPEN time, a procedure to be described in detail at a later time. Any record information coded in the *program* DCB will *not* be modified even if the DD card information is different; i.e., "hard-coded" information takes precedence. If a programmer anticipates any change in his basic record format, the volatile parameters should not be coded in the program but passed to the system via the DD card. Many assembly language shops code only the absolute minimum—DSORG, MACRF, DDNAME—parameters in the program DCB and consider this to be a normal coding standard.

Although we have no need for other parameters to describe unit records, a number of subparameters can be strung together, separated by commas, with the entire string of subparameters being enclosed in a single set of parentheses. There are no blanks within the DCB field. No blanks separate the two parameters we've looked at thus far; if a stray blank were to fall between the UNIT and DCB fields, the entire DCB parameter would be treated as comments and ignored.

Both the UNIT and DCB parameters are keyword parameters; i.e., they can be coded in any order.

Magnetic Tape

Magnetic tape is much more complex. Logical records are not restricted in format, they can be almost any length, blocked or unblocked, and records within a file need not all be the same length. A file might fill a single tape volume, but multi-volume files and multi-file volumes are a possibility. Data might be recorded at any of several densities, in seven or nine track mode.

Unlike cards and paper, tape data is often kept in a library under a catalog name. Tape is reusable, but if it is reused, any old data is lost. Because of its

---

[†] Within a program, we refer to DCB *parameters*, but the DCB is *itself* a parameter on a DD card; thus LRECL is a DCB *parameter* when it occurs within a program DCB, but it is a DCB *sub-parameter* when coded as part of a DD card's DCB parameter.

flexibility, at the end of a job step a tape might be cataloged, saved, scratched, or passed along to another step. The possibility of human error is always present—tape is not human readable—and steps to minimize this possible source of error are essential. Simple operating procedures like, "give the tape back to the programmer and let him dispose of it," are *not* adequate for tape.

The fact that tape is not human readable creates a problem in simply getting the correct tape mounted. To aid in solving this problem, most tapes are given labels, and label-checking routines inside the operating system (often a part of the OPEN macro) help to minimize this source of errors. Label checking should be simple, but not all tapes have labels and not all labels follow a standard format.

In processing tape, the programmer must provide the system with enough information to clearly define all these sources of potential variability. Specification of the physical input/output device is, of course, essential. The presence and type of labels must be identified. The serial number(s) of the tape volume or volumes to be mounted must be clearly established. The operator must be told what to do with the tape at the conclusion of the job step. If the tape is to be cataloged and stored in a library, a catalog name must be provided. Detailed record information must be communicated through the data control block, either within the program or in the DD card parameter. Any programmer who uses tape should be well acquainted with these facts; they are an important part of good job documentation. Job control language provides a formal structure for communicating these facts to the operating system.

In the discussion which follows, the various DD parameters needed for tape will be introduced from the point of view of creating a new tape data set. After the key parameters have been described, the problem of retrieving an existing tape data set will be covered.

The UNIT Parameter—Tape

The UNIT parameter for tape and the UNIT parameter for unit-record equipment are identical, with only the specific unit designator changing. UNIT = 181 is an example of the "unit-address" option, instructing an operator to mount a volume on the unit numbered 181 (channel 1, device 81). In most computer centers, the device number of each piece of hardware is clearly indicated on each device.

At the other extreme of flexibility, UNIT = TAPE9 might communicate a request for *any* nine-track tape drive while UNIT = TAPE7 might be its seven-track counterpart. Because of the varying densities and track formats of tape and the fact that most tape drives are not designed to handle all possible varieties of tape, this "group-name" form of the UNIT parameter is rarely used.

The UNIT=device-type form is most commonly used for magnetic tape. The following device types have been defined for IBM's 2400-series tape drives:

DEVICE TYPE	DESCRIPTION
2400	9 track, 800 bpi density.
2400-1	7 track, no data conversion.
2400-2	7 track with data conversion.
2400-3	9 track, 1600 bpi density.
2400-4	9 track, 800 and 1600 bpi density.
2400-5	2420 model 5 unit, 1600 bpi.

Other tape units have similar device-type designations. Using this form of the UNIT parameter, the programmer who wishes to read a nine-track 800-bpi tape would code:

UNIT=2400-4

Occasionally, when handling a multiple volume data set, a programmer may wish to request more than one tape drive. The "UNIT COUNT" subparameter is provided for this purpose. Coding

UNIT=(2400-3,3)

means that a total of three nine-track 1600-bpi drives are needed by this program. Both the device-type and the unit-count subparameters are positional in nature; i.e., the device type *must* be coded first and the unit count *must* be coded second. If a programmer were to code.

UNIT=(3,2400),

which is incorrect, the system would probably interpret this parameter as a request for 2400 tape drives of device type 3. Positional parameters derive their meaning from their relative position.

Note that, once again, the coding of more than one subparameter means that parentheses must be used. If the unit-count subparameter is not coded, a request for a single unit is assumed.

To save system time and eliminate lengthy waits by a program already in core, (a waste of valuable system resources) tape mount messages are normally given to the system operator by the job initiator program just as the job is about to enter the system. Occasionally, when probable errors or other special processing characteristics make the tape's use questionable, it makes sense to postpone the tape mount operation until the actual time of file OPEN when use is assured. Coding

```
UNIT=(2400,2,DEFER)
```

requests two nine-track, 800-bpi tape drives and postpones mounting; the DEFER option is a third positional subparameter. To postpone the mounting of a single 1600-bpi tape, the parameter

```
UNIT=(2400-3,,DEFER)
```

could be coded; the extra comma indicates the absence of a positional subparameter. Positional subparameters, to belabor a point, derive their meaning from their relative position. DEFER is the *third* positional subparameter.

The VOLUME Parameter—Tape

The VOLUME parameter, often shortened to VOL, allows the programmer to request the mounting of a specific tape volume. Individual tape volumes are normally given a unique serial number. To request the mounting of a tape with serial number MU1234, the programmer would code

```
VOL=SER=MU1234
```

where "SER = tape-serial-number" is a subparameter of the VOLUME or VOL parameter. To request the mounting of this particular tape volume on a 1600-bpi tape drive, code

```
//TSRQ    DD    UNIT=2400-3,VOL=SER=MU1234,...
```

along with other needed parameters. Note once again the absence of blanks.

This same set of parameters and subparameters can handle multiple volume files, as in

```
VOL=SER=(M01,M02,M03,M04)
```

where a request is made to mount four different volumes.

The programmer can request the mounting of a scratch or work tape by simple omitting the VOLUME parameter from his JCL card. Some installations prefer that this option not be used, insisting that a scratch tape be requested by coding something like:

```
//TAPE    DD    UNIT=2400-3,VOL=SER=SCRTCH,...
```

The VOLUME parameter is used to generate tape-mount messages. A message

```
MOUNT TAPE SCRTCH ON DEVICE 182
```

is a pretty obvious indication that a scratch tape is desired. (Just don't assign a real tape a similar serial number—SCRATCH, for example.)

The LABEL Parameter—Tape

The LABEL parameter, as you may have guessed, is used to define the type of labels on the selected volume; the OPEN macro uses this information to create labels for a new data set and to check the labels of an existing file. In addition to defining the label type, this parameter is used to specify the relative position of the desired file on a multiple-file volume—a single reel of tape containing more than one file. Other subparameters do exist, but we'll skip them for now; for our purposes, the basic form of the LABEL parameter is:

```
LABEL=(sequence-number,label-type)
```

The file sequence number is simply the relative position of the desired file on the volume—for the first file, the sequence number is 1; for the third file, it's 3. Valid label type subparameters include:

LABEL TYPE	MEANING
SL	Standard Labels
SUL	Both Standard and User Labels
NL	No Labels Present
NSL	NonStandard Labels
BLP	Bypass Label Processing.

Standard labels can be created or checked by the operating system; user labels and nonstandard labels must be checked by a programmer routine (if they are checked at all). The "bypass label processing" option implies that labels are present but, for some reason, they are not to be processed.

Normally, a single file is placed on each tape volume; to request the creation of a new tape volume with standard labels, the programmer codes:

    LABEL=(1,SL)

or

    LABEL=(,SL)

with the lone comma indicating the absence of the first positional parameter which is assumed to be 1. On a new tape data set, the OPEN macro creates a label; on an existing data set, the OPEN macro checks the label to determine if the proper file has been mounted.

The DCB Parameter—Tape

A tape data control block is just like a unit-record data control block, only a bit more complex. The purpose of a data control block is to define, for the system, the characteristics of individual records. On tape, records can be fixed or variable in length and blocked or unblocked; thus additional DCB subparameters are needed to fully define data on tape. Commonly used DCB subparameters include:

SUBPARAMETER	MEANING
BLKSIZE=	blocksize in bytes
DEN=	tape recording density
LRECL=	logical record length
RECFM=	record format

The blocksize and logical record length subparameters are pretty much self explanatory; the RECFM subparameter defines the record format, with F meaning fixed-length records, B meaning blocked records, FB meaning fixed-length blocked data, V meaning variable-length records, and so on. The density subparameter specifies the tape recording density with a code—0 for 7-track, 200 bpi; 1 for 7-track, 556 bpi; 2 for 7- or 9-track, 800 bpi; and 3 for 9-track, 1600 bpi. Why bother with a density code when density seems to be a part of the UNIT parameter? Some units can handle more than one density, and the UNIT parameter is concerned *only* with the physical device.

The DCB parameter:

```
DCB=(BLKSIZE=750,DEN=3,LRECL=75,RECFM=FB)
```

defines fixed-length blocked records, 75 bytes in length, stored in blocks of 750 bytes (10 logical records) on 1600-bpi tape. As with unit-record equipment, these subparameters might have been coded in the program DCB; the DCB parameter is always an optional part of a DD card.

The Disposition Parameter—Tape

What does the operator do with a given tape following job completion? The answer to this question is coded in the disposition (DISP) parameter. The general form of the disposition parameter is:

```
DISP=(a,b,c)
```

where:

       a = the status of the data set at the start of the job,
       b = the status of the job following successful job completion,
       c = the status of the job following abnormal completion.

All three are positional subparameters.

    If a data set is to be created within a job step, its "start of job" status is NEW. An existing data set is OLD. Some data sets, a library for example, might be accessed by more than one of the programs in core at any time. The prejob status for data sets of this type is SHR, which means share—this status is not used by a job which intends to modify data on the file. When SHR is used, the file can be accessed by two or more programs. A disposition of MOD indicates that the programmer wishes to add more data to an existing data set; the system thus positions the read/write heads at the old end-of-file marker at OPEN time.

    Following normal completion of a job step, the second disposition subparameter takes over. If there is no further need for the data, the programmer can code DELETE; a KEEP subparameter means that the data set will be retained on tape, and the tape rewound and dismounted. If the data is needed by a subsequent step within the same job, the programmer can PASS the data set. The file can be entered on a catalog (CATLG) and retained or removed from a catalog (UNCATLG) and made available for reuse.

    The desired disposition might be different following abnormal job termination; any of the normal job termination options except for PASS can be coded as the third DISP subparameter. If the third subparameter is not coded, the "normal termination" disposition is assumed to hold for abnormal termination as well.

To create a data set, pass it along to another job step, and delete it in the event of serious error, code:

```
DISP=(NEW,PASS,DELETE)
```

If a file is to be created and, normally, cataloged but in the event of an error simply kept for study or possible restart, code:

```
DISP=(NEW,CATLG,KEEP)
```

A temporary, work tape which is, in any event, needed for the life of the job step only, would have, as part of its DD card, the following disposition parameter:

```
DISP=(NEW,DELETE)
```

Since no abnormal termination disposition is coded, the second subparameter, DELETE, is assumed.

The Data Set Name Parameter—Tape

To simplify the task of retrieving cataloged or passed data sets, the programmer can give a data set a unique name by coding the DSNAME parameter (DSN is an acceptable abbreviation). A valid data set name consists of from one to eight characters (letters and numbers), starting with a letter, a $ symbol, or a # symbol. Data set names can be qualified; for example,

```
DSNAME=MU.USERDATA.SAN1
```

indicates that a data set named SAN1 can be located by referring to an index named USERDATA and that this index can be located by referring to a master index named MU. Each level of qualification must exist as an index in the system catalog.

Temporary, life-of-the-job data sets are assigned a data set name beginning with the ampersand (&) character, as in:

```
DSNAME=&&TEMP
```

Normally, to avoid possible confusion with certain system parameters, a double ampersand is used at the beginning of the temporary data set name.

Data set names for partitioned or indexed-sequential data sets are just a bit different; consult a good reference manual before working with these two varieties.

Creating a Tape Data Set—Sample DD Cards

1. Create a temporary data set and pass it to a subsequent job step:

```
//TAPE    DD    UNIT=2400-3,VOL=SER=WX2453,
//               DCB=(LRECL=145,BLKSIZE=2900,RECFM=FB),
//               LABEL=(,SL),DISP=(NEW,PASS),DSN=&&T
```

2. Create and catalog a permanent data set:

```
//MAG1    DD    UNIT=2400-4,LABEL=(,SL),DSN=TT,
//               VOL=SER=A572,DCB=(RECFM=FB,
//               BLKSIZE=1200,LRECL=120,DEN=3),
//               DISP=(NEW,CATLG)
```

3. Using a scratch tape:

```
//SCRATCH   DD   DISP=(NEW,DELETE),DSNAME=&&WORK,
//               DCB=(BLKSIZE=104,LRECL=52,RECFM=FB),
//               LABEL=(,SL),UNIT=2400-3,
//               VOL=SER=SCRTCH.
```

All of the DD parameters are keyword parameters; i.e., they can be coded in any order. (Many of the *subparameters* are positional.) Also, notice the way the JCL statements are continued onto a second, third, and fourth card—we simply break coding after *any* comma and resume on the next card. Continuation cards must begin with the // in the first two columns—this defines it as a control card—and coding must be resumed prior to column sixteen.

The DUMMY Parameter—Tape

Loading tapes is not the typical operator's favorite job, and tape jobs frequently have a very low priority. In testing his code, the programmer may wish to bypass the generation of tape load messages (and, hence, the mounting of tape). This can be done by coding the DUMMY parameter

```
//DATA    DD    DUMMY,UNIT=2400,...
```

The word DUMMY is a positional parameter and must be the first parameter in the operands field. Later, when the programmer wishes to process his tapes, the job can be resubmitted without the DUMMY parameter.

Retrieving an Existing Tape Data Set

If a data set has been cataloged or passed by a prior step of the same job, it can normally be retrieved by coding only the DDNAME and DISP parameters:

```
//TAPE1    DD    DSNAME=&&WORK,DISP=(OLD,DELETE)

//MAGS     DD    DSN=MASTO1,DISP=(OLD,KEEP)

//FILE     DD    DSNAME=MU.USERDATA.SAN1,DISP=SHR
```

Other parameters, including the data control block parameters, are part of the catalog entry for cataloged data sets and part of the operating system tables for a passed data set; thus, they need not be recoded. On many systems, however, if one of these other parameters is coded, they all must be coded. The UNIT parameter must be coded only when the "current" job step will add data requiring additional tape drives.

   In the second example cited above, a previously cataloged data set was kept following job completion; the result is to simply retain the data set and all index entries. If a *non*cataloged data set is kept, the programmer must code DSNAME, DISP, UNIT, and VOLUME parameters to retrieve it; for example:

```
//DATA    DD    DSNAME=KEEPIT,DISP=(OLD,KEEP),

//              UNIT=2400-3,VOL=SER=X12
```

The LABEL parameter is always needed for nonstandard labels. DCB information is optional, and can usually be obtained from the label at OPEN time.

Direct Access Storage Devices

Data on a direct access device is quite similar to data on tape. Numerous record formats are possible. Multi-file volumes and multi-volume files are possible, although the former is far more common. Density is *not* a variable factor. Disk space is reusable, and files can be cataloged and saved or scratched and made available to another program. The accidental or intentional destruction of data is a possibility. Disk packs and data cell bins can be mounted and dismounted according to programmer instruction, although this practice is frowned upon in many computer centers. Label checking is performed for direct access data sets. The major difference between direct access devices and tape, the possibility of direct as well as sequential access, is a function of the program and access methods and not job control language. Thus it is not surprising that most of the DD card parameters used for tape are also used for direct access data sets.

One major difference does, however, exist. Tape can be viewed as having essentially unlimited storage capacity, while direct access space is a limited resource. To insure the availability of sufficient space before initiating a direct access data set creation program, the programmer must provide the system with an estimate of his space requirements; this is done through the SPACE parameter. In the following paragraphs, we'll review the various DD parameters as they relate to the creation of a direct access file, saving the new SPACE parameter for last. Following the discussion of parameters, sample DD cards for creating and retrieving a direct access data set will be shown.

The Unit Parameter—Direct Access Files

Direct access devices are often requested by actual device type, with the 2311, 2314, and 3330 being common disk device types and the 2301, 2302, and 2303 being drum units. Coding

    UNIT=3330

represents a request for space on any 3330 disk unit.

Disk and drum are frequently used for storing the intermediate results of a data processing job. To simplify a request for such work files, many installations have defined various group names for one or more direct access volumes—typical group names include SYSDA and WORK1.

Occasionally, a programmer will request a direct access unit by actual unit address. Normally, this practice is restricted to private, mountable packs when only the correct device will do.

The VOLUME Parameter—Direct Access Files

The VOLUME parameter is used to define a specific direct access volume. On a temporary data set where the precise location of a file prior to its creation is not too important, the VOLUME parameter is not normally coded; on a permanent file, a data set is probably restricted to one and only one volume, so the parameter is needed. If a VOLUME parameter is coded, it means that the file may be stored "on this volume and only on this volume."

The LABEL Parameter—Direct Access Files

Since direct access devices are almost invariably assigned standard labels, the LABEL parameter is not normally needed. At times, often to achieve increased data set protection, user labels are used. To indicate the presence of user labels, code

```
LABEL=(,SUL)
```

which indicates the presence of both standard and user labels.

The DCB Parameter—Direct Access Files

Once again, LRECL or logical record length, BLKSIZE or blocksize, and RECFM or record format are commonly used DCB subparameters. Density is constant, so the DEN subparameter is rarely if ever needed.

The Disposition Parameter—Direct Access Files

Direct access dispositions and tape dispositions are, for all practical purposes, identical. Since disk packs are not dismounted as frequently as tapes, the operator action may be different. From the programmer's point of view, however, the dispositions are identical.

The Data Set Name Parameter—Direct Access Files

As before, the data set name or DSNAME or DSN parameter provides a convenient mechanism for retrieving a cataloged or passed data set. Qualified names are very common on direct access files.

The SPACE Parameter—Direct Access Files

On most computer systems, space on a direct access device is a limited commodity. If a program requiring ten cylinders were to be loaded and allowed to start processing at a time when only five cylinders were available, the program would either sit in core until direct access space became available or be terminated and rerun, in both cases wasting valuable system resources. To prevent, or at least minimize this problem, the programmer is required to provide the system with an estimate of his direct access space requirements through the SPACE parameter.

Space can be requested in tracks, cylinders, or blocks of data. The type of space-unit and the number of units are defined by two positional subparameters; coding

```
SPACE=(TRK,20)
```

means a request for twenty tracks, while

```
SPACE=(CYL,14)
```

asks for fourteen cylinders, and

```
SPACE=(200,10)
```

asks for ten 200-byte blocks. The type of space allocation, cylinders, tracks, or blocks, is the first positional subparameter; the number of units of space comes second.

Estimating space requirements is not always easy. To insure the availability of sufficient space, the programmer might be tempted to request a bit more space than the program could possibly need, thus, tying up a limited resource—direct access space—and, possibly, lowering the priority of the program. Fortunately, another option is available. Coding

```
SPACE=(TRK,(10,5))
```

means that ten tracks will be set aside for the use of this program; should this space be consumed, an additional five tracks will be allocated if available. The first positional subparameter, as before, represents the type of storage unit desired; the second subparameter states the number of units requested. The third subparameter is a secondary allocation, to be made available only if the program exceeds its primary space allocation. It is important to remember that the primary space allocation is made before the program begins executing, in fact, before the program is even loaded into core. The secondary allocation is filled on an as-needed, if-available basis after the job step begins executing. A job step may be cancelled for insufficient direct space, even though the primary and secondary requests are more than adequate, if space is not available at the time of the secondary request. It is to the programmer's advantage to make the primary space estimate as accurate as possible. A secondary space allocation can be repeated fifteen times. For example, the SPACE parameter

```
SPACE=(CYL,(5,2))
```

represents a request for, at most, thirty five cylinders—five primary cylinders plus two cylinders on each of a maximum fifteen secondary allocations.

The punctuation of this parameter, with nested parentheses, is a bit unusual. The use of parentheses is easy to remember if you consider the fact that both the second and third positional subparameters deal with the number of units of direct access space to be allocated and thus should be treated as a single entity.

A request for too much space can tie up a limited system resource and possibly cause the execution of another program to be postponed. The programmer can help by giving all unused space back to the system at the end of a job step; he does this by coding the RLSE or release subparameter, as in:

```
SPACE=(CYL,(5,1),RLSE)
```

This is a positional subparameter which must follow the "quantity of allocation" subparameters.

To obtain optimum disk input and output, space is sometimes requested in contiguous units, thus minimizing the amount of disk seek time needed to move from cylinder to cylinder. The parameter

```
SPACE=(TRK,(5,2),RLSE,CONTIG)
```

asks for five contiguous tracks with a secondary allocation of an additional two contiguous tracks, releasing any unused space back to the system at the conclusion of the job step. Without the RLSE subparameter, this parameter would be coded:

```
SPACE=(TRK,(5,2),,CONTIG)
```

Note the extra comma indicating the absence of a positional subparameter.

Examples—Direct Access Data Set Creation

1. A temporary data set on the system work pack:

```
//DISK    DD    DSNAME=&&TEMP,UNIT=SYSDA,
//              DISP=(NEW,PASS),SPACE=(CYL,5),
//              DCB=(LRECL=120,BLKSIZE=2400,
//              RECFM=FB)
```

2. A cataloged data set on a specific volume:

```
//RECS    DD    DSN=MU.USERDATA.SAN4,UNIT=3330,
//              VOL=SER=MIAMI3,DISP=(NEW,CATLG),
//              SPACE=(TRK,(20,5),RLSE,CONTIG),
//              DCB=(LRECL=155,RECFM=FB,BLKSIZE=1550)
```

3. A kept data set:

```
//KEEPIT   DD    SPACE=(CYL,(10,2),RLSE),
//               DCB=(RECFM=FB,LRECL=72,BLKSIZE=720),
//               VOL=SER=MYPACK,DISP=(NEW,KEEP),
//               DSNAME=MYDATA,UNIT=3330
```

Examples—Retrieving a Direct Access Data Set

1. A passed data set:

```
//DATA    DD    DSNAME=&&TEMP,DISP=(OLD,DELETE)
```

2. A cataloged data set:

```
//STUFF   DD    DSN=MU.USERDATA.SAN4,DISP=OLD
```

3. A kept data set, existing on no catalog or index, requires the UNIT and VOLUME parameters in addition to the DSNAME and DISP:

```
//DDNAME DD DSNAME = MYDATA, UNIT = 3330,
            VOL = SER = MYPACK, DISP = (OLD, KEEP)
//
```

The System Input and System Output Devices

Spooling creates two new data sets, with a system input device replacing the physical reading of cards and a system output device replacing direct communication with a printer. On many systems, a third system device is provided for spooling punched card output. Disk is often used in such spooling operations; tape is another possibility. Spooling might be done on-line or off-line. The physical volume might change from day to day or even within the same day. Since these devices are in such common use, most of the DD parameters are predefined within the operating system, leaving only token coding for the programmer.

Most programmers who have worked on IBM equipment are familiar with the card:

```
//SYSIN    DD    *
```

SYSIN is obviously a DDNAME, but what does the asterisk mean? As you may remember, a job is submitted to the system in the form of a card deck including JCL statements, perhaps one or more source modules, and data. The asterisk indicates that the data follows "this" DD card and is part of the same job stream. The entire job stream is spooled to some device; if the system is capable of finding this DD card, it can find the associated data by looking in the same place. There is, by the way, nothing sacred about SYSIN; it's a DDNAME and nothing more. The programmer may use any DDNAME for the system input device, as long as the DDNAME parameter of the program's internal data control block matches the chosen name. Many compilers and utilities, (programs not normally modified by the programmer) use SYSIN as the DDNAME of a card (or card-image) file coming from the system input device; such use probably accounts for the popularity of this particular name.

Spooling data for eventual printer output is normally done by coding:

```
//SYSOUT    DD    SYSOUT=A
```

Punched card output will be the final result from:

```
//SYSPUNCH    DD    SYSOUT=B
```

SYSOUT and SYSPUNCH, like SYSIN, are simply commonly used DDNAMEs; they have no other real significance. The programmer who codes his own data control blocks within his programs can use any DDNAME for system input and system output devices, although there is something to be said for the documentation benefits of following standard or accepted practices.

In the examples cited above, the letter "A" designated eventual printer output, while "B" meant punched cards. These designators are commonly used, but they are hardly universal; an installation can choose any set of symbols to indicate the various system devices.

Many installations limit the amount of disk space available to a single program on the system output device. When large amounts of output data are expected, this limit may be overridden by coding a space parameter:

```
//SYSPRINT    DD    SYSOUT=A,SPACE=(CYL,(5,2))
```

Job Step Qualifiers on a DD Card

Often, two or more DD cards, each in a different job step but still within the same job, are assigned the same DDNAME. This frequently happens when using a cataloged procedure for a compile, link-edit, and go. The compiler program gets its input from the system input device, so the source deck usually follows a //SYSIN   DD   * card. The GO step, assuming card input to the program, also uses the system input device for data, and the data, unless the programmer codes his own program data control blocks, is also preceded by a "SYSIN   DD   *" card. To differentiate between these two cards, the following JCL is often coded:

```
//JOBNAME    JOB    (9824,18),DAVIS,CLASS=A

//    EXEC    FORTRAN

//FORT.SYSIN    DD    *

        FORTRAN source deck.


/*

//GO.SYSIN    DD    *

        Data

/*
```

The execute card calls for a cataloged procedure named FORTRAN; this procedure contains three job steps named FORT (the compiler), LKED (the linkage editor), and GO (the program load module). FORT.SYSIN is the name of a DD card attached to the first job step which has the step-name FORT. GO.SYSIN is attached to the GO step.

Incidently, the delimiter statement, the /* card, marks the end of data submitted through the job stream. Comments may be coded beginning in card column four. Some programmers use a /* card to mark the end of each step in a multi-step job.

The PROC Statement

The JOB, EXEC, and DD statements are far and away the most commonly used job control statements, but other statements do exist. The PROC statement, for example, is used to assign default values to symbolic parameters in a cataloged procedure. Another card, the null card, is coded by simply placing slashes in the first two card columns:

```
//
```

This card is sometimes used to mark the end of a job. A comments card has //* punched in the first three card columns and anything at all punched in the remainder of the card. Comments may be inserted at any point in the JCL job stream.

A Complete Example

One of the best ways to gain an understanding of any language is by looking at and studying an actual example of its use; job control language is no exception. Our example (see Fig. 9.3) is a fairly typical multi-step job. The first job step reads and edits card data through the system input device, spooling the output to disk; the edit program is stored on a private library. Step two sorts this data, using a cataloged procedure sort routine; the output goes to tape. In the third job step, this tape file is merged with a master file on disk; errors are written to another tape, and, at the end of the job step, both tapes are cataloged. The final step is a new one for this job—it is still in the form of a COBOL source deck. This step reads the errors tape and prepares an error report which is sent to the printer.

A DD card which was not explicitly mentioned before is the STEPLIB card of Fig. 9.4; this card identifies the library on which the programs are found.

Figure 9.3 is the flowchart for our multi-step example. The actual JCL statements are coded in Fig. 9.4. Follow this example carefully; if you can

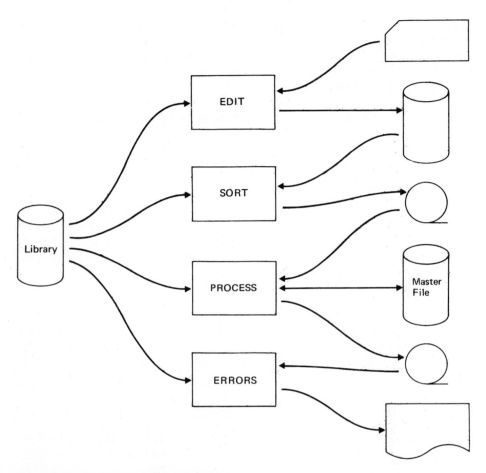

Fig. 9.3 Our JCL-example job—flowchart

understand all the parameters, you have a pretty good grasp of the material covered in the last two chapters.

Incidently, to return to the topic of libraries, all of the //STEPLIB cards of Fig. 9.4 could have been replaced by a single card

```
//JOBLIB    DD    DSN=MU.USERPGM.SAN,DISP=SHR
```

coded immediately after the JOB card. With the exception of this JOBLIB card, no other DD card may precede the first EXEC card. Also, you may have

```
//MYJOB    JOB    (9182,333),'W.S. DAVIS',CLASS=A

//STEP1    EXEC   PGM=EDIT

//STEPLIB    DD   DSN=MU.USERPGM.SAN,DISP=SHR

//OUTS  DD     DSNAME=&&TEMP,UNIT=SYSDA,DISP=(NEW,PASS),

//             SPACE=(TRK,(10,2),RLSE),DCB=(LRECL=80,

//             BLKSIZE=800,RECFM=FB)

//SYSIN    DD    *

            [Data cards]

/*

//SECOND    EXEC    SORTPC

//SORTIN    DD    DSN=&&TEMP,DISP=(OLD,DELETE)

//SORTOUT    DD    DSNAME=MYOUTS,UNIT=2400-3,VOL=SER=R712,

//                 LABEL=(,SL),DISP=(NEW,PASS),DCB=(LRECL=80,

//                 BLKSIZE=800,RECFM=FB)

//* THE NEXT TWO CARDS GIVE THE SORT ROUTINE ITS FIELDS.

//SYSIN    DD    *

     SORT  FIELDS=(1,5,CH,A)

/*      THE FIELD STARTS IN COLUMN 1, CONSUMES 5 COLUMNS,

//*     AND HOLDS CHARACTER DATA WHICH IS TO BE SORTED

//*     INTO ASCENDING ORDER.
```

Fig. 9.4 An example of the JCL for a complete job   (*Cont.*)

```
//THIRD    EXEC   PGM=PROCESS

//STEPLIB   DD    DSN=MU.USERPGM.SAN,DISP=SHR

//TAPEIN    DD    DSN=MYOUTS,DISP=(OLD,CATLG)

//MASTER    DD    DSN=MU.USERDATA.SAN5,DISP=(OLD,KEEP)

//TAPEOUT   DD    DSN=MYERRS,UNIT=2400-3,VOL=SER=E712,

//                LABEL=(,SL),DISP=(NEW,CATLG),

//                DISP=(LRECL=80,BLKSIZE=1200,RECFM=FB)

//LAST    EXEC   COBOL

//COB.SYSIN   DD    *


          [COBOL source deck]


/*

//TAPEIN    DD    DSN=MYERRS,DISP=(OLD,KEEP)

//
```

Fig. 9.4 (*Cont.*)

noticed an absence of library identification cards for our cataloged procedures; the mechanism for accessing the cataloged procedure library and certain other system libraries is a part of the operating system.

Summary

In this chapter, we've covered the parameters of the DD card for unit record, tape, direct access, and system data sets. A detailed summary of these parameters, in convenient reference form, is found in Appendix B. By far the best summary of the material in Chapters 8 and 9 is the complete JCL example shown in Fig. 9.4.

Exercises

1. Explain how a program is linked to a physical I/O device under operating system/360.

2. Explain the relationship between a program DCB and the DCB parameter on a DD card.

3. Code a UNIT parameter to reserve three 2400-series tape drives with 800-bpi capacity. Don't mount the tapes until open time.

4. Code a DD card DCB parameter for a magnetic tape file holding fixed-length, blocked records—logical records are 50 characters in length and the blocking factor is 50. It's a 1600-bpi tape.

5. Code a space parameter to reserve 20 contiguous cylinders. Allow for additional cylinders, requesting two at a time. Return unused cylinders to the system at the end of the job step.

6. Code a DD card for creating a 1600-bpi tape, serial number MYTAPE. Catalog the tape if the job step ends normally; otherwise, keep the tape for analysis. For simplicity, the tape serial number and the catalog name should be the same. Records are 125 characters each blocked in groups of 20; all records are the same length. Use standard labels.

7. Code a DD card for a temporary, work data set on the system direct access device (SYSDA). Get 10 tracks. Request secondary tracks in group of 2. They do not have to be contiguous, but do return unused tracks to the system at the end of the job step. Logical records are 100 bytes each and should be blocked in groups of 30. The data set is to be passed to a subsequent job step.

Your instructor may assign additional JCL exercises.

PART IV

Operating System Concepts

CHAPTER 10

The Functions and Objectives of an Operating System

Overview

This chapter is really an overview of the remainder of the text. In it, we'll discuss, in general terms, the functions which must be performed by a modern operating system. A number of techniques for measuring the effectiveness of data processing system are introduced, and the conflicting nature of these objectives are explored. The way in which operating system design is limited by external constraints imposed by technology, economics, and political and competitive factors is also discussed. The chapter ends with a brief preview of the various kinds of operating systems to be covered in Chapters 11 through 18.

One key idea dominates this chapter—"best" is a relative term. Good operating system design for one application might be very bad operating system design on another application. In this chapter, we'll explore the problem of conflicting objectives.

The System Resources

The purpose of any operating system is to improve, to make more effective, the utilization of system resources. The software needed to support multiprogramming is an almost perfect example of this premise; multiprogramming, as we've seen, significantly improves the utilization of the CPU by making use of otherwise wasted time. Other system resources include core storage space, registers, the input and output devices, secondary storage space, various data resources including program libraries, and, to a lesser extent, human resources including programmers, operators, and the eventual user of the results of a data processing operation; a well-designed operating system must be concerned with most if not all of these factors. A popular word in science and engineering circles is optimization. The word optimum means "the best or most-favorable degree, condition, amount, etc." (at least according to Webster). To optimize means to achieve the best possible result. The function of an operating system, simply stated, is to optimize the utilization of all the system resources.

Measures of Effectiveness

That definition sounds pretty easy, but it isn't. Let's consider an analogy. What's the optimum engine for an automobile? What is your idea of effective performance? Are you primarily interested in speed? Or safety? Or gasoline consumption? Or internal space and trunk space? Or a comfortable ride? Or cost? Or status? Or some combination? In other words, what are your measures of effectiveness, and how heavily do you weigh them? Based on the number of different models marketed in this country, different people tend to answer these questions in different ways. Tell me what characteristics you consider to be important in an automobile, then we can *begin* to discuss the precise meaning of the word optimum as used in conjunction with an automobile or an automobile engine. "Best" is a relative term.

A number of different factors can be used to measure the performance of a computer system, including:

1. *Throughput*, a measure of the amount of work going through a computer. Throughput is often expressed as a percentage, measuring actual CPU time as a fraction of total available system time.
2. *Turnaround*, a measure of the elapsed time between job submission and job completion.
3. *Response Time* is an important characteristic on time-shared systems; it's a measure of the elapsed time between a request for the computer's attention and the actual response to that request.
4. *Availability* is a measure of system accessability.
5. *Security*, which is becoming an increasingly important consideration.
6. *Reliability*.
7. *Cost*.

The perfect operating system would allow us to maximize throughput while minimizing both turnaround and response time. The system would be available to any programmer on a few moments notice. Security would, of course, be absolute, and system reliability would approach 100%. All this would be accomplished at a very low cost. Good luck.

Conflicting Objectives

Our ways of measuring computer effectiveness are, in many cases, in conflict. Throughput can be increased by overloading a system, perhaps by purchasing too small a machine—like the supermarket working with only a single checkout counter. But, what does overloading do to turnaround or response time? Conversely, turnaround and response time can be helped by underloading a system—buying considerably more computer than is needed. This, of course, clobbers throughput, since an underloaded system is bound to be idle at times.

Does this imply that turnaround and response time are always compatible? Not really. Consider a time-shared system designed to minimize response time. To achieve this objective, each program is restricted to a brief shot of CPU time, returning to the end of the job queue if this time slice isn't enough to allow the program to reach a natural break point. A ten-second program, restricted to one tenth of a second each second, would need a total of one hundred seconds of elapsed time to complete. The quest for response time can have a negative impact on turnaround.

System availability and throughput are in obvious conflict. How can a busy system be considered available?

Security is another measure of effectiveness which is in conflict with many others. The controls and checks necessitated by a concern for security take up time—both computer time and operator time. Time spent on security is time *not* spent on production. Many security procedures tend to contract rather than expand system availability. Security checks can add to run time, thus increasing turnaround. Response time can also be slowed by security arrangements.

The equipment used in our space program was among the most reliable hardware ever developed. In this program, reliability was often gained by duplicating all or part of a particular hardware subsystem—everything had its backup; this is expensive. System reliability and system cost are conflicting objectives.

In a business environment, cost often becomes an overriding objective—design a system to do the job at the lowest possible cost. A system enjoying high throughput is probably doing quite well in terms of *equipment* or hardware cost, but there are other cost factors that must also be considered. In an airline reservation application, for example, slow response time can lead to the loss of a customer, a substantial cost.

Constraints

As if conflicting objectives were not enough, the designer of an operating system faces a number of factors which severely limit his flexibility. Perhaps the most obvious constraint is technology itself; an instantaneous response is physically impossible. The limits of the electronics used in a particular machine are a constraining influence; multiprogramming software is hardly needed for an electronic tube machine but becomes almost essential with solid logic circuits.

Another technology problem arises from the fact that computers are rarely planned around a operating system; instead, the operating system is planned and designed to fit on an existing system of hardware. Throughput might be significantly improved by keeping twenty-five or thirty programs in main memory and multiprogramming; if, however, hardware design limits the equipment to a maximum core address of one million or so, there may not be enough room to hold all those programs.

Economic factors represent another valid constraint on the designer of an operating system.

Strangely, perhaps, political factors represent another common constraint. Many firms, for example, have insisted on the latest thing in computer hardware and operating systems simply because "the competition has it"; management information systems provide a good example of this phenomenon. This may be only marginally political, but where else does such a decision fit.

Other organizational decisions are more blatantly political in nature. An operating system might be designed to give priority to the type of program normally submitted by a certain department simply because of the influence wielded by its manager; other departments or functions with less political clout might find jobs typical of their department suffering from a poor priority. A strong computer operations group might succeed in pushing hated tape and disk-mount jobs to the third shift by controlling the priority decision. Every system will tend to favor the pet project of the general manager. This is an often overlooked or ignored problem, but it is an important one.

Stating System Objectives

Different applications call for different objectives. When stated explicitly, computer system and operating system objectives often take the form of target figures, as in: maintain a minimum of 75% throughput while keeping turnaround under one hour. Other targets might call for maintaining response time at a maximum of three minutes for at least 95% of system requests, or keeping average response time below two minutes. The availability parameter often takes the form of a certain level of excess capacity, (perhaps not included in throughput figures) which is made available to programmers or engineers on a demand basis. Security specifications are often written and enforcement is guaranteed by planned audits. Cost limits represent the most common type of objective—don't spend more than X dollars.

To be most effective, planning should be done for a complete system and not just the operating system. Ideally, hardware and software planning should be done together. Usually, they are not. Usually, the operating system is planned and implemented after the hardware is in place; the software objective becomes one of optimizing the utilization of system resources, *given the restriction* of the existing hardware.

The Next Few Chapters

In the chapters which follow, we'll be looking at some actual and fictional operating systems. Our basic approach will be to:

1. try to define the objectives of a system;
2. discuss any constraints or limitations placed on possible operating system software by the total system we are discussing;
3. describe the operating system as an attempt to meet the system objectives within the constraints.

The balance of Part IV is devoted to a number of general-purpose operating systems. Chapters 11, 12, and 13 are related—they represent an attempt to describe, in some detail, the operating characteristics of a specific computer and then show how two different operating systems can be designed to function in this hardware environment. The products of IBM Corporation have been chosen for this discussion. In the author's opinion, "living" systems are more instructive than "simulated" or "imaginary" systems because students can relate classroom material to their out-of-class experiences. More students are likely to have had exposure to the products of IBM than to those of any other manufacturer. Chapter 11 covers the operating principles of System/360. Chapter 12 gets into IBM's Disk Operating System (DOS), an operating system designed to support small- to medium-sized computer installations using System/360. The problems of a large computer center are encountered in Chapter 13, where we discuss Operating System/360, Multiprogramming with a Fixed Number of Tasks (MFT).

The major function of these three chapters is *not* to show how these particular operating systems work, but to show how *some typical* operating systems work; IBM is not the only builder of computers nor the only designer of operating systems. Given the background of Chapters 11 through 13, we explore some nonIBM approaches and IBM's MVT (Multiple Variable Task) operating system in Chapter 14. The final chapter of this section, Chapter 15, gets into the key concepts of virtual storage and paging.

In the final section of the text, we'll discuss a number of special-purpose operating systems where, often because of unique system requirements, a general-purpose operating system just won't do. Chapter 16 is concerned with a manufacturing process-control system in which a need for high reliability and very rapid response make many traditional operating system modules and functions just so much excess baggage; what is needed is a stripped-down made-to-order operating system. Chapter 17 gets into data base and data communications software in the context of a management information system—additions to a general-purpose operating system are needed in this application. Chapter 18 discusses multiple computer systems, using computerized supermarket checkout as an example; in this system, hardware performs many of the functions of a general-purpose operating system. All three special purpose systems describe current computer applications.

The remaining chapters are quite specific in content; read carefully.

Exercises

1. Explain how throughput and turnaround objectives can be in conflict.
2. Explain how throughput and response time objectives can be in conflict.
3. Explain how a security requirement can be in conflict with almost every other measure of system effectiveness.
4. "Best" is a relative term. Explain.
5. Discuss some of the constraints which are placed on the designer of an operating system.

CHAPTER 11

Operating Principles of the
IBM System / 360

Overview

An operating system is designed to perform within a given environment; a key component of that environment is the computer hardware. The electronic design of a computer serves to both limit and support operating system design. In this chapter, we'll take a look at some of the key design concepts of the IBM System/360 series of computers, stressing those factors which have had the greatest impact on software design; in Chapters 12 and 13, two different operating systems designed to work within this environment will be studied. Among the important concepts covered in this chapter are the program status word or PSW, the mechanism for actually controlling an input or output operation, and interrupts.

Addressing Core on the IBM System/360

Core storage is composed of a large number of tiny, ferrite cores, each capable of holding a single bit of information. As you may remember from Chapter 3, these cores are grouped together into characters or bytes (eight bits on an IBM machine), halfwords, fullwords, and doublewords. The byte, an eight-bit field capable of holding one EBCDIC character, is the basic addressable unit of core storage on an IBM System/360.

The addressing scheme of this computer is really pretty simple. Imagine every ferrite core in the machine strung, like a bunch of beads, along a single wire. The first group of eight cores is numbered byte #0, the second group is byte #1, the third group is #2, and so on in sequence until all bytes in core have been numbered. Of course, the reality is not quite this simple—core is

165

three dimensional and, on many computers, core has been supplanted by other storage media—but, from a programmer's perspective, addressing consists of little more than counting bytes.

What about halfwords and fullwords? On some computers, a fullword is the basic addressable unit of core, and a fullword might be something other than four bytes or thirty-two bits. On an IBM computer, however, the address of a halfword or fullword is simply the address of the first byte in the field.

The Program Status Word

A programmer takes a great deal for granted when submitting a job, assuming that individual statements *will* be executed in sequence unless, of course, a branch instruction is coded. It seems simple, but just how does the computer, more specifically the CPU, know which instruction to execute next? And, how is this instruction located? The answer to both questions is found in the Program Status Word or PSW.

The program status word really isn't a word at all; it's a doubleword, 64-bits in length. The PSW is the first doubleword in core storage, occupying bytes 0, 1, 2, 3, 4, 5, 6, and 7. To illustrate the function of the PSW, we'll use the following brief assembler language program segment:

CORE ADDRESS		INSTRUCTION	
1000	GO	L	3,X
1004		L	4,Y
1008		AR	3,4
1010		ST	3,Z
{ several more instructions			
1050		B	GO
{ balance of program			
1100	X	DS	F
1104	Y	DS	F
1108	Z	DS	F

and so on.

This program segment loads two binary numbers stored at core locations X and Y into registers 3 and 4 respectively, adds these two numbers together, and stores the sum at Z, eventually coming back to repeat the instructions. The actual core addresses shown on the left are expressed in decimal for convenience.

The last three bytes of the PSW (Fig. 11.1) contain the instruction address; this is the core address of the instruction which is to be executed next. As the program segment is executed, we'll follow the changing content of this PSW field.

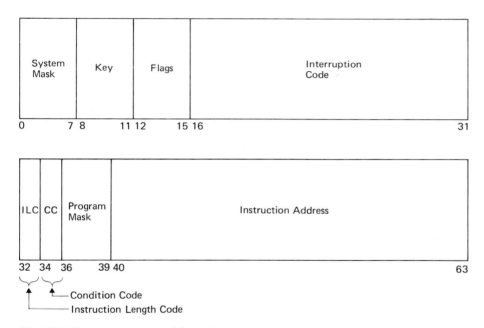

Fig. 11.1 Program status word format

In executing an instruction, the CPU goes through two distinct steps: the instruction cycle and the execution cycle. During the instruction cycle, the CPU gets one instruction from core and decodes it; during the execution cycle, the computer executes the instruction. The PSW's instruction address field is the key to the instruction cycle.

As our program segment begins, the instruction address is, we'll assume, the binary equivalent of the decimal number 1000. The CPU simply looks at the PSW which, you may remember, is *always* found at the same spot in core, and gets the address of the instruction to be executed. In this step, the selected instruction is the first load instruction which is moved into the CPU for decoding. At some time during the instruction cycle, the central processing unit bumps the instruction address field of the program status word by four (the length of the load instruction) thus causing the PSW to point at address 1004 where the next instruction in sequence is stored. After the first load is executed and the value stored at core location X is copied into register 3, the computer is ready for another instruction cycle. CPU's are not very original; the action taken is the same as before:

1. find the instruction address in the PSW;
2. get the instruction stored at that address;
3. bump up or increment the instruction address by the length of the current instruction—it now points at the "next" instruction;
4. decode the instruction;
5. enter the execution cycle;
6. go back to step number 1.

Thus the second load instruction is moved into the CPU, decoded, executed. and at some point in the instruction cycle, the instruction address is incremented by four so as to contain the address 1008, the location of the next instruction in sequence.

Following execution of this second instruction, the CPU again consults the PSW, fetches the add instruction from core location 1008, adds two to the instruction address, decodes the instruction, and adds the contents of registers 3 and 4 during the execution cycle. Note that the instruction address was incremented by only 2 instead of 4 this time. Instructions can vary in length; the "AR" instruction is only two bytes long. How can the CPU tell the difference between a two byte and a four byte instruction? More about this in a few paragraphs.

The PSW now points at the store instruction; thus, during the next instruction cycle, the store instruction is fetched and decoded while the instruction address is bumped up by 4. Continuing in its single-minded fashion, the computer executes a number of other instructions, in sequence, until finally, the instruction address points to the branch instruction. As before, the instruction stored at this address (1050) is moved into the CPU and decoded while the instruction length is incremented by 4. The execution cycle of a branch instruction is, however, a bit different. The branch instruction causes the CPU to replace the contents of the instruction address field of the PSW with the address specified in the instruction operand—in this case with core address 1000. The next instruction to be executed will be the one labeled GO.

The instruction address is three bytes or twenty-four bits long. The biggest binary number that can be stored in twenty-four bits is equivalent to the decimal number 16,777,216; this three-byte format makes it impossible for an IBM System/360 computer to address more than 16 megabytes of core (which is *far* more than most computers have anyway).

Variable Length Instructions

As we saw in the example above, not all instructions need be the same length; the main factor affecting the length of an instruction is the addressing scheme used by IBM. Registers can be addressed in four bits—the sixteen general-purpose registers are numbered 0 through 15 which is a hexadecimal "F." Core addresses require more information. Back in the second generation when core was occupied by one program at a time, the programmer could assume a start point for his job, usually address zero, and address everything from this reference point. With multiprogramming, this control disappeared; with ten programs in core at any one time, the programmer cannot assume a constant load point. The solution to this problem involves relative addressing. Programs are written as though they start at location zero, with the actual start address being supplied as the program begins its execution. The actual start address is stored in a register called the base register; byte locations relative to this base are called displacements. The absolute address of a particular byte in core can be obtained by adding the displacement to the contents of the base register. Displacements are limited to 4095 bytes (hex FFF or three half bytes) from any base; longer programs require multiple base registers.

Let's assume, using our sample program from above, that the address of the first instruction, address 1000, has been loaded into register 12 (the digit "C" in hex). The absolute and relative addresses of the instructions and storage areas in this program segment are:

ABSOLUTE ADDRESS	RELATIVE ADDRESS		INSTRUCTION
	BASE	DISPLACEMENT	
1000	C	000	L 3,X
1004	C	004	L 4,Y
1008	C	008	AR 3,4
1010	C	010	ST 3,Z

Displacements are once again expressed in decimal to simplify the discussion.

The first instruction, as you may recall, had a label—GO. The address of this label can be expressed in several ways. For one thing, it's at absolute address 1000. If this address has been stored in register twelve, another way of expressing this same core location is as a displacement of zero from base register twelve, i.e., the content of a base register plus a displacement. Since a register can always be identified with four bits and the maximum allowable displacement from a single base register is 4095 bytes which in binary is a twelve-bit number, the entire "base register plus displacement" address fits in a sixteen bit or two byte field.

Back again to variable length instructions. Some instructions (for instance, the AR or add registers instruction of our example) involve two registers. Combining a one-byte operation code with the one byte needed to identify two separate registers yields a two-byte (halfword) instruction. Other instructions, the loads and stores for example, involve the movement or processing of data between core and a register. The one byte operation code, combined with a half-byte register address and a two-byte core address, sums to three-and-one-half bytes; the extra half byte is normally used to hold an index register, giving an instruction four bytes (two halfwords) in length. Storage-to-storage operations are also possible; these include an operation code, two core addresses, and, frequently, a one-byte length field for a total of three halfwords (six bytes).

How does the CPU know the difference? If the first two *bits* of the operation code are $(00)_2$, as in the add register instruction which has as its op code $(00011010)_2$, the instruction is a register-to-register instruction. Instructions involving both a register and a storage location begin with $(01)_2$ or $(10)_2$; those involving two storage locations all start with $(11)_2$. The CPU "knows" how long an instruction is by looking at its operation code.

The PSW contains a field to indicate the length of the instruction currently being executed; this is the "Instruction Length Code" field (predictably) of the PSW and occupies (Fig. 11.1 again) bits 32 and 33. This code is set to $(01)_2$ or $(10)_2$ or $(11)_2$, for 1, 2, or 3 halfwords, respectively, at the same time the instruction address is incremented; both are hardware functions performed by the CPU. The instruction length code is used to track back to the address of the currently executing instruction should an error occur—don't forget that the instruction address portion of the program status word points to the *next* instruction to be executed.

When exactly does this updating of the PSW take place? How does the computer know whether to get two, four, or six bytes per instruction without actually getting the instruction and checking the first two bits of the operation code? The answer to these questions depends on the hardware of a given machine. On a smaller machine or on any computer designed to move information into the CPU in sixteen-bit chunks, the instruction cycle consists of two distinct operations—get the first halfword, check it, and get the rest if necessary. With this system, the time spent waiting for the "rest" of the instruction provides a perfect opportunity for updating the PSW. Other machines might be designed to move more data between core and the CPU at one time; on such a machine, it might make sense to always fetch the maximum possible instruction, simply ignoring unwanted material. At any rate, updating the PSW is a hardware function which can be performed at very high speed and in parallel with almost any other function.

Condition Codes

Have you ever wondered how the computer knows whether or not it is to branch following a conditional branch instruction? Following a comparison instruction or certain arithmetic instructions, a condition code is set; the conditional branch instruction checks this condition code and, if the condition code matches the condition indicated in the instruction, the branch is executed (the instruction-address portion of the PSW is modified). The condition code is found in bits 34 and 35 of the program status word.

Core Protection—the Core Protect Key

On the IBM System/360, core is allocated to an individual program in 2048 (2K) byte blocks. One problem with multiprogramming which you may recall from a prior chapter is the possibility of interprogram interference, i.e., one program destroying or modifying another. To avoid this problem, IBM has developed a core protection feature, the key to which is the protection "key" found in bits 8 through 11 of the PSW. As core is assigned to a program, each 2K block is given the same four-bit core protection key; later, during execution of the program, access to any 2K block not having the same core protect key is grounds for immediate program termination.

Note that a *different* core protect key is *not* assigned to each 2048 byte block in the system's core; instead, the *same* key is assigned to *all* blocks associated with the same program. The resident operating system, to cite one example, is normally assigned the protect key $(0000)_2$; if this operating system needs 50K of core, the first twenty-five blocks would *all* have protect key $(0000)_2$. Later, a 100K application program might be assigned fifty consecutive blocks all with protect key $(0011)_2$. Refer back to Fig. 11.1 for a diagram of the PSW fields.

Other PSW Fields

Thus far, we've discussed the meaning of the protection key, the ILC or instruction length code, the CC or condition code, and the instruction address portions of the PSW. Several other fields (Fig. 11.1 again) remain. Most of these fields have to do with program interruptions; thus, we'll postpone our discussion until a bit later.

Controlling I/O

Input and output devices are very slow when compared to the internal processing speeds of the computer itself; multiprogramming, as you may remember, was essentially a reaction to this problem. Back in the chapter on hardware, we discussed a partial solution to this problem—the channel. A channel is essentially a small, special-purpose computer placed between the I/O device and the computer; among its functions are buffering, counting bytes, and incrementing a core address. Since the channel is a separate hardware device, these functions can be performed in parallel with other computer operations such as the execution of another program.

How does a channel know what to do? Where does the channel get its instructions (it is a kind of computer)? How does the channel know how many bytes are to be moved between an I/O device and the computer's main memory? Where in core can the data be found (output)? Where in core is the new data to be placed (input)? This information is given to the channel and the channel communicates with the CPU through three fields called the Channel Address Word (CAW), Channel Status Word (CSW), and Channel Command Word (CCW).

Let's consider the CCW first. Like any computer, the channel needs instructions to operate; a *channel program* consists of a series of channel command words or CCW's. A channel command word is really a doubleword; it holds a command code analogous to an operation code in a regular instruction, a data address showing where data can be found (or where it is to be stored) in core, a byte count field showing the number of bytes to be moved, and a number of flags to hold channel and operation information. An operation might indicate a read or a write or a tape rewind or any other operation. A channel program consists of one or more channel command words; it is written by a programmer to control a specific I/O operation. Like any other program, it is stored in core, often as a part of an access method. The relationship of the channel command word to the channel is just like that of the assembly language statement to the central processing unit.

Much as the computer program has its program status word, the channel has its channel address word or CAW. The channel address word is found at a fixed location in main memory, byte address 72, and contains the core address of the first channel command word to be executed by the channel (Fig. 11.2). The channel program address is placed in the channel address word just prior to the actual beginning of the I/O operation; the channel uses this field to find its first command. Following this initial contact, the channel keeps track of its next command on its own. A computer may have several channels and there is no sense tying up the system's only channel address word to support one channel.

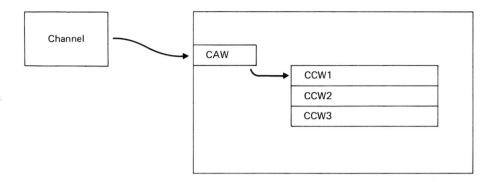

Channel Command Word

Channel Address Word

Fig. 11.2 The channel address word and the channel program

Information relating to the status of a channel is passed to the computer through the channel status word or CSW (Fig. 11.3). Like the channel command word, it's really a doubleword; the channel address word is the only *word* in this group. The CSW contains, in addition to the address of the channel program being executed, the data address, and, byte count, a status field where a binary code is used to indicate such information as device busy, channel-end, device-end, or a program check—in other words, the status of the input or output operation. Both the channel address word and the channel status word contain the program's core protection key, allowing for core protection checks during an input or output operation.

Let's review I/O control one more time. A channel program, consisting of one or more channel-command words (CCW's) has been previously written by a programmer and stored somewhere in core. Just prior to the beginning of an I/O operation, an operating system module places the address of this channel

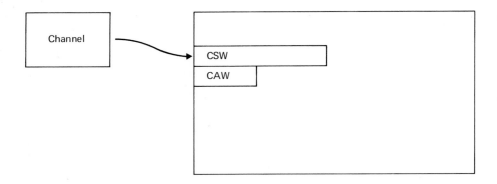

Channel Status Word

Key		Command Address	Status	Byte Count

Fig. 11.3 The channel status word

program in the channel address word (CAW) which is found at byte 72 in core. This same operating system module completes the channel command word or words by inserting the data address and byte count and places the core protection key in the channel address word. The channel, at some later time, reports its status to the computer through the channel status word (CSW) which is found at core address 64.

There are two types of channels—selector channels and multiplexer channels. A selector channel is designed to operate in burst mode, transmitting data between a device and core in a continuous stream. High-speed devices such as tape, disk, and drum are normally attached to a selector channel. A multiplexer is much more complicated, being designed to operate in an overlapped mode, getting a byte or two from a card reader, sending a byte to a printer, and so on. Low-speed devices such as card readers, printers, card punches, consoles, and terminals are usually attached to a multiplexer channel. Multiplexing involves substantial logic—the channel must keep track of byte counts and core locations for a number of different devices at the same time. On some smaller or slower computers, these logical functions are actually performed by the central processing unit, with the multiplexer channel "stealing" an occasional CPU cycle or two. In any case, the channel can deal directly with core without actually involving the CPU; this is called "direct memory access."

Privileged Instructions

On a computer system running multiple programs and several channels at the same time, the result of a policy allowing each program to completely control its own I/O could be disastrous; a better approach is to funnel all input and output operations through a single operating system module. This sounds great in theory, but what about the programmer who "cheats"?

On the IBM System/360, there are only four instructions for actually communicating with a channel; these instructions are: Halt I/O (HIO), Start I/O (SIO), Test CHannel (TCH), and Test I/O (TIO). These instructions are privileged; i.e., they can be executed only by an operating system module. This principle is enforced by the core protection feature; the operating system, as you may remember, is given a protection key of $(0000)_2$ and privileged instructions can be executed *only* when the protection key field of the PSW is $(0000)_2$.

In order to start an I/O operation, the programmer must first branch or link to an operating system module. This system program can then take over, set up the CAW and the channel program CCW's, issue the privileged Start I/O instruction, and test the channel-status word (CSW) for error or successful start

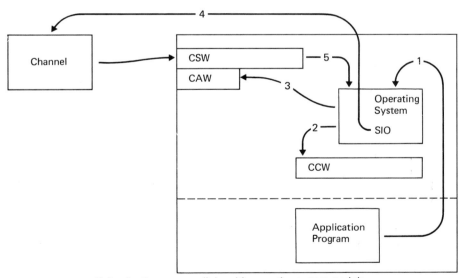

1) Application program links with operating system module.
2) Channel program completed.
3) Address of channel program placed in channel address word.
4) Start I/O instruction issued.
5) Channel reports status through channel status word.

Fig. 11.4 Operating system and channel communication

(Fig. 11.4). A few, rare programmers still insist on coding their own channel programs, but even they must surrender control to the operating system in order to start the I/O operation.

The Interrupt Concept

Exactly how does a programmer link to an operating-system module? Labels won't work, because a label is translated into a relative address by a compiler or an assembler and has meaning only within a load module. A branch to a fixed absolute address isn't practical; for one thing, the operating system has a different protection key. An external reference of some kind might provide a solution, but the interrupt concept provides a better one.

The interrupt concept works by switching PSW's. To visualize the workings of an interrupt, let's look at core storage in a typical system and highlight a few key fields:

1. our program,
2. the operating system module which will start an actual I/O operation,
3. the PSW (Fig. 11.5),
4. two additional doublewords known respectively as the Old PSW and the New PSW (Fig. 11.5).

The CPU is executing the application program by following its usual pattern—look at the PSW to find the address of the next instruction, find that instruction and decode it, execute the instruction, look at the PSW for the address of the next instruction, and so on. At some point in time, the programmer is ready for an I/O operation, so he codes a special instruction. On the IBM computers, this is a Supervisor Call (SVC) instruction. This instruction, like any other instruction, is found by the CPU through the PSW, moved into the central processing unit, decoded, and executed. What happens when the instruction is executed is, however, a bit different.

The SVC instruction, when executed, causes an interrupt to occur. An interrupt is implemented by system hardware. It's a two step operation. First, the current program status word is copied into the Old PSW field. The New PSW has as its instruction address field the address of the first instruction in the operating system module; this New PSW is moved into the current PSW field during the second step of this hardware operation. The central processing unit now enters its next instruction cycle, looking for the instruction to be executed at the address specified in the current program status word; this next

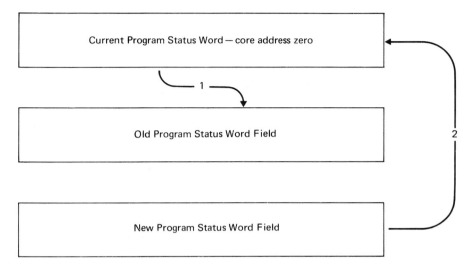

Fig. 11.5 The interrupt concept

instruction is in the operating system. The New PSW, since it allows linkage to an operating system module, probably contains $(0000)_2$ in its core protection key field, thus allowing privileged instructions to be executed. Later, control is returned to the application program by moving the Old PSW back into the current PSW location. Figure 11.5 summarizes these steps.

Let's review this interrupt concept again, step by step, using Fig. 11.6 as a guide. Our program is loaded in core beginning with core location 50,000; the operating system module which will eventually handle our I/O is loaded starting with address 1000. The New PSW field, which is found at a fixed location in core, has zeros as its protect key and 1000 as its instruction address (Fig. 11.6a); the Old PSW, as we begin this operation, contains "who knows what." The current PSW, the key to CPU functioning, is the first doubleword in core and contains a protect key of $(0010)_2$, the key of our program; the instruction address reads 50,500 which is, let's assume, the address of the instruction immediately following a supervisor call (meaning that the supervisor call is currently executing).

The supervisor call instruction is like any other instruction during the instruction cycle; not until the execution cycle does the actual interrupt occur. First, the current PSW is copied into the Old PSW field which is found in a fixed location in core (Fig. 11.6b). As soon as this step is completed, the New

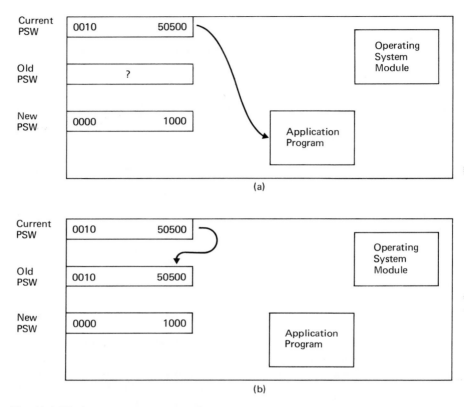

Fig. 11.6 The interrupt concept, step by step

PSW is electronically copied into the current PSW field, the first doubleword in core (Fig. 11.6c). This completes the interrupt.

The central processing unit is now ready for its next instruction cycle. Not being a particularly original thinker, the CPU looks for its next instruction at the address specified in the last three bytes of the first doubleword in core which now contains 1000, the address of the desired operating system module. The operating system module thus begins executing; since the protection key is $(0000)_2$, privileged instructions are allowed. Later, after the input or output operation has been started, the Old PSW field is moved into the first doubleword in core (the current PSW) by the last instruction in the operating system module (Fig. 11.6d); the next CPU cycle will once again fetch an instruction in the application program.

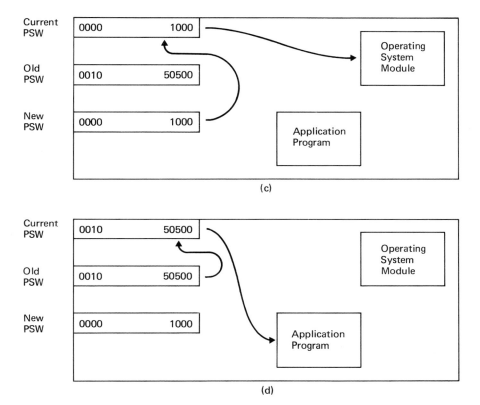

Fig. 11.6 (*Cont.*)

That's really all there is to it, the interrupt concept is that simple. Don't try to look for complicating factors just because you're sure that interrupts "must be confusing"; there aren't any.

Interrupt Types

The IBM System/360 recognizes five distinct types of interrupts; they are:

1. external,
2. supervisor call,

3. program,
4. machine-check,
5. input/output.

External Interrupts

An external interrupt can come from any of three sources:

1. The operator's console,
2. Another CPU or some other control device,
3. The timer.

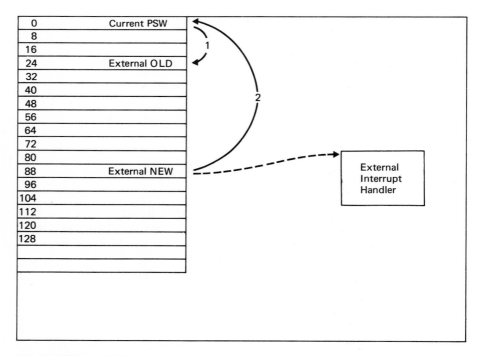

Fig. 11.7 External interrupts

Of prime importance to the average programmer is the timer interrupt; this is the mechanism for controlling a time-shared system or for terminating a program which has exceeded its time estimate.

An external interrupt is an electronic signal to the central processing unit. As the interrupt signal is received by the central processing unit, hardware takes over, dropping the current program status word into the Old External PSW field (core address 24, the fourth doubleword in main memory) and, shortly thereafter, moving the New External PSW into the current PSW field (Fig. 11.7). Incidentally, if the interrupt should arrive while the CPU is executing an instruction, the processing of the interrupt is delayed until the instruction is complete; i.e., external interrupts are recognized between instructions.

Bits 16 through 31 of the PSW contain an interrupt cause code. As part of the interrupt process, this sixteen-bit field is set in the Old PSW, giving the external interrupt handler routine in the operating system the ability to identify the exact cause of the interrupt.

Supervisor Call (SVC) Interrupts

On the System/360, the programmer does not directly control any I/O operations, needing the help of the operating system—the core resident portion of the operating system is known as the supervisor. The programmer links to this operating system module through the supervisor call or SVC interrupt.

The supervisor call interrupt is a bit different, starting with a program instruction. The SVC instruction is pretty straightforward, with, for example,

```
SVC    17
```

representing a request for supervisor module number 17 which might be a read or a write or an OPEN or a CLOSE or any other operating system module. The SVC interrupt handler routine starts with a branch table which gets us to the right module—each individual routine has its own number. Most programmers don't code their own SVC's, this instruction usually being buried in a macro or an access method.

During the execution cycle of an SVC instruction, the interrupt's hardware functions take over, dropping the current program status word into the Old SVC PSW doubleword (core address 32), moving the New SVC PSW (core address 96) into the current PSW field (address 0), and moving the operand fields of the SVC instruction, the 17 in our above example, into the interrupt code field of the Old SVC PSW (Fig. 11.8). If you're getting tired of reading about PSW switching, that's good—you're learning it.

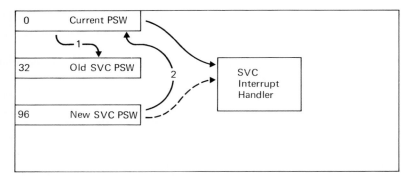

Fig. 11.8 Supervisor call interrupts

Program Interrupts

It's a rare programmer who doesn't soon learn about program interrupts—zero divides, invalid data, overflows, addressing, protection exceptions, and so on. A program interrupt is brought on by a programming error; the CPU recognizes such errors as they occur and implements hardware functions which copy the current PSW into the Old Program PSW field (address byte 40), copy the New Program PSW (byte 104) into the first doubleword in core (the current PSW), and move the interrupt cause code into the Old program status word (Fig. 11.9). There are a total of fifteen different program interrupt cause codes which are summarized in Fig. 11.10.

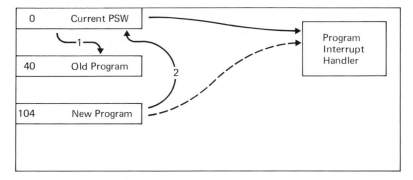

Fig. 11.9 Program interrupts

CODE		
DEC	*HEX*	*MEANING*
1	0001	Operation—invalid operation code.
2	0002	Privileged operation—programmer attempted to execute a privileged operation outside protect key 0000.
3	0003	Execute—an EXECUTE instruction led to another EXECUTE instruction.
4	0004	Protection.
5	0005	Addressing.
6	0006	Specification—incorrect word boundary or register.
7	0007	Data—invalid data.
8	0008	Fixed-point overflow.
9	0009	Fixed-point divide—often a zero divide.
10	000A	Decimal overflow.
11	000B	Decimal divide.
12	000C	Exponent overflow—floating-point exponent too big.
13	000D	Exponent underflow.
14	000E	Significance—a floating-point addition or subtraction yields an all zero fraction.
15	000F	Floating-point divide.

Fig. 11.10 Program interrupt cause codes

Machine-check Interrupts

A machine-check interrupt indicates that the self-checking circuitry of IBM's System/360 series has detected a hardware failure. If an instruction is executing when a machine-check occurs, the instruction is terminated—there is no sense trying to perform any computations or logical operations on a computer known to be malfunctioning. As a result of a machine-check interrupt, the current PSW is copied into the doubleword starting at core address 48 (the Old machine-check PSW), the New machine-check PSW is copied into the current PSW field, and, under control of the operating system, the state of internal circuitry is copied into core. The New Machine-check PSW is found in the doubleword beginning at core address 112; this interrupt is described in graphical form in Fig. 11.11.

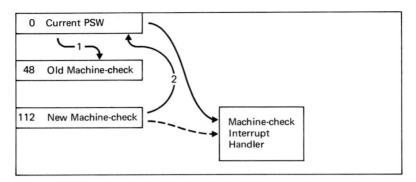

Fig. 11.11 Machine-check interrupts

Input/Output Interrupts

Channels and the central processing unit work independently—the fact that a channel can free the CPU from the need to directly control an I/O operation is the primary justification for its use. Since the channel is working independently, it must have a mechanism for signaling the CPU when an operation is completed. This mechanism is the input/output interrupt.

When a channel completes input or completes output or, for some other reason requires the attention of the central processing unit, an interrupt is sent. Note that the input/output interrupt originates in the channel. An I/O interrupt causes the current PSW to be copied into the Old Input/Output interrupt doubleword (address 56), the New Input/Output PSW to be moved up to the current PSW location, and the channel and device address of the unit causing

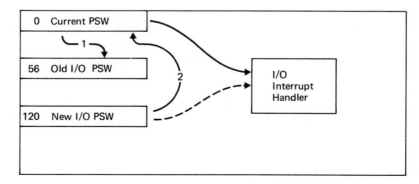

Fig. 11.12 Input/output interrupts

the interrupt to be dropped into the interrupt-cause-code field (bits 16 through 31) of the Old program status word. The channel status word is also set by the interrupt hardware. If the central processing unit is executing an instruction at the time of the interrupt, that instruction is completed before the interrupt is recognized. The input/output interrupt is summarized in Fig. 11.12.

Permanent Storage Assignments

Throughout our discussion of the program status word, channel status word, channel address word, and interrupts, we indicated that these important fields are found in fixed core locations; these permanent storage assignments are summarized in Fig. 11.13. Since these locations are fixed, the system programmer need not worry about the location of key information.

ADDRESS			
DECIMAL	HEXADECIMAL	LENGTH	PURPOSE
0	0	doubleword	Current PSW
8	8	doubleword	Initial program load CCW1
16	10	doubleword	Initial program load CCW2
24	18	doubleword	External old PSW
32	20	doubleword	Supervisor call old PSW
40	28	doubleword	Program old PSW
48	30	doubleword	Machine-check old PSW
56	38	doubleword	Input/Output old PSW
64	40	doubleword	Channel status word
72	48	word	Channel address word
76	4C	word	Unused
80	50	word	Timer
84	54	word	Unused
88	58	doubleword	External new PSW
96	60	doubleword	Supervisor call new PSW
104	68	doubleword	Program new PSW
112	70	doubleword	Machine-check new PSW
120	78	doubleword	Input/Output new PSW
128	80	variable	Diagnostic scan-out area— following machine-check.

Fig. 11.13 Permanent storage assignments

Masking

The typical data processing system has more than one channel—perhaps one multiplexer and two or three selectors; these channels operate independently and, often, simultaneously. It is possible that two or more I/O interrupts might occur, from different channels, in a very brief span of time, perhaps even at the same instant of time. Let's see what might happen if two I/O interrupts were to arrive at the central processing unit within a few microseconds of each other.

As we begin this exercise, an application program, Program A, has control of the CPU. The first of our input/output interrupts arrives at the central processing unit (Fig. 11.14a), dropping the current program status word into the Old I/O interrupt slot and moving the New I/O interrupt PSW into the current PSW doubleword. A brief instant later, a second interrupt arrives while the first one is still being processed. Hardware, in its automatic way, drops the current PSW into the Old I/O PSW and moves the New I/O PSW to the

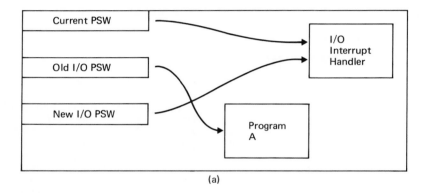

(a)

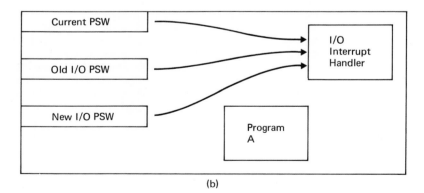

(b)

Fig. 11.14 The problem with multiple input/output interrupts in a brief span of time

current position (Fig. 11.14b). What happens to the link back to the program? Eventually, the operating system will return control to the original application program, but, as a result of the perfectly normal system action in handling the second interrupt, the PSW showing where to resume the program has been wiped out. We've lost the ability to resume processing where we left off. This cannot be allowed to happen.

The system mask, the first eight bits of the PSW, provides a mechanism for getting around this problem (a diagram of the PSW fields is repeated in Fig. 11.15 for convenience). The first bit is associated with channel zero, usually the multiplexer; if this bit is a binary 1 the central processing unit can accept an interrupt from this channel, while a binary 0 indicates that the interrupt cannot be accepted and must be kept pending in the channel. Bits 1 through 6 have the same meaning for channels 1 through 6—selectors; a 1 means that an interrupt can be accepted by the CPU and a 0 means that the interrupt must be kept pending. If the New I/O PSW has binary zeros in its first seven bit positions (Fig. 11.16), no additional input/output interrupts can be accepted as long as this PSW is in control; as soon as the operating-system module which handles the interrupt finishes processing and, as its last act, moves the Old I/O PSW back to the current position, a pending I/O interrupt can be recognized.

The eighth bit (bit number 7 since our count starts with 0) is used to mask external interrupts for much the same reason—one external interrupt might be closely followed by another. Much less likely, but still possible, is the occurrence

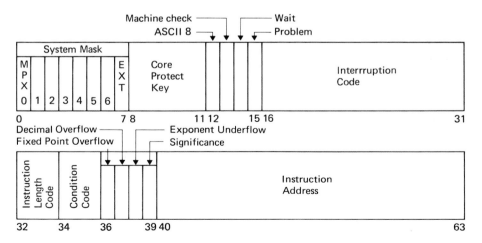

Fig. 11.15 The program status word

Current PSW	Mask 0000 0000	Key 0000		I/O Interrupt Handler Address

Old I/O PSW	Mask 1111 1111	Key 0101		Application Program Address

New I/O PSW	Mask 0000 0000	Key 0000		I/O Interrupt Handler Address

Fig. 11.16 Masking input-output interrupts

of an external interrupt closely followed by an input/output interrupt closely followed by another external interrupt (or an I/O, external, I/O sequence), which could destroy a key program status word in the Old External field even if external interrupts masked out all other external interrupts. To prevent this from happening, both input/output and external interrupts are normally masked during the handling of *both* external *and* input/output interrupts.

What about the other three interrupt types? What happens if a supervisor call, a program interrupt, or a machine-check were to happen during the processing of some other interrupt? As far as simultaneous interrupts of the same type are concerned, both the SVC and program interrupts arise from a program instruction and, since the CPU can only process one instruction at a time, simultaneous interrupts can't occur. If the operating system is handling an interrupt of any kind, it has no need for an SVC interrupt since the machine is already in a supervisor state; thus, an "SVC and something" problem can't occur. Conflicts with a program interrupt are unlikely since, ideally, the operating system can't program check. If a machine check occurs, why worry about simultaneous interrupts? A machine check indicates a machine malfunction, and it's senseless to attempt to continue processing on a machine known to be in some way defective.

Incidently, machine checks can be masked, usually during the processing of another machine check—PSW bit 13 controls this function.

The Program Mask

Following a program interrupt on most systems, normal system action is to terminate the program causing the interrupt, perhaps producing a dump. At times, the programmer may wish to override this standard procedure, providing a special subroutine to handle such potential problems as overflows or underflows—PL/1's ON CONDITION options are a good example. Bits 36 through 39 allow for the suppression of fixed-point overflows, decimal overflows, exponent underflows, and significance exceptions.

Program States

The computer, at any one time, is either executing a problem program or a supervisor program; i.e., it is either in the problem state or the supervisory state. Bit 15 of the PSW (Fig. 11.15) is used to indicate the computer's state—1 means problem and 0 means supervisory. This bit, along with the core protection key, provides a double check for priviledged instruction execution.

A given program is, additionally, ready to resume processing or waiting for the completion of an input or output operation; i.e., it's either in the ready state or the wait state. Bit 14 of the PSW is used to indicate a program's readiness.

The only program status word bit we have yet to mention is bit number 12; this bit is used to indicate whether EBCDIC or ASCII–8 codes are being used.

Interrupt Priority

"If it can happen, it will." At some point in the life of a computer system, all five types of interrupts will hit the central processing unit at precisely the same instant of time. Which is handled first? When faced with such a pure priority decision, almost any answer will do; the important thing is having some procedure, *any* procedure, ready.

On the IBM System/360, the machine-check will be serviced first—no sense trying to handle a supervisor call on a malfunctioning machine. Once the machine-check is out of the way, here's what happens (Fig. 11.17):

1. The *program* interrupt is accepted, dropping the PSW of the application program into the Old Program PSW doubleword.
2. The *external* interrupt is accepted, dropping the current PSW, which points to the program interrupt handling routine, into the Old External PSW.
3. The *input/output* interrupt is accepted, dropping the external interrupt's program status word into the Old I/O PSW.

Since no more interrupts are pending (or if pending on a channel can't be accepted because of masking), the input/output interrupt handler, which is pointed to by the current program status word, begins processing. Following completion, the Old I/O PSW is moved into the current PSW position, allowing

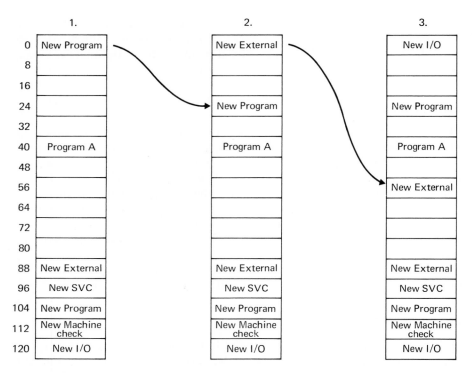

Fig. 11.17 Simultaneous interrupts

the external interrupt handler to take over. This module, by making its old program status word current, transfers control to the program interrupt handler which, through the same mechanism, gets us back to the original program.

Incidently, step number one above could have described either the program or the supervisor call interrupt; they can't possibly occur simultaneously. Why?

A Typical Example

To illustrate the interrupt concept in a slightly different light, let's consider a simple example. Our program, the only problem program in core, is about to issue a supervisor call requesting the start of an input operation; the initial current PSW (Fig. 11.18a) points to the SVC instruction. During the CPU's instruction cycle, this instruction is moved into the central processing unit and decoded, and the instruction address is incremented by two bytes (the length of an SVC instruction).

The execution of an SVC instruction causes a hardware interrupt, dropping the current program status word into the Old SVC PSW and making the New SVC PSW current (Fig. 11.18b). The central processing unit continues to follow its same pattern, entering an instruction cycle by fetching the instruction stored at the address specified in the current program-status word; following the interrupt, this instruction is in the supervisor call operating system routine (Fig. 11.18c).

After the supervisor call handling routine gets control, it:

1. sets up a start I/O (SIO) instruction;
2. completes the byte count and core address fields of one or more channel-command words (CCW's) in the channel program, using the information specified in a program data control block;
3. places the address of the first CCW into the channel address word (CAW);
4. issues the SIO, thus starting the physical input operation (Fig. 11.18d).

Before returning control to the initial program, the operating system module repeatedly checks the channel status word (CSW) until the channel reports either a successful or unsuccessful beginning; this is illustrated in Fig. 11.18(e). If unsuccessful, the operating system module either retries or reports the reason for its failure; if successful, the channel assumes further responsibility for the transfer of data and the operating system module is finished. As its last act, the control program moves the Old SVC PSW back into the current position (Fig. 11.18f), making sure to first set bit number 14 to a binary 1 indicating that, since the input operation has not yet been completed, the program is in a wait state.

With the current PSW indicating that the program in control is in a wait state, the CPU does nothing for a while. Finally, at some later time, the channel completes the input operation and sends an input/output interrupt to the CPU, dropping the current PSW into the Old I/O PSW location and making the New I/O PSW current (Fig. 11.18g). The new current PSW has bit number 14 set to a binary zero indicating a run state; it points to the first instruction in the input/output handler routine, so that routine begins executing. The channel status word is checked to make sure that the operation was successfully completed, while the interrupt cause code portion of the Old I/O PSW shows the channel and device address of the interrupt source—not too critical in our single program example but, as we'll see in later chapters, an important cross-check item in a multiprogramming system. After ascertaining that all is well with the requested input operation, the I/O interrupt handler sets bit number 14 in the Old I/O PSW to zero (run state) and moves this program status word

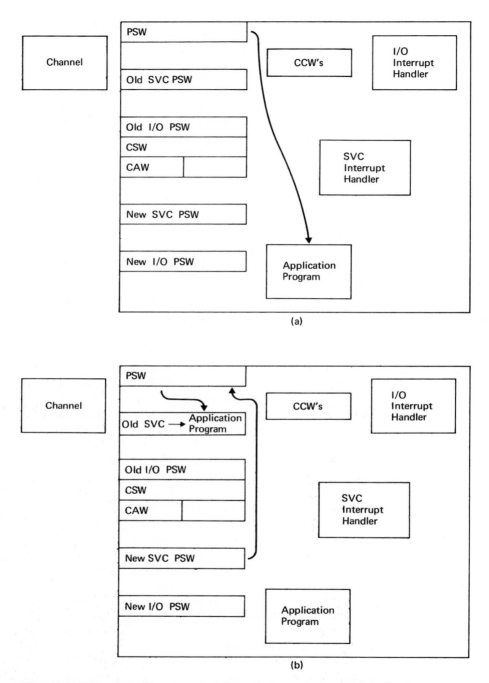

Fig. 11.18 An example of interrupts and channel communications. (a) application program about to issue SVC; (b) PSWs switched as a result of SVC interrupt.

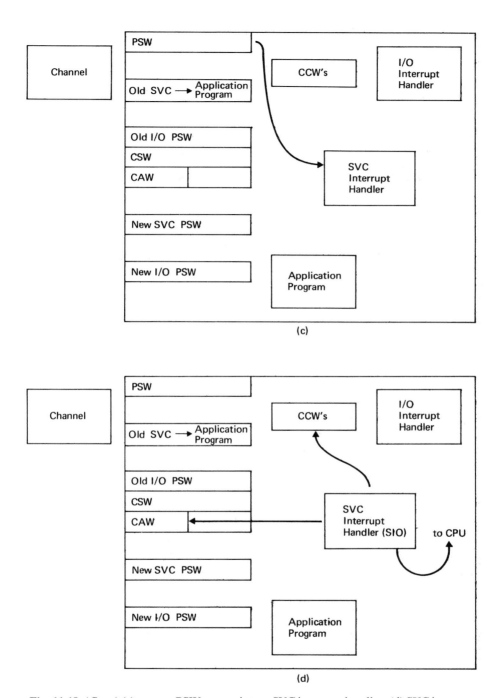

Fig. 11.18 (*Cont.*) (c) current PSW now points to SVC interrupt handler; (d) SVC interrupt handler routine completes CCWs, placing address into CAW

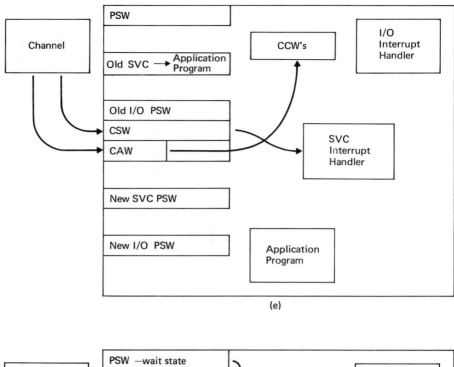

(e)

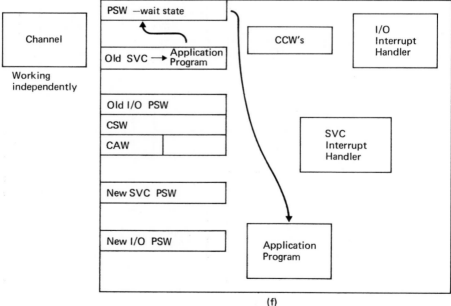

(f)

Fig. 11.18 (*Cont.*) (e) channel locates its program through the CAW and reports status through CSW; (f) program in wait state, channel works independently

194

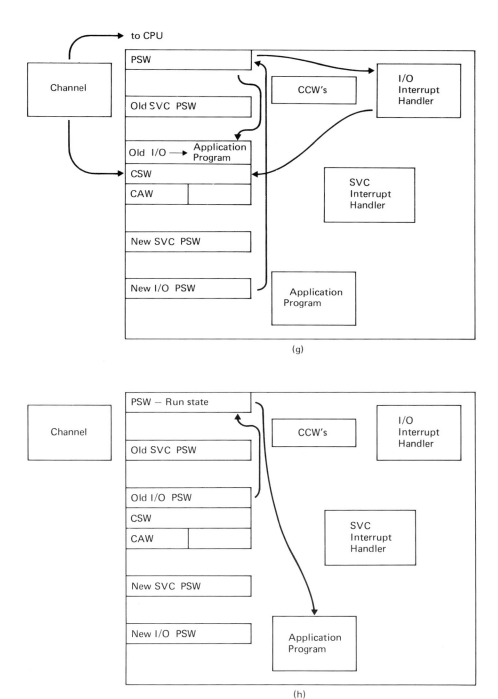

Fig. 11.18 (*Cont.*) (g) I/O interrupt occurs some time later, channel status reported through CSW; (h) original program resumes control

195

back to the current position, thus returning control to the original program (Fig. 11.18h).

With multiprogramming, of course, the problem is a bit more complex. During the time our computer spent in the wait state in the above example, a multiprogramming system would have started another program; since there is only one old and one new program status word field for each interrupt type, starting another program means that the latest PSW for the "waiting" program must be saved if a return trail is to be preserved. How this can be done is one of the topics covered in the two next chapters.

Other Manufacturers—Other Approaches

There are no patents on the basic concepts underlying the program status word or interrupts or channel linkage; all manufacturers do essentially the same things, though often in very different ways. Consider, for example, the program status word. No law says that the basic control and status information used to direct the actions of a central processing unit must occupy the first sixty-four bits of core storage; often, one or more special registers are set aside to hold this information. The PSW or its equivalent can be located at any fixed spot, as long as the CPU can find it. Often, the functions of instruction location, condition code setting, masking, and interrupt support are broken into discrete pieces, yielding a number of program status "words" or registers. Even the definition of a "word" varies from manufacturer to manufacturer, ranging from 12 bits to 64 bits and beyond; some machines even support a variable-length word.

One of the most important differences between the various suppliers of computer mainframes lies in the way they handle interrupts. Some computers are designed to handle only one or two different types of interrupts; IBM can handle five on its System/360 and System/370 series; the Xerox Data Systems Sigma 5/7 series is capable of working with up to 224 interrupt levels. As an upper limit, imagine one interrupt for each different I/O device, a separate SVC-like interrupt for starting an I/O operation with each individual device attached to the system, at least fifteen different program interrupts (one for each type), and so on. The big advantage to multiple interrupts is speed—it is possible to link directly to the specific operating system module designed to handle a particular variety of interrupt rather than first going to a general module (perhaps a branch table) whose only function is to link to the desired routine. The cost of the multiple-interrupt approach is measured in a loss of some flexibility. The interrupt is normally implemented through hardware; hardware is fast but a bit tougher to change than a program.

The sheer number of interrupts is not the only place where manufacturers differ; the IBM approach of Old PSW's and New PSW's for each interrupt type is not universal. One popular variation involves maintaining stacks or queues of pending interrupts in special registers or in core; as each additional interrupt arrives, it is simply added to the list. Many different approaches have been tried; let's take a quick look at two of them.

Stacking interrupts is somewhat analogous to a last-in-first-out inventory policy. Imagine that in our computer system we have a current PSW, a single Old PSW, and an amount of core set aside to hold an interrupt stack. An application program is in control as we start our look at the system. An interrupt occurs—any interrupt—and the current PSW is copied into the Old PSW field as the interrupt takes over. While this interrupt is being processed, three more interrupts (we'll call them B, C, and D) occur in quick succession. Rather than interrupt the current interrupt, these three will be kept pending in core. An address pointer identifies the first available spot in the stack; as interrupt B hits the system, it is stored at this location and the address pointer is incremented by the length of the New PSW. Interrupt C, by going through the same procedure, is stored just after interrupt B. After interrupt D is accepted, the pointer is looking just beyond this last "pending" interrupt. As soon as that first interrupt completes its processing, the system scans the interrupt stack, discovers that there are pending interrupts, decrements the address pointer to the start of interrupt D, moves this information into the current PSW, and handles the interrupt. If no additional interrupts occur, interrupt C is taken next, followed by interrupt B; additional interrupts would be placed at the end of the queue and would therefore be executed before any interrupts already present. Finally, when the queue is empty, the application program with control information stored in the Old PSW field regains control; in effect, the Old PSW field is the first position on the stack.

Interrupt queues normally involve two address pointers, one showing the location of the interrupt which is to be processed next and another tracking the next available location for an incoming interrupt. It's a bit like a first-in/first-out inventory system.

Queueing and stacking algorithms can get very complex, taking into account such factors as time in queue and interrupt priority among others. The IBM approach of masking I/O and external interrupts isn't needed here—there is no Old PSW to be destroyed. One key advantage lies in the handling of multiple levels of interrupts, with a 200-interrupt level system needing only as much space as perhaps a 10-interrupt system using the Old and New PSW approach of IBM. Where does the New PSW come from? Some might be maintained in an IBM-like New PSW queue, while others might come from the interrupt source itself—imagine each I/O device sending an interrupt containing the core address of the operating system module which is to handle the interrupt. Specific algorithms and techniques may vary, but the underlying concept of an interrupt remains pretty much the same.

The mechanism for communicating with a channel can vary significantly among manufacturers as well. In Control Data Corporation's CYBER series, for example, the central processing unit shares the spotlight with a number of peripheral processors one of which handles all the problems of input and output. The peripheral processors are all independent and can work in parallel with the central processing unit; the logical equivalent of CCW's, the CAW, CSW, and the SIO instruction can be set up and executed while the central processor is handling other business, as can the handling of the eventual I/O interrupt.

Throughout this chapter, we've been concentrating on the IBM System/360. Our objective has not been one of trying to promote the products of this firm. What we wanted to do was to illustrate, in some detail, the actual workings of interrupts, basic program controls, and channel linkage on some computer—any manufacturer's equipment would have served as well. Why then IBM? For most readers, IBM provides the most relevant source of examples. In Chapter 12, we'll take a look at an operating system written specifically to support the IBM System/360—DOS; in Chapter 13, OS/MFT will be discussed. While reading these chapters take special note of how the material we've just covered provides a framework for the operating system.

Summary

In this chapter, we have covered several topics including the format and function of the program status word, the interrupt concept, and the mechanism used by IBM for controlling physical input and output operations. In effect, the topics covered in this chapter provide a bridge between the pure hardware and the pure software components of a computer system, allowing a program to communicate with a channel or the central processing unit.

The key fields in the program status word (PSW) include: the system mask for masking I/O and external interrupts, the core protection key, the interruption code, the instruction length code, the condition code, the program mask for masking certain program interrupts, the instruction address, and the individual bits which indicate the program state. The current PSW is *always* the first doubleword in core.

Channel operations are controlled by a channel program, stored in core and consisting of a series of channel command words (CCW's). The channel finds its first channel command word by looking at the channel address word

(CAW) which is always found at address 72 in core; the channel reports its status back to the main computer through the channel status word (CSW), byte address 64. Starting, terminating, and testing a channel are some of the functions performed by a number of privileged operations which can be executed only by an operating system module. The CPU is able to recognize an operating system or supervisor module in two ways: the core protect key in the current PSW (the only program status word the central processing unit cares about) is all zeros and the problem state key, bit 15 in the PSW, is also zero.

The five types of interrupts recognized on an IBM System/360 are: External, Supervisor Call, Program, Machine-check, and Input/Output. All interrupts are handled by dropping the current PSW into the Old PSW field and moving the New PSW to the current position—the first doubleword in core. The cause of the interrupt is placed in the Old program status word at the end of this hardware process—the interrupt handler routine will find the proper interrupt cause code in the Old program status word as it begins processing.

A Final Note

Interrupts are actually handled by programs once the hardware functions of switching PSW's is complete. Except for the fact that they are hopefully well-written and use a number of privileged instructions, these operating system modules are much like any other program.

Exercises

1. On the IBM System/360, all I/O operations are forced through an operating system module. How is this process enforced?

2. How does System/360 handle an interrupt?

3. Describe the contents of the interrupt cause code field of the Old PSW following each of the five types of interrupts allowed on System/360.

4. An application program has just issued an SVC to request the start of an I/O operation. Describe everything that happens between the SVC and the return of control to the original program.

5. Explain interrupt queueing and interrupt stacking—approaches used by manufacturers other than IBM.

6. Why is it necessary to mask off I/O and external interrupts during the processing of an I/O interrupt?

7. The contents of certain fixed locations in core are:

ADDRESS	CONTENTS IN HEXADECIMAL
0	FF04000B D001 3000
8	00000000 00000720
16	00000000 00000000
24	00510082 C0026400
32	FF510008 C0031424
40	FF51000B C003F340
48	00510000 C004A000
56	00510003 C00422FA
64	00000000 00000000
72	00000000 00000000
80	00000000 00000000
88	00040000 0001A000
96	FF040000 00017000
104	FF040000 0001 3000
112	00040000 00011000
120	00040000 00015000

Sketch a map of core showing the location of each of the interrupt handling routines. What kind of interrupt has just happened? What is the address of the "bad" instruction? Can an I/O interrupt happen now? How do you know? Can a privileged instruction be executed?

CHAPTER 12

IBM System/360
Disk Operating System

Overview

IBM's Disk Operating System (DOS) is a software package designed to control an IBM System/360 or System/370 computer. It includes modules to handle interrupts, coordinate job-to-job transition, communicate with channels, handle I/O operations, maintain a series of libraries, compile and link-edit programs, and in general supervise a multiprogramming operation. All of these functions must be performed within an IBM System/360 or System/370 environment. The operating system must provide a mechanism for smooth coordination between the programmer's application module and the PSW, interrupt-handling, and channel-communication concepts which are built into this computer series. In this chapter, we'll study the key operating system modules which handle these functions.

DOS is used on smaller computers. The operating system is somewhat limited in scope—the small user is rarely interested in software intended to be "all things to all people," preferring an operating system designed to be efficient in his environment. This limited scope makes DOS an ideal operating system for our purposes here—it's great for introducing basic concepts. In Chapter 13, we'll be building on these basic concepts as we move into a much more complex operating system—OS/MFT.

DOS System Geography

Under DOS, a computer's main storage is divided into a number of fixed-length partitions as shown in Fig. 12.1. The first partition, beginning at core location 0, holds the supervisor program. This first partition is itself subdivided. Starting at core address 0, we find the current PSW, old and new

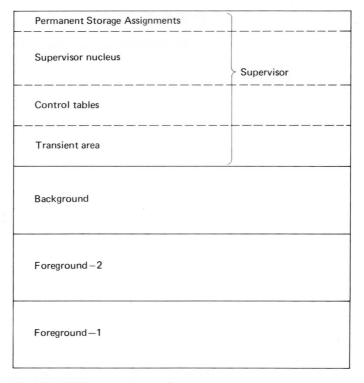

Fig. 12.1 DOS system geography

PSW fields, CAW, CSW, and the other permanent storage assignments described in the prior chapter. Following these permanent fields, we find the supervisor nucleus, a series of core-resident modules which take care of such things as interrupt handling, channel scheduling, program loading, error recovery, core protection, and job accounting. Following the nucleus is a series of control tables, giving the resident supervisor a mechanism for keeping track of I/O device assignments. We'll take a close look at the contents of these tables a bit later in the chapter. The final piece of the first partition is a transient area which holds, as you might expect, transient modules. These are operating system modules whose expected use is not sufficiently high to justify placing them in a core-resident state; instead, they are kept on disk (usually) and loaded into core when needed.

What remains of main memory is divided into from one to five problem-program partitions (in the late-1975 DOS release). The first of these is called the Background partition. In our example (Fig. 12.1), the Background partition is followed by a Foreground-2 partition, which is followed by a Foreground-1 partition; the number is an indication of partition priority, with Foreground-1 having top priority and the Background partition having lowest priority. If our system were supporting a full complement of six partitions (one for the operating system plus five problem-program partitions), Foreground-4 and Foreground-3 would be found between the Background and Foreground-2 partitions in our example, with the priority sequence being F-1, F-2, F-3, F-4, and, finally, the Background partition.

Getting Started—System Generation

An operating system and system configuration such as the one pictured in Fig. 12.1 does not simply spring into being; it must come from somewhere. The source is a procedure known as SYStem GENeration (SYSGEN).

The manufacturer (in this case, IBM) maintains a complete master copy of the operating system. When a customer decides to purchase or lease a computer, representatives of both IBM and the customer get together and plan the detailed content of the operating system for the customer's own operating environment. By analyzing typical applications and by identifying the specific devices to be attached to the system, it is possible to pinpoint those operating system modules which are of greatest importance to this specific installation; these key modules can be concentrated in the supervisor nucleus, the portion of the operating system which is core resident, while less-used modules are given transient status. Tables are created to support the specific I/O devices and the partition configuration chosen by the customer. This "made to order" version of the DOS operating system is then copied to a SYStem RESidence device, usually a disk pack; this SYSRES pack, when transferred to the customer's computer, is the source of the operating system.

Initial Program Load

As long as the operating system, even a *disk* operating system, remains on a disk pack, it does little or no good; if the operating system is to perform useful work, it must be copied from the SYSRES device into core. This objective is achieved through a procedure called Initial Program Load (IPL).

The first step in the IPL sequence is to mount the system-residence pack on a disk drive. A series of control cards containing special job control language statements is then placed in the system card reader. Next, the operator sets switches on the computer control panel to indicate the channel and device address of the SYSRES device and pushes the LOAD button on the control panel. As a result of this series of steps, the core resident portion of the supervisor, the supervisor nucleus, is read from the system residence device into core. Before turning control over to the supervisor, the operator has an option to change certain system parameters by entering commands either through a card reader or the operator's console.

Once the supervisor has been loaded, the copy of the core-resident portion serves as backup. Since the system residence pack contains supervisor transients and system libraries in addition to a copy of the nucleus, SYSRES normally remains mounted when the system is running; if the computer goes "down" for any reason—hardware malfunction, program bug, or according to plan—the IPL procedure is simply repeated (although many operators would object to the use of the word "simply").

Loading Application Programs—Single Program Initiation

Once IPL has been successfully accomplished, the computer system is ready to accept application programs. One core resident supervisor module is called the Single Program Initiation (SPI) Routine (Fig. 12.2); by passing control statements to this routine through his console, the operator can request the loading and execution of a specific application program in a foreground partition. The operator can make device assignments and request program execution through console commands which are quite similar to the job control statements we studied back in Chapter 7.

The Job Stream Approach

With few exceptions, job-to-job or job-step-to-job-step transition is pretty trivial—an execute statement and, perhaps, a few device assignments. To insist that a human operator type these instructions each time a job is run is a very inefficient way of managing a computer system.

By using job-control cards, individual control statements can be keypunched and subsequently read by a card reader, a procedure which consumes far less time than typing every one. A programmer can prepare his job deck, using a JOB card to mark the beginning, a "/&" card to mark the end, EXEC cards to identify individual job steps, and ASSGN cards to make I/O device assignments; this job deck thus becomes a self-contained series of program statements and system commands requiring little or no operator intervention (beyond, perhaps, mounting tapes or disks and responding to program messages) from program start to job completion. Job-step-to-job-step transition is handled by job control cards instead of by operator messages, a significantly more efficient procedure.

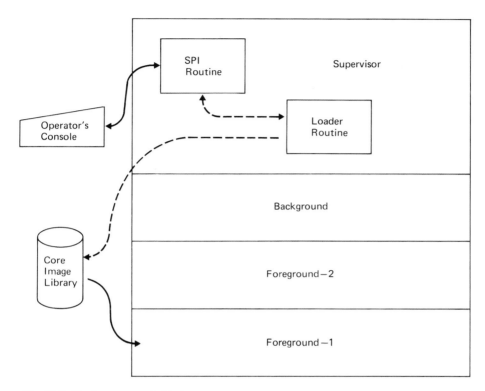

Fig. 12.2 Single program initiation

Why stop with one job? There is no reason why any number of jobs can't be loaded, back to back, into the system's card reader and processed in sequence, one job after another. JOB cards and "/&" cards serve to separate jobs, and, within a job, the EXEC cards serve to identify individual job steps. Using such a "job stream" approach, job-to-job transition can be handled smoothly and efficiently by a program written to interpret job control statements, with a minimum of operator intervention required.

The Job Control Program

If you read the previous paragraph carefully, you probably noticed the following statement: "job-to-job transition can be handled smoothly and efficiently *by a program* written to interpret job control statements"; we've simply added italics this time. Program loading and program initiation are not automatic. In the

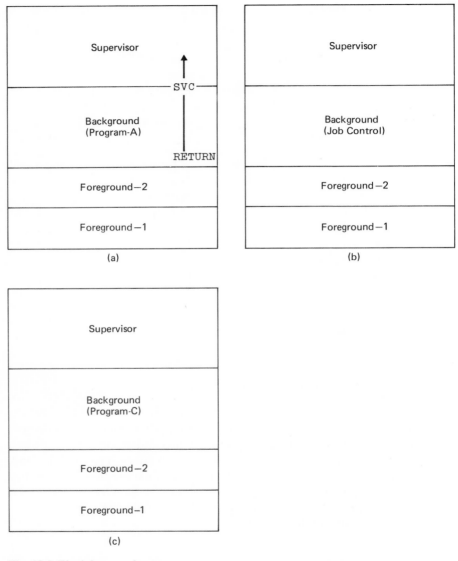

Fig. 12.3 The job control program

single program initiation mode, these functions are performed by the SPI routine; the Job Control Program takes care of things in a job-stream approach.

The job control program is not a part of the resident operating system; instead, when a job transition point is reached (end of job step), the resident supervisor loads the job control program into the newly freed partition and passes control to this module. Job Control then reads control cards, makes any necessary device assignments, prepares the partition for the execution of an application program, and handles other housekeeping functions. When the job control program encounters an EXEC card, it asks the resident supervisor's program-loading routine to read in the requested program and give it control.

Let's review this process through an example, following Fig. 12.3. In Fig. 12.3(a), a program in background partition has just reached successful completion, and this fact has been communicated to the resident operating system through a RETURN macro. The operating system loads a copy of the job control program from the SYSRES Pack into the background partition. This program overlays the problem program (which has just completed anyway). The job control program, once in core, (Fig. 12.3b) reads job control cards for the next job step, performing any requested services. Normally, the last control card in the job step is the EXEC card; when this card is encountered, the job control program turns control back to the resident operating system which loads the requested program from either the system or a private core-image library into the background partition, overlaying the job control program (Fig. 12.3c).

Job-stream operation is standard in the DOS background partition; it can also be used in foreground partitions if the proper parameters are selected at SYSGEN time. With the possible exception of an on-line data collection program or an information storage/retrieval program which is initiated first thing in the morning and allowed to run continuously for an entire shift or even all day, the use of job streams and operating system control of job-step-to-job-step transition allows for much more efficient use of a computer than does single program initiation. No human operator can type control statements as fast as a card reader can read them. Granted the control cards must be keypunched by someone, but the programmer keypunching a control card isn't forcing a $100,000 machine to wait while he hunts for the letter "E" on a keyboard; time wasted off-line on a keypunch is much less expensive than time wasted on-line on an operator's console.

Spooling

Implicit in our discussion of job streams was the source of control cards and the job stream itself—a card reader. The card reader, as we should know by now, is one of the slower I/O devices. Spooling involves reading job streams to a faster device, usually disk but sometimes tape, either off-line or during slack periods on the computer (when all active programs are in a wait state, for example); once this has been done, actual application programs and the job control program can read card *image* data from a high-speed device rather than work directly with the low-speed device. This helps throughput.

Spooling is also used at the other end of the data processing cycle—output. Rather than writing records directly to a low speed (relatively) printer, a program running on a system with spooling writes records to high speed disk or tape; later, again either off-line or during otherwise slack periods, the data is dumped from the high-speed device to the printer.

A number of spooling programs are available today; some are provided (for a fee) by the manufacturer, others are marketed by independent software firms. Generally, these spooling routines occupy a foreground partition, often foreground-one. Later in this chapter, we'll show how the operating system and the job control program can be made to look for job streams on a spooled data set; in Chapter 13, we'll consider the actual functioning of a spooling operation under OS/MFT, a slightly higher-level IBM operating system.

Multiprogramming and the Physical I/O Control System

Now that we've seen how the supervisor program is loaded via IPL and application programs are loaded by SPI (single program initiation) or the job control program (job streams), we're ready to consider how DOS handles the multiprogramming problem. I/O, more specifically, the disparity between the speed of an I/O device and the computer's own internal processing speed, is, as you may recall, the key to multiprogramming—rather than forcing a high-speed CPU to wait for a (relatively) slow I/O device, the CPU switches its attention to another program. By executing several programs concurrently, both throughput and turnaround time can be improved.

Since I/O is the key to multiprogramming, it follows that a study of the input and output functions as handled by a given operating system should provide excellent insight into multiprogramming controls. The Physical Input/Output Control System (PIOCS for short) of IBM's Disk Operating System does provide such an insight.

PIOCS is implemented through three macros: the CCB macro which creates something called a command control block, the EXCP or execute channel program macro, and the WAIT macro. To use PIOCS, the programmer must first write his own channel program using channel command words or CCW's as described in the prior chapter. This channel program is stored somewhere in his program partition (Fig. 12.4a). Also in his program, usually in among storage-area definitions, the programmer must code a CCB macro.

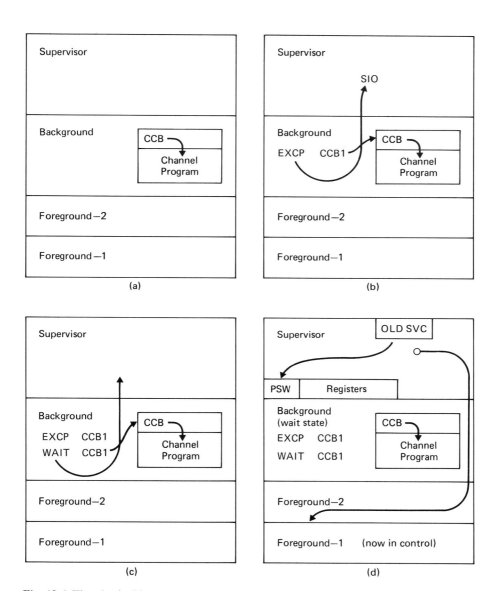

Fig. 12.4 The physical input/output control system

This macro creates a command control block, containing such information as the symbolic name of the actual I/O device, the address of the first CCW in the channel program, and various flags which are set by the user program or the operating system to indicate the status of an I/O operation—the CCB is a twenty-four byte or sixteen byte (programmer option) control block.

When the programmer is ready to request an I/O operation, he issues an EXCP macro (Fig. 12.4b); this macro results in a supervisor call (SVC), transferring control to the operating system. The reason for this transfer of control is simple—only the supervisor is allowed to issue the SIO instruction needed to actually start an input or output operation. The only operand needed on an EXCP macro is the address of the CCB which, you may remember, contains the symbolic unit address and the address of the associated channel program.

Following execution of the services requested by the EXCP macro, the supervisor returns control to the application program (Fig. 12.4c). Usually, this program quickly reaches a point where it is unable to continue until the requested I/O operation is completed, and issues a WAIT macro (again, referencing the CCB). This is another supervisor call. Its purpose is to tell the operating system that the issuing program is unable to continue until the operation described in the referenced CCB is completed. The supervisor is thus in a position to place the program into a wait state, remove its most current PSW (the Old SVC PSW) from the interrupt queue, save the program's registers, and attempt to turn control over to another application program (Fig. 12.4d). Incidently, in a foreground partition, the Old PSW and registers are saved in a special region set up in the partition; for the background partition, this information is saved in the supervisor's partition.

What if two or more programs are ready to go when our program enters a wait state? This is where partition priority comes in. Foreground-1 has high priority, followed by F-2, F-3, F-4, and the background partition; the program in the highest priority partition will go first.

The Logical Input/Output Control System

Very few application programmers are interested in writing their own channel programs, and, in fact, most DOS programmers do not, directly, use PIOCS. Instead, they rely on a series macros known, collectively, as the Logical Input/Output Control System (LIOCS).

The programmer using the logical input/output control system must code a DTF macro for each file accessed by his program. The DTF (define the file) macro generates a DTF table for the file containing detailed information about the data to be accessed—logical record size, block size, record format (fixed-length, variable-length)—and other descriptive information which defines the access method needed to process the data. The final stage in the generation of the macro involves setting up a series of address constants which, eventually, will link the DTF table and the access method logic module.

The linkage editor resolves these "external references" during the link-edit step. In building the load module, a copy of the proper access method logic routine is "grafted" onto the program object module; the actual address of this access method routine replaces the address constants generated by the DTF macro. Once the program load module (or phase in DOS) is loaded and begins running, the programmer's GET and PUT or READ and WRITE macros reference the DTF table, resulting in a branch to the access method module included by the linkage editor (Fig. 12.5).

There are three key components to an access method logic module. First, it contains the actual channel program. The second key element of the access method module is the PIOCS instructions (CCB, EXCP, and WAIT macros)

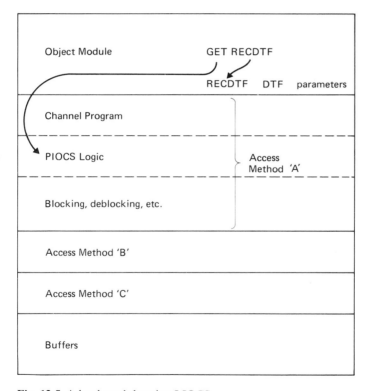

Fig. 12.5 A load module using LIOCS

needed to support the requested operation—LIOCS *uses* PIOCS. Finally, the LIOCS module contains instructions to support blocking, deblocking, and buffering.

Multiprogramming Summary

DOS supports multiprogramming. In this mode, as you may recall, a number of programs (a maximum of five under DOS) are loaded into core at the same time; the CPU processes these programs concurrently, switching its attention from one to another much as a chess master handles concurrent opponents. On a computer, multiprogramming takes advantage of the wide disparity between I/O and internal-processing speeds. When a program in the foreground-1 partition issues a request for input or output, the time required to fill this request is relatively long. Most of the time, the program will be unable to continue until the request is filled. Rather than force the entire computer system to wait, this single program is dropped into a wait state and control of the CPU is given to the foreground-2 partition (or some other partition if the F-2 program is also in a wait state).

The key to controlling this kind of multiprogramming is, obviously, I/O. On IBM's System/360, the instruction which actually begins an I/O operation, the SIO or Start I/O instruction, is privileged, meaning that it can be executed only by an operating system module in the first (core protection key 0000) partition; thus the programmer *must* surrender control to the operating system. Once the supervisor has control, multiprogramming can be implemented.

Under DOS, the physical input/output control system is the programmer's direct link to the multiprogramming functions of the operating system. The CCB or command control block macro creates a block of information and status flags allowing for communications between the processing program and the supervisor's PIOCS logic modules. By coding an execute channel program (EXCP) macro, the programmer causes an SVC instruction to transfer control to the supervisor which issues an SIO instruction and returns control to the processing program. A third PIOCS macro, WAIT, allows the programmer to surrender control to the operating system which can, subsequently, transfer control of the CPU to another partition.

Most programmers do not actually code PIOCS macros. Instead, they code logical LIOCS macros—DTF's, GET's, PUT's, READ's, WRITE's— which link to an access method module grafted onto the load module by the linkage editor. This access method module contains the channel program, PIOCS logic, and blocking/deblocking routines needed by the program.

Incidently, in many DOS installations application programmers do not code their own DTF's. Instead, the DTF's are written as system macros or simply prewritten and included in the programmer's source module through a COPY statement, thus allowing the programmer to concentrate on program logic rather than the details of an I/O operation.

Core Allocation

Now that we've considered how multiprogramming can be implemented under DOS, it's time we took a look at some of the problems created by multiprogramming. One of these is core allocation—when core contains a number of unrelated programs, how is this key resource broken up and allocated. DOS is a fixed-length partition operating system; at system generation time core is divided into a number of fixed-length partitions. The operator, at IPL time, can change the standard configuration, but, once the system starts running, core allocation is fixed and constant.

Core protection is a related problem—how can the system prevent a program in the background partition from destroying data or instructions in the foreground-1 partition? The answer is equally simple—each partition gets its own, unique, core protection key, and any attempt to execute an instruction which would destroy the contents of any storage location outside a program's own protection key region results in a protection interrupt and, most likely, program termination.

I/O Device Control

What if two programs both request input from the same tape drive at roughly the same time? When core can contain a number of unrelated programs, this problem can exist, and the operating system must be able to handle it. The Disk Operating System uses three key tables to control I/O device allocation.

The first of these three tables is the Physical Unit Block or PUB table. Each physical device attached to the system has a single, 8-byte entry in the PUB table; the first byte identifies the channel number, the second identifies the device number, the other six hold various pointers and flags. This table, stored in the table region of the supervisor partition, is created at system generation time and is maintained in channel sequence, with devices attached to channel 0 (the multiplexer) coming first, followed by channel 1, and so on.

As you may recall from the chapter on DOS job control, the programmer rarely refers to a physical I/O device, using instead, a symbolic name. These symbolic names are kept in a Logical Unit Block or LUB table—there is one such table *for each partition* active on the system. Individual LUB table entries are stored in a fixed sequence as shown in Fig. 12.6. These entries are each two bytes long, with the first byte pointing to a PUB table entry.

SYSRDR	Input unit for job control statements.
SYSIPT	Input unit for application programs.
SYSPCH	Unit for punched-card output.
SYSLST	Unit for printed output.
SYSLOG	Unit for operator messages.
SYSLNK	Disk extent for linkage-editor input.
SYSRES	System residence area.
SYSCLB	Private core-image library.
SYSRLB	Private relocatable library.
SYSSLB	Private source-statement library.
SYSREC	Disk extent for error logging.
SYS000– SYSmax	Other units. Exact meaning is installation dependent.

Fig. 12.6 LUB table sequence

Probably the best way to visualize the functioning of these two tables is through an example (Fig. 12.7). Let's assume that a program in the background partition has just issued an I/O request referencing a device known as SYSIPT. To find the actual device being referenced, the supervisor first looks at the Logical Unit Block (LUB) table for the background partition; since SYSIPT is

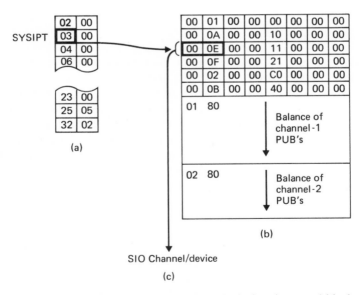

Fig. 12.7 The relationship between the logical unit-control-block table and the physical unit-control-block table. (a) the LUB table; (b) the PUB table; (c) the SIO instruction

always the second entry in any LUB table, attention is focused on this second block (Fig. 12.7a). The first byte of this entry identifies Physical Unit Block (PUB) table entry number 03 as the one containing the information giving the physical device assigned to SYSIPT for the background partition—it's channel 0, device 14 (OE in hex, Fig. 12.7b). As you may recall from Chapter 11, the Start I/O instruction contains in the operands field the channel and device address of the unit, the PUB table entry is where this information comes from (Fig. 12.7c). Assuming that the channel is free, the channel/device address is moved into a SIO instruction, the instruction is executed, and the channel takes over.

But, what if the channel is *not* free? Rather than keep the system waiting, an I/O operation which cannot be started because of a channel-busy condition is placed on a channel queue, a third key I/O control table, for later processing. Later, when an I/O interrupt signals the end of an I/O operation, the supervisor checks the channel queue table to see if any additional operations are pending for the channel; if there are, the supervisor starts the pending request before resuming normal processing.

Individual channel queue entries are four bytes in length; they contain the address of the command control block (CCB) in the requesting program and a pointer to the next channel queue entry. One of the fields in the individual physical unit block (PUB) entries points to the channel queue. Channel queues allow the system to avoid the problem of simultaneous (almost) access to the same device. Other fields in the PUB entry allow a specific device—a tape drive, for example—to be assigned to a given partition for the life of a job, a request which is communicated through an ASSGN statement. Since every I/O operation must go through the PUB table, this gives pretty good control.

This *could* cause a problem. Card input is common to many programs; let's assume that the foreground-1, foreground-2, and background partitions all require card input. Why not attach three card readers to the system? There is, don't forget, one LUB table for *each* partition; in F-1, SYSIPT might be assigned to PUB entry 1 and thus, indirectly, to channel 00 device 01 (Fig. 12.8), while in F-2, SYSIPT is tied to PUB entry 2 and channel 00 device 02. In the background LUB, SYSIPT points to PUB #3 and, indirectly again, channel 00 device 03 (Fig. 12.8).

Spooling is implemented in much the same way. Assuming that the spooling routine resides in the F-1 partition, SYSRDR and SYSIPT for this partition refer to an actual card reader; in all other partition LUB tables, SYSRDR and SYSIPT refer to the spooled file created by the spooling program. Thus the programmer is not aware of the actual source of his data on a spooled system.

Throughout this discussion we've been refering to the supervisor in general terms as we discussed the logic of controlling I/O; actually, there are a number

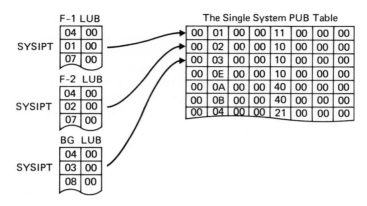

Fig. 12.8 Three-card readers for three partitions

of easily identified supervisor *modules* involved. The programmer requests the help of the supervisor through a supervisor call interrupt which is handled by an SVC interrupt handling routine. The LUB and PUB table relationship, channel queueing functions, and the issuing of SIO instructions are handled by a channel scheduler module. I/O interrupts are handled by an I/O interrupt handler routine which links to the channel scheduler which checks for possible pending I/O operations for the "just freed" channel before returning control to a processing program. These few examples serve to illustrate the point that an operating system is a collection of program modules.

Librarian Functions

DOS supports three levels of program libraries. A source statement library, as the name implies, holds source code (assembler or compiler language source statements) in modules called "books." Macro expansions are usually stored on a source statement library; when the macro is referenced in the programmer's source code, the associated book is simply added to the module and compiled or assembled along with the programmer's code. Data structures might be precoded and added to the source module through the use of a COPY statement. The system source statement library resides on the system residence pack; private source statement libraries are also supported, and can reside on almost any secondary storage device.

A relocatable library holds object modules. Access method logic, which is added to an object module by the linkage editor as it builds a load module, usually resides on the relocatable library. Subroutines can be added to a module by using the INCLUDE statement we discussed back in Chapter 7.

Relocatable library object modules are read by the linkage editor and used in building a load module. As with source statement libraries, the system relocatable library resides on SYSRES. Private relocatable libraries are also supported by DOS.

A load module, the output of the linkage editor, represents a module of machine-level code ready to be loaded and executed—it's a complete, ready to run program. Load modules are maintained on a core image library. An EXEC statement references a core image library member (called a phase under DOS), instructing the supervisor to load the phase into a core partition and execute it. The system core image library is found on the system residence device and, once again, private core image libraries are supported.

DOS provides a number of special programs which maintain, service, and copy library members. These programs support such functions as: the addition, deletion, or renaming of members, maintaining library directories, the listing or punching of library members, the creation of new private libraries, library reorganization, and other functions.

Summary

IBM's Disk Operating System (DOS) is a general-purpose operating system designed to support multiprogramming in an IBM System/360 hardware environment. Under DOS, core is divided into a number of fixed-length partitions (maximum—operating system supervisor plus five application-program partitions) at system generation time, when a copy of the operating system is made using the manufacturer's master copy and the specific option choices of the customer as a guide. The resulting SYSRES pack is subsequently mounted on a drive at the customer's location and, through a procedure known as Initial Program Load (IPL), the core resident portion of the operating system, known as the supervisor, is copied into core; at this time, the core assignments made at SYSGEN time can be changed by the operator if desired.

The supervisor occupies the first partition in core. This partition is subdivided into supervisor, table, and transient regions; little-used operating system modules are read into the transient region on an as-needed basis.

The remainder of core is divided into a number of problem program partitions, with a background partition being followed by one or more foreground partitions. The foreground partitions have highest priority. Programs are loaded into a partition either by the operator through the single program initiator module of the supervisor or, more commonly, under control of job control cards in a job stream. In this latter mode, the job control program is first loaded into the application program partition where it reads and acts on job control cards before causing the supervisor's loader routine to load the application program from a core image library.

The key to DOS multiprogramming is the physical input/output control system (PIOCS) which is implemented through three macros—CCB which creates a command control block, EXCP which instructs the supervisor to execute a channel program, and WAIT which returns control to the supervisor so that another program partition can be given control. Few programmers actually use PIOCS, preferring the DTF, GET, and PUT macros of the logical input/output control system (LIOCS). The access method modules of LIOCS are grafted onto a load module at link-edit time; these modules contain the necessary channel programs, PIOCS code, and blocking/deblocking and buffering logic.

I/O device allocation is controlled through a number of system tables. The physical unit block or PUB table holds one entry for each I/O device attached to the system. The logical unit block (LUB) table relates symbolic device assignments as used by the programmer to the actual device assignments in the PUB table. If a channel is busy at the time an input or output operation is requested, the request can be kept pending in core by placing it in a channel queue; later, when an I/O interrupt occurs, the interrupt handler routine turns control over to the channel scheduler routine which checks for pending I/O requests on the channel, starting the next one before returning control to a processing program.

The final subject covered in this chapter was that of libraries. DOS supports source statement, relocatable, and core image libraries, both system and private.

In the next chapter, we'll be studying a more complex operating system designed to function in the same hardware environment—OS/MFT. We'll be building on many of the concepts introduced in this chapter.

Exercises

1. Sketch the DOS system geography for a system with four active foreground partitions in addition to the supervisor and background partitions. Show the subdivisions of the supervisor partition.

2. What is the difference between SYSGEN and IPL?

3. Describe the steps involved in loading a program through the job stream utilizing the job control program.

4. How is multiprogramming implemented through PIOCS?

5. Relate LIOCS to PIOCS.

6. DOS is a fixed partition operating system. What does this mean?

7. Explain DOS I/O device allocation. Include the relationship between the PUB and LUB tables in your discussion.

CHAPTER 13

IBM System / 360 Operating System Multiprogramming with a Fixed Number of Tasks

Overview

In this chapter, we'll be discussing another operating system designed to support multiprogramming on an IBM System/360 or System/370 computer; it's known as the IBM System/360 Operating System, Multiprogramming with a Fixed Number of Tasks (MFT). We'll see how, through software, such problems as scheduling, core allocation, CPU access, I/O device control and allocation, data management, and others are handled when core is occupied by more than one program. Since this is an IBM operating system written to support an IBM computer, software is restricted and limited by IBM's hardware design; thus, the operating system must be able to deal with interrupts, program status words, and the channel-linkage fields.

The intent of this chapter is to illustrate, in general terms, how a typical operating system works. To do this, we'll have to analyze the operating system in some detail, but we are not really interested in a complete, "bit level" understanding of what is really nothing more than one solution to a fairly common data-processing problem; thus no attempt will be made to cover the detailed function of each and every operating system control block. Hopefully, this chapter contains enough detail to illustrate what happens while staying below the level of total confusion often felt by students attempting, for the first time, to wade through a passage on the seemingly infinite series of control blocks and pointers at the core of an MFT operating system.

In reading this chapter, try to concentrate on OS MFT as a *solution* to the multiprogramming problem, and not as a separate problem in itself.

The Basic Structure of MFT

IBM's System/360 and System/370 Operating System, Multiprogramming with a Fixed Number of Tasks—from here on, simply MFT—is nothing more than a collection of programs, tables, and indexes designed to support multiprogramming within the hardware environment of an IBM System/360 or System/370 computer. A number of these modules are core resident, while others reside on secondary storage and are read into core on an as-needed basis—the "Resident Area" and the "Linkage Area" respectively in Fig. 13.1.

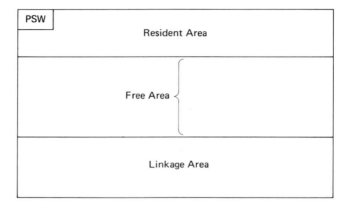

Fig. 13.1 Basic MFT core structure

The remaining free area is available for application programs. The computer operator, at IPL time, divides this region into anywhere from two to fifteen partitions, indicating, for each, the partition size and the job class or classes which are to run within the partition. Partition assignments can be changed by the operator, but until this human intervention takes place, the number of partitions and the size of each partition are fixed—hence, multiple *fixed* task.

To illustrate this concept further, let's set up the computer system we'll be using in many of our examples throughout this chapter. Our computer has 300K bytes of core storage. The resident and linkage areas take up a total of 80K, leaving 220K for application programs (incidentally, there is no deep significance to the fact that the resident area is in low core and the linkage area is in high core; that's just the way the original operating system design team decided to set things up). We run three different classes of programs on this system. Class A jobs, the most common type, are short-running jobs requiring no more than 90K of core. Longer running jobs and jobs needing more than 90K are run under Class B. Class C is for jobs requiring tape mounts. The operator creates two partitions through his console—a 90K partition restricted to Class A jobs and a 130K partition restricted to Class B and Class C jobs. The geography of this sytem is illustrated in Fig. 13.2.

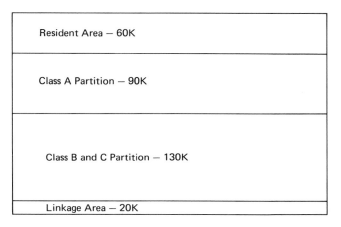

Fig. 13.2 Core assignments for a three partition (supervisor and two application programs) MFT system

To help improve the efficiency of the system, application programs are spooled to a disk queue (Fig. 13.3); an operating system module performs this spooling function, while another operating system module moves program load modules from the queue and the various libraries into core. Once in core, other operating system modules handle interrupts, control communications with the input/output equipment, and perform other services for the application program. In the balance of this chapter, we'll be studying how the application programs and these operating system modules "fit together." We've already discussed, in general terms, most of these operating system modules in prior chapters; the functions will not be new, although the program and table names chosen by IBM may be. In the next few pages, we'll concentrate on IBM's program names and terminology, relating the individual MFT operating system components to the general functions of an operating system as described in Chapters 5, 6, and 10. Once the key modules have been identified and defined, we'll consider the interrelationship of the operating system and two application programs by analyzing a few seconds of actual system time.

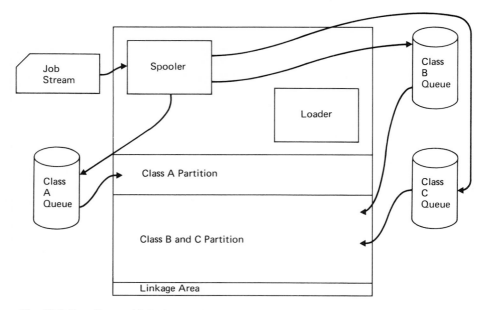

Fig. 13.3 Spooling and job classes

Jobs and Tasks

To a programmer interested in checking and testing a program, the functions of compiling and link-editing a job are pretty much beside the point—all he wants is a job listing and a set of program results. To the computer, this rather simple job involves three distinct steps, with the compile step accepting source deck input and producing object module output, the linkage-editor reading the object deck and producing a load module, and the load module being loaded and executed in the third step. The programmer looks at a job; the computer sees three job steps or *tasks*.

Within the operating system, the individual modules concerned with getting a job into the computer, including the functions of loading and starting the routines requested by individual job steps (EXEC cards), are grouped under the general term of "Job Management." Once a program or routine has been loaded, "Task Management" takes over the responsibility for operating system support of the program, basically handling interrupts. After the program completes, job management once again takes over, cleaning up the remnants and preparing the partition for another program.

Let's go over that again, step by step, following the flowchart in Fig. 13.4; we'll use a compile, link-edit, and go job in our example. First, job management

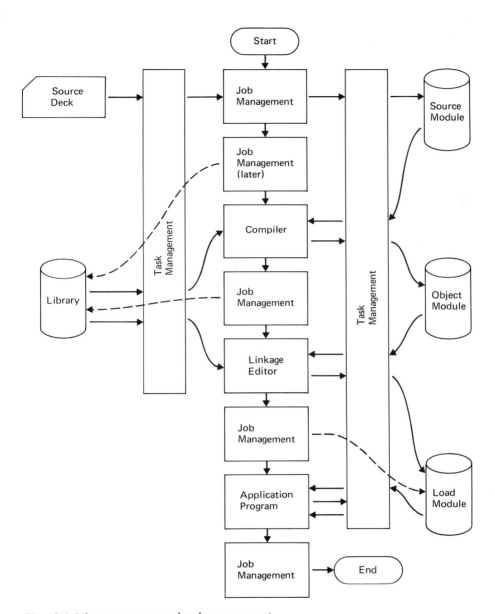

Fig. 13.4 Job management and task management

reads the source deck, spooling it to a disk file. Some time later, another job management routine, recognizing the fact that a partition is free, reads the first EXEC card for the job and loads and starts the compiler program. Should the compiler require the help of the operating system (a supervisor call to request the start of an I/O operation for example), help is provided through task management. As its last act, the compiler writes an object module to disk (with the help of task management, of course), after which job management takes over again and cleans up the partition. Job management can now load and start the linkage editor which reads (through task management) the object module and creates and writes, again with the help of task management, a load module. Job management then cleans up, loads the load module, and starts it. As the application program runs, the various interrupts are handled by task management. Upon completion, job management finishes up.

Let's take a closer look at the operating system modules which constitute job and task management.

Job Management—the Master Scheduler

Which job, or specifically job step, should be given control next? This question is answered by the master scheduler routine (Fig. 13.5). Most of the time, jobs are scheduled according to a preset rule (like first-in-queue, first-out) or by priority; at times, operator intervention is desirable. The operator can communicate with the master scheduler routine; using this facility, the operator can override standard system action, perhaps giving a "hot" job top priority or cancelling a job giving unacceptable intermediate results or locked in an obvious

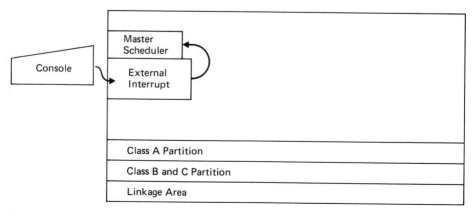

Fig. 13.5 The master scheduler

internal loop. The operator's console, as you may remember, is linked to an IBM computer through the mechanism of an external interrupt; once the interrupt handler routine recognizes the specific cause of the interrupt, it simply turns control over to the master scheduler through a branch instruction.

Job Management—the Reader/Interpreter

The reader/interpreter, as the name implies, reads jobs and places them on the job class queues (Fig. 13.6). As the job is read, JCL statements are scanned for accuracy and, if they are undecipherable, the job is cancelled at this point. Cataloged procedures are added to the job stream. A series of core tables listing programs by class and within class by priority is created and maintained. Since input-card data is part of the job stream, the system input device (SYSIN) comes from this job management function.

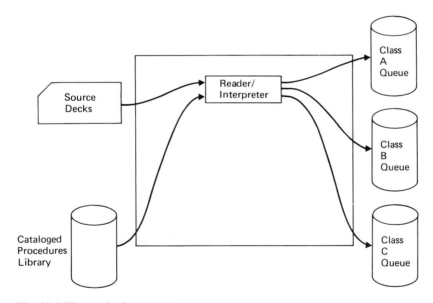

Fig. 13.6 The reader/interpreter

Job Management—the Initiator/Terminator

As a partition becomes available, the initiator routine takes a new job step from a class queue, loads it, and starts it. In the MFT system, there is one initiator/terminator for each and every partition. Like the job control program of DOS, the initiator/terminator is a transient module, occupying the application program's partition between job steps. The terminator portion of this module, as you've probably already figured out, performs the clean-up functions at the end of a job step.

When the operator sets up the partitions, he indicates the job class or classes which are to run in the partition; the initiator/terminator for that partition works with the designated job class queue or queues only. Once the initiator has loaded and started a job step, task management takes over as the operating system's representative. The terminator routine comes into play at the conclusion of the job step.

To summarize, the job reader works with the complete *job*, reading all the cards and enqueueing them, while the initiator/terminator concentrates on individual *job steps* (the EXEC card), fetching them one at a time from the job class queue, performing the essential functions of loading and starting the individual job steps, and, following job-step conclusion, cleaning up the partition. The functions of the initiator/terminator are illustrated in Fig. 13.7.

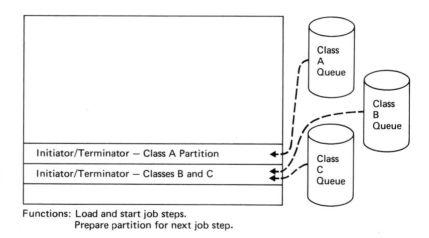

Functions: Load and start job steps.
         Prepare partition for next job step.

Fig. 13.7 The initiator/terminator

Job Management—the Output Writer

Remember spooling? Programmers do not normally communicate directly with slow output devices like a printer or a card punch; instead, such output is spooled to a faster device like disk or tape for later printing or punching. The output writer is the routine that dumps the system output devices to the proper medium (Fig. 13.8).

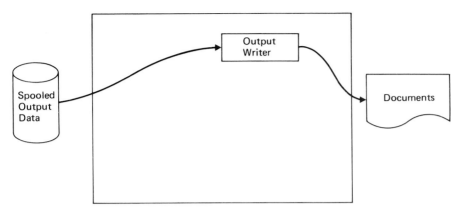

Fig. 13.8 The output writer

Job Management—Summary

Job management is concerned with starting and finishing things. Under the control of job management, a given job is spooled, scheduled, loaded (by job step), and started. Once an individual job step begins executing on its own, job management is no longer involved; any needed operating system support is provided by task management. Once the application program completes, job management once again takes over, preparing the partition for the next job step.

Task Management

The function of task management is to support an application program while it is running. A task management routine starts as a result of an interrupt. The SVC interrupt allows the programmer, through an SVC instruction, to initiate a link to an operating system module which can get an input or output operation started. The I/O interrupt allows the channel to control an I/O operation without the help of the computer, thus freeing the computer to work on another task; the channel simply signals the CPU when an operation is completed. Program errors and timer interrupts are handled by the program interrupt and external interrupt handlers, respectively. Programs are protected from machine errors by the machine-check interrupt handler routine.

We read about these interrupts back in Chapter 11. All the interrupt handler routines grouped together make up task management. Task management routines gain control of the computer as the result of an interrupt; following the completion of a task management routine, control is returned to the original program or, should that be unwise due to a program or timer interrupt or normal program termination, to job management.

Interrupts, as you may remember, are implemented through the switching of program status words, with the Old PSW field providing a link back to the original program. There is only one Old PSW field for each of the five types of interrupts. When a program enters the wait state—following the start of an I/O operation for example—this link must be removed from the PSW queues and stored somewhere in core; if it isn't and another program is allowed to gain control, this link back to the initial program might be destroyed by a subsequent interrupt of the same type. Task management does this—we'll look at the mechanism in a few paragraphs. Controlling program status is a task management function.

Tying Things Together—Basic MFT Control Blocks

To execute a single job step, it is necessary to coordinate a number of job management, task management, and application program routines; how can all these separate subprograms and modules be made to work in concert? These separate routines are tied together and coordinated through a series of control blocks and pointers.

The key to finding most of the important system control blocks and pointers is the Communication Vector Table or CVT (Fig. 13.9). The CVT is essentially a table of addresses; it contains the address of most of the key control blocks. The communication vector table is itself pointed to by the address stored in the

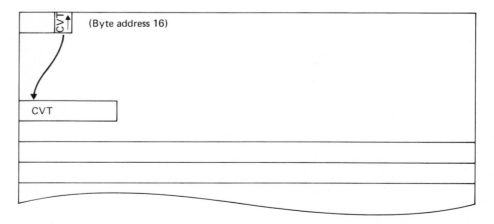

Fig. 13.9 The communication vector table

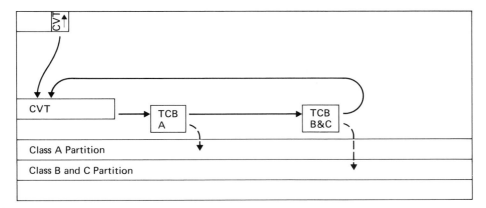

Fig. 13.10 The task control block queue

third doubleword field in core storage—core address 16; this, as you may remember from Chapter 11, is one of the system's permanent storage assignments. It was previously identified as the initial program loading CCW2; once initial program loading is complete, this field is free for some other use and the address of the CVT is placed here.

Activities within a partition are coordinated by a task control block or TCB. There is one TCB for each partition (Fig. 13.10). The communication vector table points to the first TCB which contains a pointer to the second TCB (Fig. 13.10)—this is called the TCB queue. On a system with more than two partitions, the CVT points to the first TCB which points to the second TCB which points to the third, and so on. If two or more programs are ready to start at the same instant of time, which one goes first? Answer: the one whose TCB shows up earliest on the TCB queue. In our example, since the task control block for the Class A partition is the first one on the queue, Class A jobs have a higher internal priority than do Class B or Class C jobs.

The contents of a given partition are described by a series of "request blocks" spun off the task control block (Fig. 13.11). The existence of an active program within the partition is indicated by a Program Request Block or PRB. If a supervisor call interrupt is being processed in support of the partition, this fact is indicated by the presence of a Supervisor Request Block or SVRB. In a simple read-a-card, process-the-data, and print-a-line program, using the system input and output devices, it is not at all unusual for three request blocks to be active at one time—a PRB to indicate the presence of an active program and two SVRBs to show that access methods are in the process of blocking or deblocking physical records.

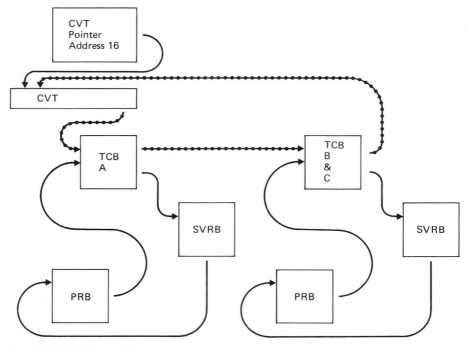

Fig. 13.11 The request block queue

Request blocks identify active modules executing in (or in support of) a partition; if the request block queue is empty, so is the partition. One of the specific functions of the terminator module is to wipe out these request blocks following task completion. Job management finds an empty partition by finding a task control block with no request blocks attached.

An Example

One of the best ways to gain an understanding of these control blocks and pointers is to follow them through a few seconds of computer time. Our computer system is the one we've described earlier in this chapter—two partitions: 90K for Class A and 130K for Class B and Class C. The CVT points to the Class A task control block (Fig. 13.12), giving these jobs top internal priority. As we start our example, both partitions are empty (no request blocks) and a number of programs have already been spooled to the job class queues (on disk). As we start, the master scheduler routine has control (Fig. 13.12).

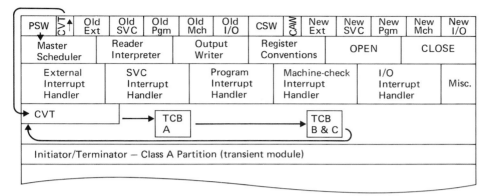

PSW	CVT↑	Old Ext	Old SVC	Old Pgm	Old Mch	Old I/O	CSW	CAW	New Ext	New SVC	New Pgm	New Mch	New I/O

Master Scheduler	Reader Interpreter		Output Writer		Register Conventions		OPEN		CLOSE		

External Interrupt Handler	SVC Interrupt Handler	Program Interrupt Handler	Machine-check Interrupt Handler	I/O Interrupt Handler	Misc.

CVT ────▶ TCB A ──────────────── TCB B & C

Initiator/Terminator — Class A Partition (transient module)

Fig. 13.12 Our system as we begin our example

The master scheduler is going to try to get something started. In the absence of any operator commands, the master scheduler begins looking for an empty partition. The communication vector table is found through the address stored at core address 16; the CVT points to the first task control block (Class A). The partition controlled by this TCB is free; there are no active request blocks present. Thus the master scheduler causes the initiator/terminator module for this partition to be loaded and transfers control to this job management routine.

The Initiator/Terminator (Fig. 13.13) creates a program request block and attaches it the TCB for this Class A partition. A job is read from the class A

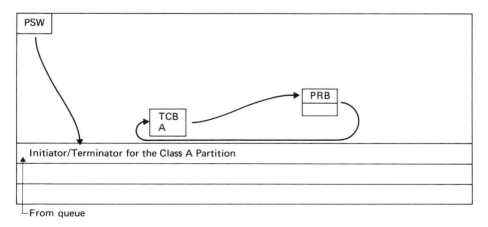

PSW

PRB

TCB A

Initiator/Terminator for the Class A Partition

From queue

Fig. 13.13 The initiator/terminator in control

queue and loaded into the partition (for simplicity, we'll forget about the time delay inherent in reading the initiator/terminator and the job step from disk queue and assume that both happen in an instant). As its last act, the initiator routine branches to the application program's entry point.

After executing several instructions, the application program finds itself in need of data, so it issues a supervisor call instruction (Fig. 13.14), causing an SVC interrupt and passing control to the SVC interrupt-handler routine, a part of task management.

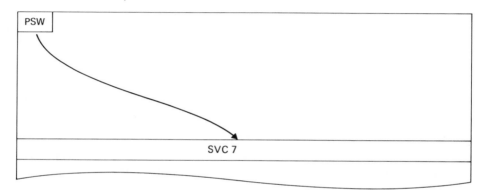

Fig. 13.14 The application program in control

This task management routine starts by attaching a supervisor request block (SVRB) to the request block queue (Fig. 13.15), thus indicating that an operating system module is active in support of this partition. The input operation is started in the usual way, with channel command words and the channel address word being initialized and a start I/O instruction executed. The routine then waits until the channel reports its status through the channel status word. Assuming that the status is positive, the channel takes over the responsibility for the input operation, and the original program is placed into a wait state; this change in state is accomplished by the SVC interrupt handler which changes the wait-state bit (bit 14) in the Old SVC PSW. This old PSW is then copied into a doubleword space in the program request block, and control is returned, via a branch, to the master scheduler.

The master scheduler once again tries to get something started. In the absence of specific operator instructions, it begins looking for either an open partition or a program in the ready state. The CVT is once again the starting

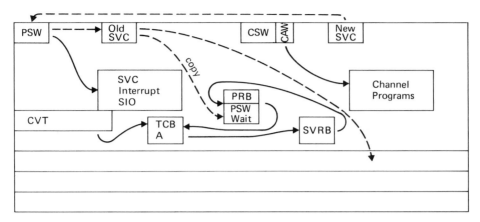

Fig. 13.15 The SVC interrupt handler takes over

point, pointing to the TCB for the Class A partition. The presence of request blocks indicates that the partition is in use; a quick check of the PSW field in the program request block indicates that the program is in a wait state (Fig. 13.16). The TCB also contains a pointer (the address) of the next task control block on the TCB queue; since nothing can be done with this first partition, the master scheduler moves along.

Since there are no request blocks chained off this second TCB, the Master Scheduler "knows" that the partition is empty. The initiator/terminator routine

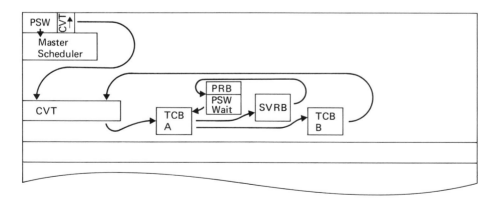

Fig. 13.16 Back to the master scheduler

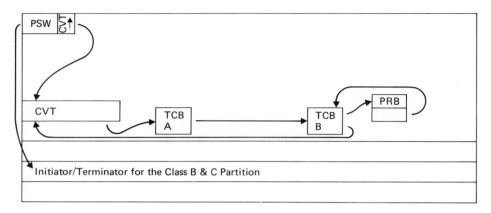

Fig. 13.17 The class B initiator/terminator

responsible for this partition (Fig. 13.17) is loaded, and in turn loads and starts a task or job step from the Class B queue—the program request block (PRB) shown in Fig. 13.18 was created by the initiator/terminator to show that a task is now active in this partition. The PSW of Fig. 13.18 shows that the application program in the second partition is in control.

Suddenly, an I/O interrupt occurs, indicating the end of the input operation previously started for the program in the Class A partition; as a result of PSW

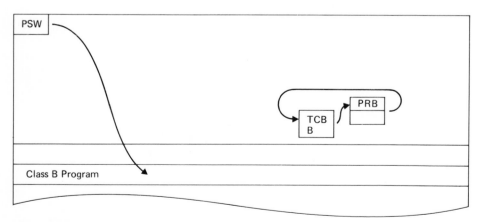

Fig. 13.18 A second application program begins

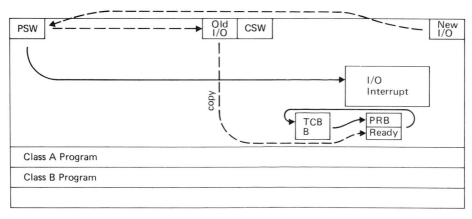

Fig. 13.19 An I/O interrupt occurs

switching, the I/O interrupt handler, a task management routine, takes control (Fig. 13.19). The Old I/O PSW field, don't forget, still points to the Class B program, and this program is in a ready state; even so, it's copied to the PRB. The interrupt handler identifies the program connected with the interrupt, program A, and, by following the CVT/TCB/PRB chain, locates its most current program status word and resets its fourteenth bit to indicate a ready state (Fig. 13.20). Once again, control is returned to the master scheduler which begins

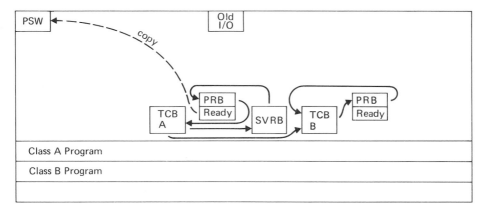

Fig. 13.20 Class B is still ready, but Class A gets control

its usual search of the TCB queue. Discovering that the most current PSW of the Class A program indicates a "ready" state, this PSW is copied from the program request block to the current PSW location (Fig. 13.20 again), thus transferring control to the Class A program. Notice that a supervisor call routine is still actively supporting this partition—you can tell by the presence of an SVRB on the request block queue. This particular I/O operation involved a standard, queued access method, and there are a number of unprocessed logical records left in the buffer.

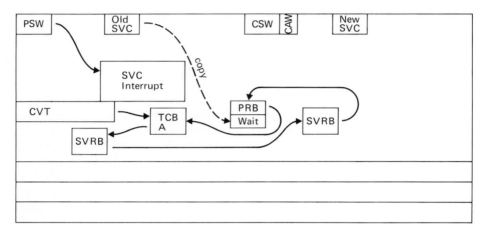

Fig. 13.21 An SVC interrupt gets us back to task management

After some time and several instructions, the Class A program reaches the point where output data must be sent to the printer and, thus, issues an SVC interrupt. As a result, control is passed to the SVC interrupt handler (Fig. 13.21) which creates another SVRB, starts the output operation, sets the Old SVC PSW's fourteenth bit to indicate a wait state, moves this PSW field into the program request block for the Class A partition, and turns control back to the master scheduler (Fig. 13.22).

The master scheduler, once again, begins searching the TCB queue looking for something to start. The program in the first partition is in a wait state, so the master scheduler moves along to the Class B partition. Discovering that the program in this partition is in a ready state, the PSW found in the program request block is simply moved into the current PSW location, thus returning control to the Class B program (Fig. 13.23).

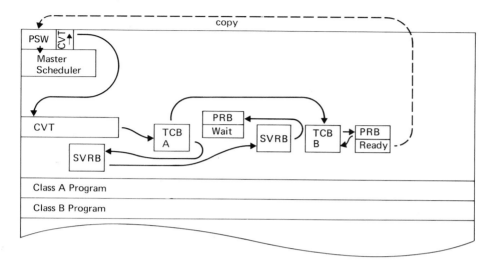

Fig. 13.22 The master scheduler

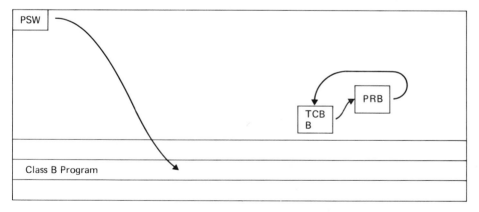

Fig. 13.23 The Class B program regains control

After a bit of time, the Class B program issues an SVC for input data. Task management, specifically the SVC interrupt handler, takes over (Fig. 13.24), creates an SVRB, starts the input operation, sets the Old SVC PSW to a wait state, and moves this Old PSW to the Class B PRB. And again, it's back to the master scheduler (Fig. 13.25).

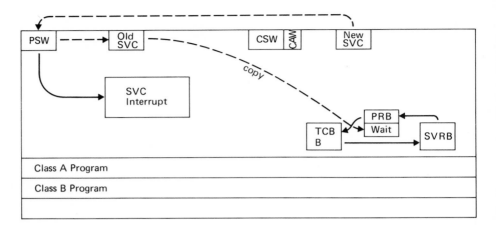

Fig. 13.24 An SVC is issued

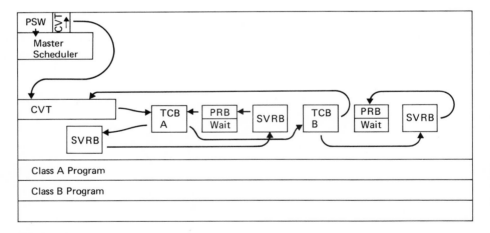

Fig. 13.25 Back to the master scheduler

By tracing a path through the CVT, the TCB queue, and the RB queues, the master scheduler discovers that both partitions are active and both contain programs in the wait state. Since no application program is ready to go, control is passed to the reader/interpreter function of job management (Fig. 13.26) which starts the operation of spooling one more card from the card reader to disk, returning control to the master scheduler (Fig. 13.27). Once again, all

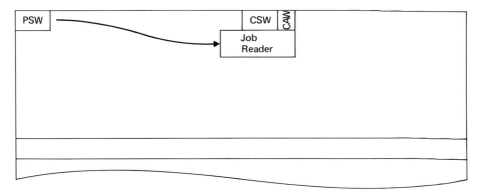

Fig. 13.26 Job management—the reader/interpreter

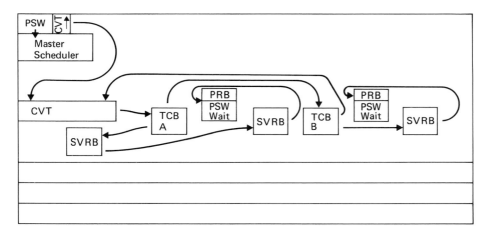

Fig. 13.27 The master scheduler again

partitions are full and waiting. As a last resort, control is passed to the output writer (Fig. 13.28) which starts an output operation, dumping one record from the system output device to the printer, again returning control to the master scheduler (Fig. 13.29). Everything is now waiting, so the system settles into a hard wait (Fig. 13.30) with four I/O interrupts pending.

Finally, an I/O interrupt occurs, starting the task management routine (Fig. 13.31); it's for the Class A program, so the fourteenth bit in the program

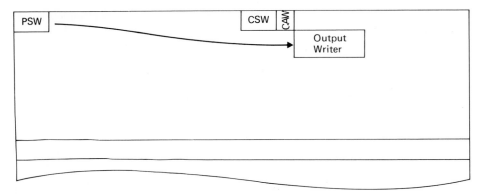

Fig. 13.28 Job management—the output writer

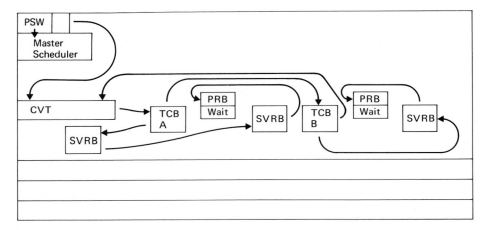

Fig. 13.29 Again, the master scheduler

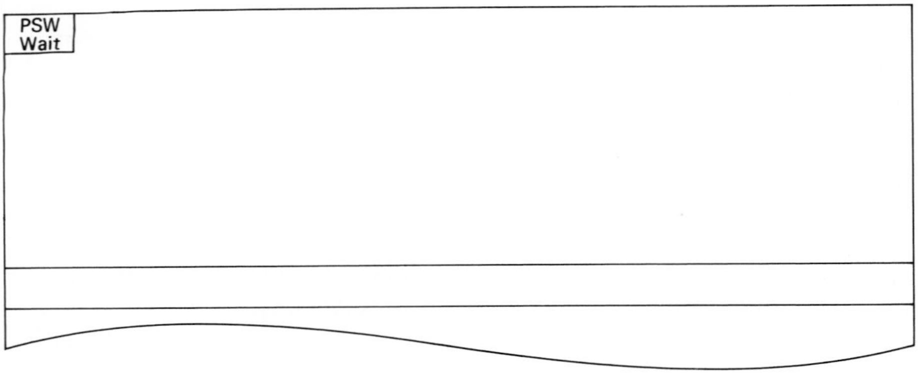

Fig. 13.30 The whole system waits

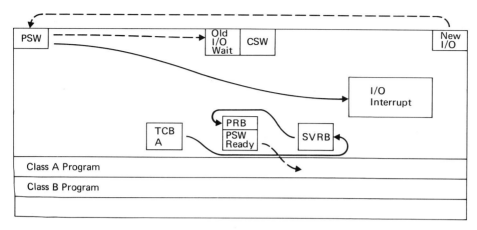

Fig. 13.31 An I/O interrupt occurs

request block's PSW field is set to a ready state. In this case, let's assume the output data was sent with a blocking factor of one, meaning that the supervisory functions associated with this SVC are completely finished; the SVRB is wiped off the request block queue, the PSW found in the program request block is made current, and Program A once again takes control (Fig. 13.32).

But only for a while—two instructions into the program is a zero divide; the resulting program interrupt turns control back to task management (Fig.

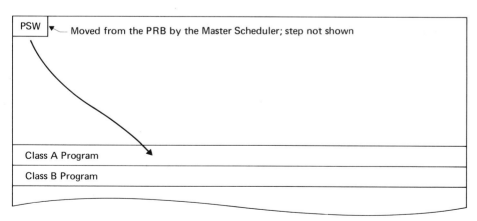

Fig. 13.32 The Class A program resumes

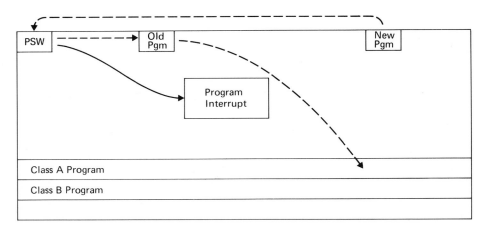

Fig. 13.33 But quickly program checks

13.33). The program interrupt handler prepares a dump and turns control over to the terminator routine for the partition. The terminator (Fig. 13.34) wipes out all request blocks and once again links back to the master scheduler. The job management routine resumes its eternal quest to "get something started," following the CVT/TCB chain to the first partition, discovering, through the lack of request blocks, that this partition is available (Fig. 13.35), and linking to the Class A initiator/terminator.

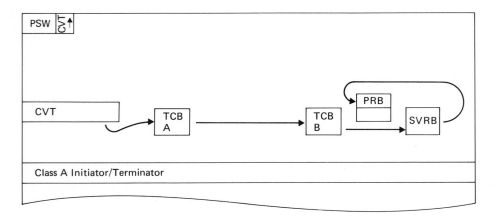

Fig. 13.34 The terminator routine prepares the partition for the next program

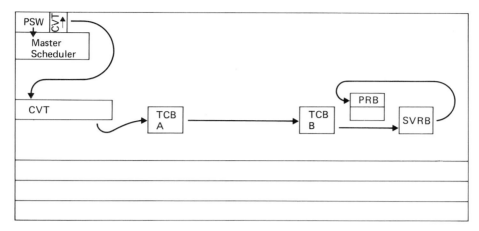

Fig. 13.35 We leave the system as the master gets ready to start another Class A program

Our Example—a Summary

In this example, we have followed the changing state of the program status word and other pointers through a few seconds of computer time on a multi-programming machine. Let's try to relate some of the things that happened to the general functions of an operating system as discussed in prior chapters.

Scheduling helps to improve the utilization of all the system resources by minimizing time delays due to necessary setup. One key element in implementing any scheduling system involves grouping similar jobs; under MFT, this function is performed by the reader/interpreter routine, a part of job management. The class parameter assigned by the programmer through a job card identifies many of the key characteristics of the job; once the job reader has spooled the job to a queue, the master scheduler routine, another part of job management, can, as its name implies, implement scheduling.

Internal priorities were seen to be a potential problem on a multiprogramming system—when two or more programs are ready to go at the same time, which one goes first? This problem is also handled by the master scheduler routine through the simple expedient of causing this program to search the CVT/TCB chain in a fixed sequence as it looks for a ready program.

Register protection—a program which enters a wait state *must* find expected values in the registers when it resumes—is implemented through standard register conventions; although we didn't mention them in our example, register conventions are a part of each operating system module. There is room in both the task control block and in the supervisor request block for saving registers.

Spooling was shown to be at least a partial solution to the problem of dealing with slow speed input and output devices; under MFT, the job reader and the output writer handle spooling. Because of the fact that third generation equipment is so fast, on-line spooling is possible, with these two spooling functions being started when the CPU has serviced all available application programs and has nothing else to do anyway.

The use of channels was shown to be a big help in minimizing the impact of slow I/O operations; essentially, the channel assumes all responsibility for actually controlling the operation, freeing the CPU to do other work in parallel. Task management ties the channel and the computer together by handling the request for the start of a channel operation through an SVC interrupt and taking care of I/O interrupts, the channel's signal that an operation has been completed.

Task management also handles program interrupts. Core protection, a topic not covered in our example, is implemented by having the CPU check to make sure that the sending and receiving addresses of a potentially destructive instruction (like a move) both lie in the same partition, i.e., both have the same protect key (remember the PSW's protect key field?). If they don't, it's grounds for a program interrupt—task management. Timer interrupts, a hedge against endless loops, are one variety of external interrupts and are handled by this task management function. Operator intervention through the console also causes an external interrupt resulting in a branch to the master scheduler, a job management routine.

The potential problem of two or more programs wanting the same input or output device at the same time is handled by job management; two jobs requesting the same tape drive are simply not loaded into core at the same time. The exact procedure for implementing this control will be discussed within the next several pages. Data management is another topic we'll cover soon.

In short, MFT is nothing more than a collection of programs, program modules, and routines designed to implement the functions which must be performed by a multiprogramming operating system on an IBM System/360 or System/370. The module names and the structure of the various control blocks and pointers are unique to MFT, but the functions being performed are common to all multiprogramming operating systems.

I/O Controls Under MFT

In a serial-batch system, all input and output devices are available to the program in control of the system. As soon as we progress to multiprogramming, conflicts are inevitable. These conflicts must be resolved, and they are—by the same job and task management routines we've already discussed. To implement these I/O device controls, the operating system builds and maintains a series of special control blocks and pointers; we'll look at some of the key ones in the next few paragraphs.

I/O Control—the Unit Control Block

If an operating system is to control the allocation and scheduling of input and output devices, it's only reasonable that the operating system have a list of available devices; this list is provided through the Unit Control Block (UCB), specifically through a chain of UCB's (Fig. 13.36). Under MFT, each device attached to the computer has its own unit control block. Each UCB contains such information as channel and device address, the device type (2314, 3330, 1403, etc.), and various sense and status fields. This table is created at system generation time. There is one UCB for each and every I/O device attached to the system; a device without a unit control block is, as far as the operating system is concerned, nonexistent.

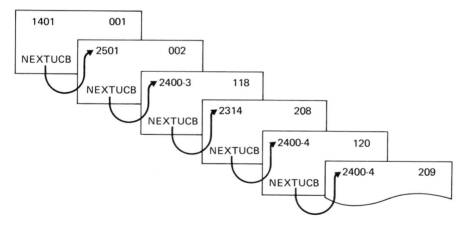

Fig. 13.36 Unit control blocks

As a job is read by the reader/interpreter, requests for I/O support (made via DD cards) can be checked against the UCB queue; if a request is made for a device which is not on the system (probably an error in coding the JCL statement), there is no sense in even spooling the job. As a job or job step becomes ready for loading, the initiator/terminator can check the UCBs to make sure that a given device is available before loading the step. Should a job step require exclusive use of a device—a tape drive, for example—the fact that the device is not available for other jobs can be noted in the UCB, thus informing other initiator/terminators (one per partition, remember) that a job step requesting "this" device should not be loaded but, instead, be kept waiting a bit longer. Job management works with the unit control block to make sure that two or more jobs do not try to use the same I/O device at the same time.

I/O Control—the Task Input/Output Table

The Task Input/Output Table (TIOT) is created by job management just prior to the loading and starting of a job step or task; essentially, it's a list of all the DDNAMEs on all the DD cards included in the job step. Along with the DDNAME is a series of pointers which allow the system to find all the parameters coded on the DD card. A schematic of a TIOT is shown in Fig. 13.37.

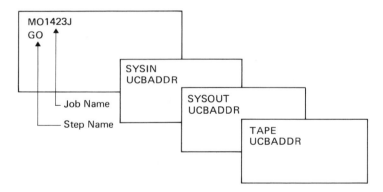

Fig. 13.37 The task input/output table

I/O Control—the DCB and DEB

We've already looked at the data control block in some detail—it's a series of constants, coded within the programmer's own module, describing such things as the access method to be used in a given I/O operation, the logical record and blocksizes, record formats, the DDNAME assigned to the JCL card describing the physical device, and other characteristics of the data. There is one data control block for each device accessed by the job step.

The Data Extent Block (DEB) is an extension of the data control block. While the DCB is entirely within the programmer's own region and thus subject to programmer modification and control, the DEB is not generally programmer-accessible.

I/O Control—the OPEN Macro

Most programmers are aware of the OPEN macro in a negative sense—if I don't code it, my program blows up on the first read. The OPEN actually performs a much more positive function. When the programmer codes an OPEN, he is indicating that the program is about ready to begin requesting input or output operations on a particular device. Within the application program, the OPEN takes the form of an SVC instruction coupled with some constants and addresses identifying the data set (through the DCB) to be opened—the programmer usually sees just the word OPEN, especially in a high-level compiler language, but the pointers and the SVC are there. The SVC instruction causes an SVC interrupt, thus signaling the operating system of the programmer's intentions.

You may remember, from our discussion of the DD card, that not all data control block parameters need be coded within the program DCB; many can be coded in the DCB parameter of the DD card. It is necessary to get these DD card DCB subparameters into the program data control block at some time; this is one of the functions of OPEN. You may also remember that it is not normally necessary to code any DCB parameter on a DD card when retrieving an already existing data set; this is because such information as logical record length, blocksize, record form, and others can be found in the data set label. Moving this information from the label into the program DCB is another OPEN function.

The OPEN works something like this. First, any parameters coded as zero in the program data control block (uncoded fields are zero fields) are filled from the DCB parameter of the associated DD card. The DDNAME is one parameter which must be coded in the program DCB; thus the OPEN routine has the "associated" DDNAME and the proper DD card can be located through the task input/output table which contains a list of all the DDNAMEs (and thus DD cards) included in the job step's JCL.

After merging in the DCB parameter fields from the DD card, the OPEN routine performs its label checking functions; at this time, any DCB fields which are still zero can be filled from label information on an existing data set.

(Incidentally, the OPEN creates a label for a new data set). Following execution of the OPEN routine, the basic I/O control blocks are complete and ready to support an input or output operation (Fig. 13.38).

The OPEN routine is a part of task management; it gains control as the result of a supervisor call interrupt. The OPEN routine is usually one of the resident operating system modules.

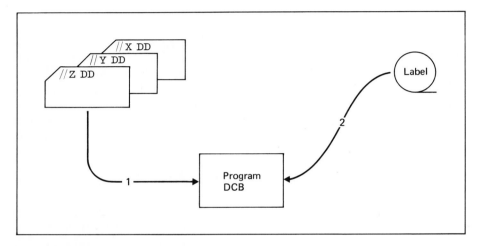

Fig. 13.38 The OPEN routine builds basic control blocks for supporting I/O

I/O Control—the Application Program/Channel Program Link

Actual physical I/O operations are, as we know, controlled by a channel; the channel gets its instructions from a channel program—one or more CCWs. Individual channel programs, for (hopefully) obvious reasons, are not the type of software routines that the typical programmer should be allowed to modify or change. For this reason, channel programs are placed either in the region of core assigned to the operating system or in the access method routines grafted onto the load module by the linkage editor. The programmer must have some control over the I/O operation, of course; the data control block is within his partition and can be modified. These pieces must be linked together.

We've already looked at the data extent block or DEB; it's basically an extension of the data control block. One key function performed by the DEB is to provide a link between the DCB (the application program) and the unit control block identifying the specific input or output device involved in this operation (Fig. 13.39). The DCB and the channel program are tied together by another control block, the Input/Output Block or IOB (Fig. 13.39 again); we haven't discussed this control block in detail, and we won't. The important point to remember is that we now have a complete link between the application program and the channel program; the routine requesting an I/O operation and the routine which will actually implement this request have been tied together.

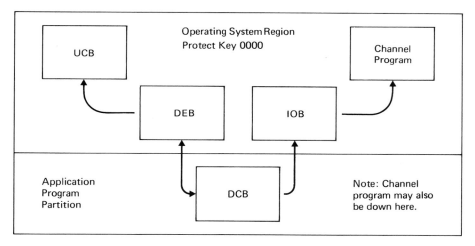

Fig. 13.39 I/O control blocks

Data Management

Data management is concerned with such things as access methods, libraries, catalogs, and so on. MFT supports all of these concepts.

Much of data management—access methods and buffering techniques in particular—is added to an actual load module by the linkage editor; the code for these routines is often found on a direct access library. To simplify access to several key libraries, an activity normally calling for a JOBLIB or STEPLIB DD card, information needed to achieve a linkage is stored in the communication vector table. The SYS1.LINKLIB (a DSNAME, nothing more) is one such library, containing routines used by the linkage editor. Another library accessed through the CVT is the SYS1.SVCLIB which holds SVC and other operating system routines not part of the resident operating system.

SYSIN and SYSOUT, the system input and system output devices, are a part of data management. These two data sets provide an excellent example of the difficulty involved in separating functions into neat, clean categories. Data is placed on the system input device by a job management routine. It is moved from the device into core under the control of task management. Yet, the system input device is part of data management. Direct communication between the various pieces of the operating system is the rule rather than the exception.

System Geography

The MFT operating system is composed of three distinct regions. First is the resident operating system—those routines which reside in core at all times; this part is called the *Nucleus*, and it occupies low core, i.e., from byte zero up to byte number whatever. A second region contains the various control blocks needed by the operating system; these are maintained in the *System Queue Area* (Fig. 13.40) which follows the Nucleus. The third portion of the operating system consists of all those operating system modules which do not reside in core but instead are maintained on a direct-access file (SYS1.SVCLIB) and brought into core on an as-needed basis. The portion of core set aside to hold these transient modules is called the *Link Pack Area* (Fig. 13.40 again). What's left is called the *Free Area*; this is the core available for application programs.

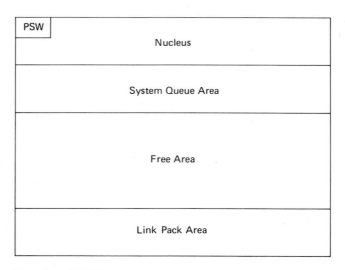

Fig. 13.40 MFT System Geography

System Generation and Flexibility

What operating system modules should be included in the *nucleus*? One possible answer, recognizing the inherent time delays involved in moving a module from a direct-access device into core, is "all of them." Unfortunately, operating system modules, like any software routine, take up space and the more core we assign to operating system modules, the less we have available for application programs. Computers do not exist for the purpose of running an efficient operating system; computers exist to execute application programs and the operating system performs a support function.

The other extreme is to keep most or all of the operating system on disk or drum and bring modules in as needed; this frees core, but the time delay arising from direct-access I/O each time an operating system module is needed leads to inefficiency. This is done on some smaller computers using a disk operating system, but on a larger, faster computer, it's impractical.

Somewhere between these two extremes is the "best" solution. On a large computer running numerous, small, brief programs, the "best" solution might be close to the "all in core" alternative. A scientific machine running long, compute-bound programs might lean toward a minimum-nucleus operating system. MFT was designed by IBM to be a general-purpose operating system, capable of supporting both types of applications.

The modular nature of MFT is the key to this flexibility. Certain routines and control blocks *must* be core resident; beyond this, individual modules may be made resident or part of the system library at the option of the user. IBM provides the basic system and options; the user builds his own system during system generation.

Generally, the nucleus is maintained on a direct access device. During initial program load (IPL), the nucleus is copied into core, queue and linkage areas are set up, and the operator defines partitions in the free area. The fact that a copy of the system exists on an external device (usually a direct-access device but sometimes tape) serves as a backup. The data set holding a copy of the nucleus has the data-set name SYS1.NUCLEUS.

MFT Limits

Multiprogramming exists because of the speed disparity between the computer and its I/O devices; by placing a number of programs in core storage at the same time and allowing the CPU to switch its attention from program to program, much of what would be wasted "wait" time can be utilized. The operating system exists to handle the inevitable conflicts.

We've been looking at a system with two programs in core. In a two-program system, there will be times when both are waiting; additional system efficiency could be gained by introducing a third program. The same argument might be used to justify a fourth program, a fifth, and so on. As the number of programs in core increases, the amount of time when the computer is left with nothing to do (because all programs are waiting for something) must drop. There is a limit—eventually, interference between programs will become so great as to offset the advantages of adding more programs—but, up to this point, the more programs we have in core, the greater the utilization of the computer.

Under MFT, there are a few more-practical limits. The first one is core. The address of the last byte in the largest possible IBM System/360 machine is, in hex, $(FFFFFF)_{16}$, a limit arising from the use of three-byte or 24-bit addresses in the PSW and throughout the machine; that's about sixteen million bytes, not an important limit but still a limit. The number of programs which can be loaded into core at any one time is more realistically restricted by the amount of core actually available; a megabyte computer with a 200K operating system has space for only eight 100K partitions.

There is one other limitation. Each partition must have its own protection key. The protection key field in the PSW is four bits long. There are only sixteen different combinations of four bits, (0000) through (1111). The operating system uses protect key (0000), leaving keys for fifteen application-program partitions.

Summary

IBM System/360 Operating System, Multiprogramming with a Fixed Number of Tasks, better known as MFT, is an operating system designed to support multiprogramming on an IBM System/360 (or System/370) computer. Under this system, core is divided into a number of partitions; these partitions are set up by the operator and can be almost any size but, once set up, they remain fixed until further operator intervention.

The operating system consists of a number of programs designed to handle the problems caused by having more than one program in core. Job management routines are responsible for getting programs into core and starting them. The reader/interpreter performs a spooling function. Individual job steps are scheduled for execution by the master scheduler routine which also handles operator communications. Job steps are loaded and started by the initiator/terminator routine—one per partition—which also cleans up after the job is finished. The output writer handles output spooling. Once a program is in core, it is supported by task management which handles interrupts. The usual data management functions are also part of MFT. The various operating system modules rely on a series of control blocks and tables; key control blocks and tables include: the communication vector table, task control blocks, request blocks, the data control block and data extent block, unit control block, input/output block, and the task input/output table.

MFT is a general-purpose operating system intended to cover as many different types of system requirements as possible—not surprising when you consider IBM's market. To implement this flexibility, the operating system has been written in modular form, with the user selecting those modules which will be core resident and those which will reside on a library and be brought into the computer on an as-needed basis; the user requiring rapid operating system response can thus have the needed core resident modules, while the user needing significant amounts of core can go with a minimum resident system.

Exercises

1. What is the difference between a job and a task?

2. What are the responsibilities of job management?

3. What are the responsibilities of task management?

4. How does the master scheduler discover if a partition is free or busy? Mention all the pointers, control blocks, and tables involved in this process.

5. Describe the series of control blocks involved in linking an application program to a unit control block and a channel program. What is the function of each of these control blocks?

6. How are DD card DCB subparameters and label information merged with the program DCB?

7. OS/MFT, as a multiprogramming operating system, is designed to support several concurrent programs in core. Discuss some of the limits on the number of such programs.

CHAPTER 14

Multiprogramming with Dynamic Core Allocation

Overview

The use of fixed-size partitions is an excellent approach to multiprogramming whenever the job mix of an installation can be predicted with fair accuracy; unfortunately, such predictions cannot always be made and, when job needs are more variable, the MFT type of system has some flaws. In this chapter, we'll discuss several techniques for making better use of the system's resources under more variable demands. Key topics include: the use of variable-size partitions or regions, dynamic core allocation, roll-in and roll-out, subtasking, parallel processing, foreground/background systems, and multiprocessing.

Some of the examples in this chapter will be based on the IBM System/360 and System/370, Multiprogramming with a Variable Number of Tasks (MVT) operating system; we've already discussed the relevant hardware features of this family of machines and the MFT operating system, providing a good base for continued study. Our intent in this chapter is to introduce some important concepts and *not*, as in the previous chapters, to delve into the details of any single system. It is important to remember that an operating system is not an IBM exclusive—all computer manufacturers provide them. Throughout this chapter, nonIBM operating systems will be mentioned and compared, on a functional level, with IBM's OS/MVT system. The basic function of an operating system is to maximize the utilization of system resources within the hardware constraints of a particular computer system; hopefully, this chapter will help to illustrate this idea by pointing out that competitive operating systems are really performing the same functions on a different set of hardware.

Improving Core Efficiency

Multiprogramming is concerned with improving the utilization of the central processing unit, achieving this objective by maintaining several programs in core and switching from program to program. The amount of available core space sets a limit on this process. An operating system based on the assignment of fixed-size partitions can be very effective when program sizes are predictable and relatively consistent, but an MFT-like operating system can lead to extreme inefficiencies in the utilization of core storage when program sizes are more variable.

Consider, for example, an assemble/link-edit/go job submitted by a student as part of a homework assignment. The assembler program requires 60K of core (Fig. 14.1a), the linkage editor needs 120K (Fig. 14.1b), and the "Go" step

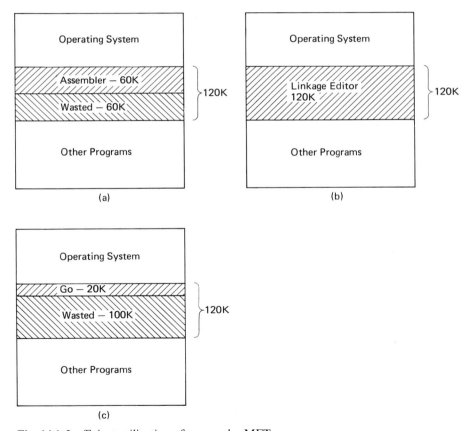

Fig. 14.1 Inefficient utilization of core under MFT

needs a mere 20K (Fig. 14.1c); if this job is to execute under MFT, a 120K partition must be set up. During the assembler step, 60K of core is wasted; during the link-edit step, the entire partition is used; during the "Go" step, fully 100K is wasted. By anyone's definition, that's an inefficient utilization of core storage, and this problem is repeated in each partition.

Why not assign each task exactly the amount of core it needs; i.e., set up variable length partitions? Under such a variable system, the 60K that *might* have been wasted in partition A and the 60K that *might* have been wasted in partition B can be made available to another program; the net effect of improved core utilization is to add another program or two to the multiprogramming queue, thus improving CPU utilization without increasing the total amount of core.

Most computer manufacturers can supply such an operating system to their customers—variable partition allocation is not an IBM exclusive. We will use an IBM operating system—OS/MVT (Multiprogramming with a Variable number of Tasks)—in introducing this concept simply because MVT is a logical extension of MFT which we've already covered in some detail; after covering the IBM solution to variable core allocation, we'll spend some time looking at the products of other computer firms.

OS/MVT

Under IBM's MFT operating system, partitions are assigned by the operator at IPL time and remain fixed in size and location until the operator once again intervenes. Under MVT, the size and location of a partition is determined by the initiator/terminator routine just prior to the loading of a task (in MVT, what was called a partition is now called a region). In our assemble/link-edit/go example, job management might discover a 60K block of core at address 250,000 and load the assembler program. Some time later, after the assembler has completed, the linkage editor might be loaded into a 120K block starting at core location 175,000. Once this job step completes, this 120K block becomes available to the system, leaving plenty of space for the go step (Fig. 14.2). By giving job steps only as much core as they need, the problem of wasted or unused space is minimized. Figure 14.2 shows other job steps running under various classes packed tightly into core—the net result is an extra task or two in the same amount of main memory.

The old adage, "What you get for nothing is nothing," holds in operating system design as it does in most areas; an operating system like MVT is inherently more complex than MFT. The initiator/terminator cannot simply load a program, start it, and forget it until the terminator gains control. This job management module must be capable of scanning core to find a sufficiently

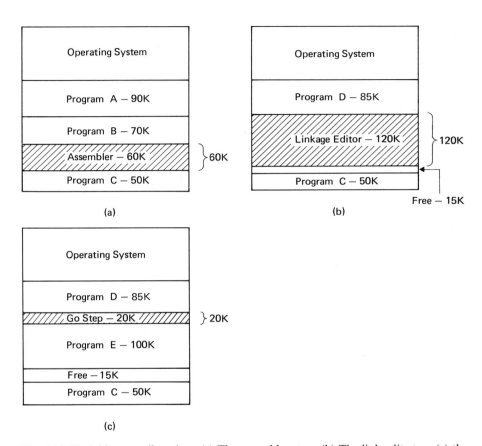

Fig. 14.2 Variable core allocation: (a) The assembler step; (b) The link-edit step; (c) the GO step.

large region and keeping track of the start address, end address, and length of a region, in addition to the MFT-level functions. Keeping track of region boundaries means additional control blocks and/or more-complex control blocks. An MVT operating system will occupy more core than an MFT system, and the more-complex modules will take longer to execute.

Under MFT, a complete job is normally executed step by step before the next job is started. This is standard operating procedure under MVT as well, but this rule may be violated in order to gain even more efficient core utilization. Let's assume, for example, that the 60K assembler program has just completed and that, at this instant of time, there are no 120K regions available for the linkage editor. Obviously, the second step in this job cannot be loaded and started until a 120K block becomes free; thus the link-edit step is postponed for a time, and the operating system must be able to keep track of this fact.

There is, however, a 60K region available—it held the assembler program just completed. And what better way to fill this space than with another assembler step from another job? Using this approach, it is not impossible to find four or five or more jobs running under the same job class either in core or on a queue in a partially completed state—a bunch of object modules waiting for sufficient space to run the linkage editor. The operating system must be capable of keeping track of all these partially completed jobs, which adds to its complexity. The functions are the same as those of MFT; variability makes them a bit more complex.

Dynamic Program Relocation

The whole point of a variable task type of operating system is to cut down on the dead spaces in core, thus making better use of this resource. The MVT approach helps, but does not totally eliminate the problem; at any given instant in time, core storage might look like Fig. 14.3, with unusable 10K, 12K, and other small chunks of memory spread throughout. If these empty spots could be compacted into a single, contiguous region, another task might be loaded and started. This is the intent of dynamic program relocation; application pro-

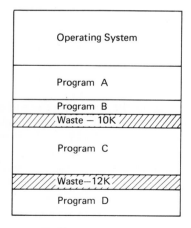

Fig. 14.3 Dead spaces in core under MVT

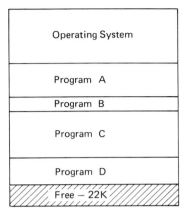

Fig. 14.4 Core following dynamic program relocation

grams are simply shifted up to fill any dead spaces, resulting in the concentration of any such spaces at the end of core (Fig. 14.4)—now, enough space exists for the loading of another task.

On an IBM computer, the implementation of this technique is not quite as simple as the definition in the previous paragraph might imply. Registers on an IBM System/360 or System/370 are available for general-purpose use; i.e., a given register can be used for arithmetic at one time and for addressing at another. When a program is relocated, every memory location in the program is shifted by a constant relocation factor (moving a program from core location 152K to core location 148K means subtracting 4K from every address in the program); every register used for addressing must be modified by this factor, but arithmetic registers may *not* be modified (imagine the impact of a decision to subtract 4096 from the contents of a register used as a counter in a statistical analysis program). The problem can be overcome by the imposition of tight register conventions or by restricting the programming department to compiler languages which (normally) store register contents immediately following arithmetic computations. Undoubtably, there are installations which have done this, but dynamic program relocation is not a standard feature of MVT.

Other manufacturers have an easier time of it. Many firms have designed their computers around separate addressing and arithmetic registers, often with only limited programmer access to the addressing registers. Given this hardware design, dynamic program relocation can be achieved by simply incrementing or decrementing the addressing registers.

Parallel Processing

When a program requests the help of the operating system in starting an input or output operation, the program is normally placed into a wait state following the successful beginning of the I/O. Although the wait state is normal, it is not *always* desirable. At times, a programmer may wish to complete some other processing after the input or output operation has started and before it is completed; in effect, some programmer routine is to run *in parallel* with the I/O operation. The logic or this type of processing is illustrated in Fig. 14.5.

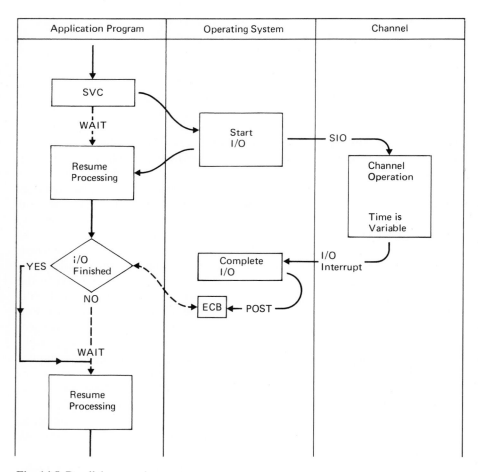

Fig. 14.5 Parallel processing

The most serious problem in parallel processing is event synchronization. To use an admittedly unrealistic but understandable example, let's imagine that a programmer wishes to have the operating system start an I/O operation and, while the channel is controlling the operation, wants to regain control and execute a number of instructions in a computational subprogram. If both the I/O operation and the subprogram complete at the same instant of time, there is no problem. If the I/O operation completes first, again there is no problem—in both cases, the application program can continue normally. What happens, however, when the subroutine finishes before the I/O operation? If you think about it, you'll see that the application program must wait until the I/O is finished before continuing (Fig. 14.5 again).

How can the computer know which of two parallel modules has completed first? This is important! On the IBM System/360 and System/370, this problem of event synchronization is handled by a special control block called an Event Control Block or ECB. In our example, the fact of I/O completion would be noted in an ECB through the execution of a POST macro (probably by an operating system module). The application program, upon completion of the "parallel" subprogram, checks the ECB. If it has been "posted," the parallel operation is finished and processing can continue; if not, the application program issues a WAIT macro and drops into a wait state.

This kind of parallel processing is not found in most everyday application programs; more often, it's done in the operating system itself. (Why not do some housekeeping while waiting for a channel to return its status following the execution of an SIO instruction, for example?) In the next section, we'll take a look at a class of applications in which a certain amount of parallel processing might be desirable.

Subtasking

Remember from our discussion of second-generation overlay structures back in Chapter 5 what happened with overlays? Basically, due to limited core space, it was necessary to load only part of a program at one time, bringing in needed modules on an as-needed basis. On a modern computer even with adequate core, it is sometimes desirable to load less than one-hundred percent of some application program. Consider, for example, a master file update program which occasionally (once a month or so) is expected to handle some unusual condition. The subroutine to handle this condition might occupy 20K of core, and it makes little sense to keep this 20K of normally useless core in an active state on a daily basis. A more reasonable approach would be to keep this subroutine on a library and write the main program in such a way that (with the help of the operating system, of course) a copy of the routine is read into core only when needed. The operating system keeps track of this new task by creating a new task control block and ATTACHing (through an ATTACH macro) it to the main task control block for the region. Where does the extra core come from in a variable task type of system? A GETMAIN macro is executed, and if space is not available, the application program waits until it is.

This process is made-to-order for parallel processing. If the application program is well planned, there is no reason why the need for the subtask can't be recognized long before the processing of the first subtask instruction. If this is the case, the programmer can (through his instructions) turn control over to the operating system, get the required core, start the process of reading the subprogram from a library, regain control, continue executing instructions until the subprogram is actually needed, eventually check an event control block, and either branch to the subprogram or drop into a wait state.

The application cited above is not, of course, the only possible example of subprogramming and multitasking. Outside the realm of application programs, to cite another example, the operating system is constantly subtasking as it gets nonresident operating system modules from a library and brings them into the link pack area for execution.

Roll-in and Roll-out

Some advanced operating systems have a roll-in and roll-out feature; basically, it works something like this. Let's assume that core is full. Suddenly, an extremely hot job arrives—for some reason or other, it *must* be processed immediately. One option would be to simply cancel a number of active jobs and restart them. The roll-in and roll-out feature gives us another option; one or more application programs are simply copied to disk (rolled-out), freeing space for the higher priority routine. Sometime later, the original program is copied back into core (rolled-in) and allowed to continue.

The implementation of this concept is, as you may expect, a bit more complex than the definition. At a minimum level, the operating system becomes responsible for keeping track not only of programs in core and those in queue waiting to start but also a number of partially completed tasks on disk or some other auxiliary storage device—even more control blocks and tables. Some machines with a roll-in/roll-out feature require programs to be "rolled-in" to exactly the same core locations initially occupied; in other systems, these transient routines can be dynamically relocated to other core locations as they become available, adding another level of complexity to the operating system.

A very good example of the value and implementation of a roll-in/roll-out feature can be found by studying almost any terminal oriented, time-sharing system. Let's assume, for our example, a rather small time-shared system capable of supporting up to fifty terminals at the same time. Two problems stand out in trying to analyze such a system. First, we are dealing with fifty different users, and our operating system must be capable of keeping track of all fifty. Imagine the amount of core needed to support fifty independent programs—a mere 25K per user (a pretty small partition) would mean that we would need 750K of core for programs alone, not counting the operating system! The second key factor is the I/O speed and transaction rate we can expect from each of these users. They are going to be using keyboard type terminals, which are slow. There will be considerable "head scratching" time if this group of users is at all typical. In other words, we might expect thirty seconds, a minute, even more to transpire between a computer-generated message and the human response; on a computer capable of executing over one million instructions per second, that's an awfully long time.

Roll-in/roll-out logic is an obvious fit in such an environment. For starters, let's assign five different users to each of ten 25K partitions (a total of only 250K of core); we'll concentrate on users "A" through "F" who are sharing our first partition. User "A" has control first and, after a brief flurry of activity, finds it necessary to provide additional data and, so, issues a read instruction. The computer "knows" that it will take user "A" at best thirty seconds or so to figure out exactly what is needed next, type his response, and send it to the computer; this is more than enough time to roll user "A's" program out to disk and roll-in user "B's" program. In fact, the computer is *so* fast that, in all likelihood, all five users will have had a shot at core before the first one is ready with his response—a computer has very little trouble keeping up with five human beings working at human speeds.

An even better approach involves dynamic relocation of user programs as they come back from disk or drum. Very few time-sharing users are interested in programming at the assembly language level, with most working in BASIC or FORTRAN or APL or terminal PL/I or some other compiler language. Few compiler languages use registers as accumulators or counters, thus eliminating one of the major problems of dynamic relocation. Using this dynamic approach, the possibility of drawing an unlucky "busy" partition would disappear. Assuming that the average user would require the computer for one full second (a pretty long shot of time) between I/O operations, it would be theoretically possible to support up to thirty users in a *single* partition and still be able to respond to each and every user's normal thirty-second cycle (we're probably overestimating our user's capabilities here) without any delays.

Responses, of course, are not regular (this is a good queueing theory problem), but four or five regions should be more than adequate for our fifty-user system.

Before leaving this topic, let's consider one more problem—what happens when one terminal user loads and starts a long, compute-bound program like a statistical analysis routine? We might have forty-nine other users sitting at their terminals waiting for this module to complete. One simple solution to this problem involves the WAIT macro—a compiler preparing load modules to execute under this system simply inserts one after every "so many" instructions, thus forcing the program to surrender control of the computer at fairly regular, brief intervals. More sophisticated systems use a timer, either software or hardware, and restrict programs to a single "time slice" of a fraction of a second before forcing a wait state (perhaps through an external interrupt).

Foreground/Background Processing

In introducing the basic ideas of roll-in and roll-out in a time-shared environment, we discussed an admittedly extreme case in which terminal users controlled the CPU for as much as one full second between I/O operations. It is very difficult, on a line-by-line terminal, to provide enough information in a single transaction to keep a modern, high-speed computer busy for anything near that long; one-tenth or even one-hundredth of a second per transaction would be much more typical. Let's use one-tenth of a second as we attempt to formulate a more realistic example.

Our system supports fifty users. Each user is capable of one transaction—typing and entering one line, responding to one system question, etc.—every thirty seconds on the average; that's two per minute. The average transaction takes one tenth of a second; thus, each of our fifty users needs the computer for 0.2 seconds per minute. Taking all fifty users into account, this time-shared system can be supported in $50 \times (0.2)$ or 10.0 seconds per minute of CPU time, meaning that fully fifty seconds per minute can be used for some other activity without negatively impacting system performance. It's not quite this simple, of course—program interference, the timing of requests, and system overhead detract from system performance—but a time-shared, terminal-oriented application characterized by widely spaced (in a computer's time frame) requests for support and brief shots of actual computation can often be supported in but a fraction of available CPU time.

Why not use this time for some other purpose? This is, as you may remember, the underlying motive behind multiprogramming—put another program or two in core and transfer control to these extra modules when not busy. There is only one problem; if the extra program is a longer-running routine needing four or five seconds between I/O operations, the ability of the time-shared system to respond rapidly to user transactions (the basic motivation behind a time-shared system) may be seriously impaired.

The foreground/background approach provides the best of both worlds, so to speak. Basically, programs requiring quick response are placed in the foreground partition while other programs needing lesser response times are placed in the background. Following *any* interrupt, the operating system attempts to give control to the foreground region first; the background gets control *only* when there is no ready program in the foreground. In a terminal-oriented system with dozens of users sending I/O interrupts into the system at fairly random and unpredictable intervals, the chances of a background partition grabbing and keeping control for a long period of time are slim at best. In some systems, a timer routine or, occasionally, a WAIT macro helps to ensure foreground response.

Basically, the foreground/background idea is a priority scheme. On an IBM System/360 or System/370, this can be achieved by simply ensuring that the master scheduler routine of job management always checks the foreground partition or region first, even when the program which had control at the time of the interrupt is still ready.

This type of system operation is not restricted to time-sharing or terminal applications; often, a typical batch-processing program will be placed in the foreground with compute-bound jobs relegated to the background, allowing the batch job to execute normally while the background job utilizes the time between the multiple I/O operations typical to batch jobs. Some manufacturers have designed their computers around this concept, with the higher priority of the foreground job being implemented through hardware; we'll examine a few of these a bit later in the chapter.

A good example of a foreground/background design can be found in IBM's CALL-OS system which is designed to run under their MVT operating system. One region of the computer's core is assigned to CALL-OS; within this region, the CALL-OS system, sort of an operating system within an operating system, takes command, allocating its core among the many users, performing roll-in and roll-out functions, keeping track of programs, and so on. Running at a lower priority are a number of other regions—the background.

Multiprocessing

When two or more programs occupy core at the same time and share the resources of a single CPU, we call it multiprogramming. When two or more processors are involved, it's called multi*processing*. The former, multi*programming*, is a software concept; multi*processing* is a hardware concept. An operating system is a collection of programs or software; why discuss hardware in a software book? The answer to this question is simple—many of the functions performed through a modern operating system can be implemented by either hardware or software means.

One very common multiprocessing application is the master/slave combination depicted in Fig. 14.6. When an application requires significant amounts of I/O, particularly when this I/O can come from numerous sources, the "master" computer is often used for the express purpose of coordinating all this I/O and maintaining queues, leaving all the high-powered processing to the slave machine; this approach is particularly valuable in a time-shared operation with numerous, often remote users communicating with the system through terminals. The "master" computer is often a mini or a smaller machine with the ability to handle multiple levels of interrupts; the "slave" is often much larger and much more expensive.

Some manufacturers have designed their computers around what is essentially a multiprocessing concept. In the next few pages of this chapter, we'll take a look at some nonIBM computers including a few of this variety.

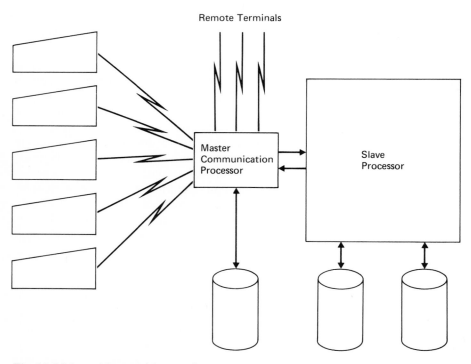

Fig. 14.6 Master/slave multiprocessing

Other Manufacturers

IBM is not the only manufacturer of computers around today; many other firms are doing an outstanding job in this field. In the next few paragraphs, we'll take a brief look at several of them, concentrating on key factors in their hardware design and major operating systems they supply. We'll try to keep details to a minimum; it's just a survey.

Burroughs Corporation offers an operating system called the Master Control Program or MCP in support of their 6700 and 6800 series of computers. This operating system is designed to support batch, multiprogramming, time-sharing, and real-time applications. Burroughs has always been an innovative company when it comes to software and hardware design, and such concepts as both hardware and software interrupts, interrupt stacking, dynamic storage allocation, and storage hierarchy (to be discussed in Chapter 15) are part of this product.

Control Data Corporation sells both large and small computers and, thus, offers a number of different operating systems. The Master Operating System (MOS) is designed to run in support of their 3300/3500 series of computers. This is a multiprogramming system capable of handling up to five job classes; the system is designed in such a way that it always tries to keep at least one job from each class active.

To support their 6400/6500/6600 series of computers, CDC has their disk-oriented Scope 3 operating system. The interesting thing about the CDC 6000 series, however, lies in its hardware design. In addition to the main processor or CPU, a CDC 6000 computer has a number of peripheral processors—in effect, additional computers which work in parallel with the main processor. One of these peripheral processors holds the operating system's Monitor program, roughly equivalent to IBM's master scheduler, initiator, and terminator modules. A second peripheral processor handles communications with the operator's console, while a third is responsible for I/O control. All peripherals are independent; i.e., they can function simultaneously. On such a system, once a request for I/O is recognized through the equivalent of an SVC, the request can simply be turned over to the proper peripheral processor and the equivalent of such functions as channel communications, the execution of an SIO instruction, and checking the channel status word can be done while the main processor is busy with other work. An operating system designed to support this computer series will be quite different from IBM's software, but the functions to be performed are pretty much the same.

Digital Equipment Corporation is well known as a supplier of smaller computer systems, particularly in the time-sharing market. One of their smaller machines, the PDP-8, can be used to support from four to thirty-two concurrent users under their Time Sharing System (TSS/8). The computer actually holds one program at a time in core, with roll-in and roll-out taking care of the multiple-user problem. The system uses time slicing as a means of preventing any single program from controlling core for an excessive period of time.

To support a series of larger computers, the PDP-11/40 and PDP-11/45 family, Digital Equipment Corporation has their Resource Sharing Timesharing System/Extended (RSTS/E). This is a legitimate multiprogramming system, capable of keeping track of a number of different core resident programs at any one time. The system uses stack processing concepts for handling interrupts, with hardware doing most of the work of maintaining the push down stacks. The system also makes use of virtual storage concepts, a topic we'll cover in detail in the next chapter. DEC has other, more-batch-oriented operating systems to support this particular family of computers as well.

Digital's PDP-15 computer is another example of a computer designed around the multiprocessing concept. This machine has five processors: the CPU, an integrated floating-point processor, an I/O processor, a graphics processor, and a peripheral processor; all are independent and capable of running in parallel. DEC has four operating systems designed to support processing on this machine, all, obviously, bearing little resemblance at the detailed coding level to an IBM operating system.

Before its purchase of General Electric's computer division, Honeywell was best known for its smaller and midsized computers; GE added larger computers to the product line. In support of its 200 series of machines, Honeywell offers something called the MOD 4 operating system. This system is capable of handling up to twenty independent partitions and multiple job classes in a manner similar to the MFT system we studied a chapter ago.

The Honeywell 600 series (615/625/635) is derived from equipment previously marketed by General Electric Corporation; the General Electric Comprehensive Operating System (GECOS III) supports this series of machines. GECOS III is a general-purpose operating system, with features designed to support local batch processing, remote batch processing, and time-sharing. Memory is normally assigned to programs in a manner analogous to IBM's OS/MVT, with dynamic program relocation and roll-out options being used to get high priority programs into core. The system supports thirty-two different interrupt vectors, four of which are I/O. The equivalent of IBM's Old PSWs and interrupts are maintained on a dispatcher queue capable of holding up to sixty-three entries; programs are selected from this queue and executed in priority order.

Like GE, RCA is no longer in the computer business, but their computers are still in use. The Spectra 70 Tape-Disk Operating System (TDOS) is probably the best known of their software products. This system was designed to be disk resident until scheduled and loaded by the operator, then remaining core resident until the entire job stream is processed. TDOS can handle as many as six concurrent programs in variable sized partitions.

UNIVAC has an operating system known as EXEC 8 which is marketed in support of their 1108 series of computers. It supports batch, interactive, and real-time applications.

Xerox computers are interesting if for no other reason than their heavy emphasis on multiple interrupts; their SIGMA 2 series, for example, can handle up to 134 different interrupt levels! The Real-Time Batch Monitor (RBM) is one operating system designed to support this series. It multiprograms using MFT-like, fixed-size foreground and background partitions. Individual programs are connected to interrupts; in effect, what IBM called an Old PSW and stored on a request block queue is called an interrupt and stored on an interrupt dispatching queue or stack in a Xerox machine. Each level of interrupt has its own priority level which determines the order in which modules will be executed. In a larger machine, the SIGMA5/7 series, Xerox is capable of handling as many as 224 interrupt levels. The Batch Time-Sharing Monitor (BTM) supports, as the name implies, both batch and time-sharing applications on this computer series. The foreground/background approach is an integral part of this system, with the time-shared applications occupying, as you might suspect, the foreground partition. Incidentally, as of mid1975, Xerox no longer markets computers.

Summary

In this chapter, we've studied, on a functional level, a number of fairly advanced operating system concepts. We started with an analysis of IBM's OS/MVT which, as we saw, was developed in an attempt to make better, more-efficient use of core. Following this discussion, we covered the basic concepts of dynamic core relocation, parallel processing and event synchronization, subtasking, roll-in and roll-out logic, foreground/background processing, and multiprocessing. The chapter ended with a discussion of mainframe suppliers other than IBM, including: Burroughs, Control Data Corporation, Digital Equipment Corporation, Honeywell, RCA, UNIVAC, and Xerox.

Exercises

1. Why is space often wasted under a fixed-partition operating system? How does a variable-partition (or region) system help?

2. What is dynamic program relocation?

3. What is subtasking?

4. How can CPU processing and parallel channel operations be synchronized?

5. A time-shared system often involves parallel processing, foreground/background processing, and roll-in/roll-out logic. Discuss how these ideas are related.

6. What is multiprocessing?

7. The CDC 6000 series of computers utilizes multiple "peripheral" processors in addition to the main processor. What are some of the advantages of this approach?

CHAPTER 15

Segmentation, Paging, and Virtual Memory

Overview

Multiprogramming, as we should certainly know by now, involves placing several programs in core at the same time and allowing them to share the resources of the CPU in an effort to improve the degree of system utilization. The limiting factor on this process is usually core and not CPU time, a problem which becomes more and more acute as computers become faster and faster. In this chapter, we'll take a look at program segmentation and paging, two techniques which tend to improve the utilization of core. Using these two concepts as a base, we'll develop the key ideas of virtual memory.

Core Efficiency

As we've already seen in our discussion of multiprogramming, the more programs we can load into core, the greater is our utilization of the central processing unit's time. There is a limit, of course—eventually, program interference begins to overwhelm any gain in efficiency—but this point, except in the case of a relatively few well-planned and well-run systems, is rarely reached. In general, adding another program to core means improving system efficiency.

This was the whole point of MVT—improve the utilization of core so that additional programs might be added. It did represent an improvement over fixed-partition operating systems, but, as you may remember, had a nasty habit of leaving small chunks of storage spread here and there throughout core—the fragmentation problem. Dynamic program relocation helps, but creates problems of its own, particularly when hardware has not been designed with this facility in mind. First, we have the problem of address translation—addressing,

271

but not arithmetic registers, must be relocated. A second problem, perhaps of even greater impact, is the fact that the computer must literally stop doing useful work during the relocation process. Some machines are designed to handle dynamic program relocation through hardware; these can do the job quickly and with a minimum of lost time. Other machines do not have this feature and must implement dynamic relocation through software. At best, variable partitions or regions, even with dynamic relocation, will leave an occasional 2K or 4K or 10K chunk of unused core.

As electronic technology advances, computers become faster and faster; this ever increasing speed makes the problem of core efficiency even more crucial—to cite a fairly simple example, a ten-program system, which previously was able to utilize only 50% of available CPU time, suddenly drops to a mere 25% utilization on a machine which is twice as fast. Is it any wonder, then, that so many manufacturers are offering hardware and software packages designed to improve core utilization along with their solid logic and monolithic circuit computers?

Segmentation

Why must a program always occupy contiguous regions in core; why not break it into pieces and place individual segments wherever they fit in core (Fig. 15.1)? Many programs are composed of individual modules and subroutines anyway, with relative addressing being of a critical nature only *within* a given segment and not across segments. Individual segments would certainly be smaller than complete programs without segmentation, and these smaller pieces would be better able to fit into small openings in core, yielding the advantages of dynamic program relocation without the disadvantages. The extra 10K chunk (or two or three) of unutilized core left behind by even the best MVT-type system can be used to hold an extra program or two with no increase in total core, thus improving system efficiency at a relatively low cost.

There are, however, some costs—mostly in the area of addressing. In a program written as a contiguous whole by some programmer, how are the addressing problems caused by noncontiguous program loading handled?

One approach is to simply leave it to the programmer. Most programs have a number of separate and obvious (to the programmer) logical functions to perform; a good programmer, or one writing under a set of good program standards, can break these functions into segments that make sense. Each segment can be assigned a different base-addressing register to be initialized at program load time. Since all addresses can be computed relative to the base register, addressing within a segment is not a problem. In assembly-level languages, setting up a separate base register and a control section for each of

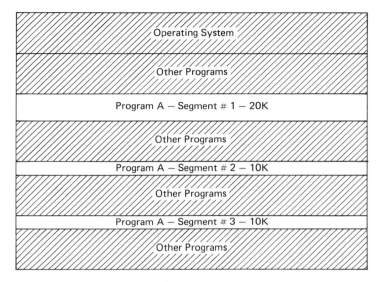

Fig. 15.1 Program segmentation

several segments is common practice. Some higher-level languages either have this facility or can easily implement it through the compiler—PL/I's BEGIN block feature is a good example.

Leaving things to the programmer is not always the best idea. Why not let the operating system take on some if not all the responsibility for program segmentation? If the programmer uses BEGIN blocks or subroutines, great—this gives the system an obvious and logical segment break point. Even if he doesn't, there are still some obvious break points—work spaces, input and output buffer areas, and the program logic are three such "naturals." Other standards might be imposed by an operating system or through a compiler—a limitation on maximum segment size is common.

Addressing under segmentation is different. One addressing scheme involves breaking an address into two pieces (Fig. 15.2), a segment number occupying the high-order bit positions and the displacement within the segment

Segment	Displacement

Fig. 15.2 Program segmentation addressing

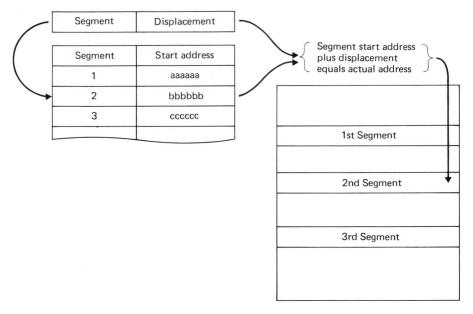

Fig. 15.3 Dyanmic address translation

filling the low-order bits. As a program is loaded, a segment table (Fig. 15.3) is built, containing the segment number and the actual core address of the first memory location in each segment. During program execution, addresses are dynamically translated, with the segment number being converted to a base address through a table look-up operation and the actual, absolute core address being computed by adding the displacement portion of the address to the base address. (Fig. 15.3).

Sometimes it's easier to see exactly what is going on by following an example. To keep things as simple as possible, let's use a sixteen-bit minicomputer as our model—on this machine, all addresses are sixteen bits long. We'll assign the following meanings to these sixteen bits:

1. the high-order four bits hold the segment number.
2. the low-order twelve bits hold the displacement.

A four bit segment number means that we have room for at most 16 segments (0000 through 1111). The twelve bit displacement allows for 4096 (0000 through 4095) storage locations in each segment. Before going any further, it is important that we take note of the arbitrary nature of this addressing scheme—we might just as well have chosen a two-bit segment number and a fourteen-bit displacement or a three-bit segment number and a thirteen-bit displacement or any other combination that strikes our fancy. Ideally, the segment size should be small enough to actually utilize random pieces of free core, large enough to hold a full complement of program logic, and flexible. It should be a reflection of the kinds of programs (the job mix) actually run in a given installation—which is easier to say than to do.

At any rate, we've chosen an addressing scheme involving a four-bit segment number and a twelve-bit displacement for our installation; once the decision has been made, all we must do is follow it consistently. In Fig. 15.4, we'll be tracking the segmentation process on our minicomputer.

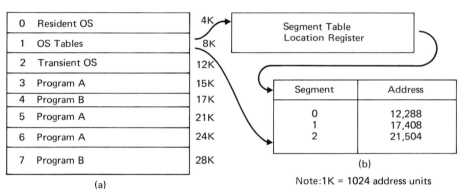

			4K		
0	Resident OS			Segment Table	
1	OS Tables		8K	Location Register	
2	Transient OS		12K		
3	Program A		15K		

Segment	Address
0	12,288
1	17,408
2	21,504

(b)

Note:1K = 1024 address units

Program loading table:

0	Resident OS	4K
1	OS Tables	8K
2	Transient OS	12K
3	Program A	15K
4	Program B	17K
5	Program A	21K
6	Program A	24K
7	Program B	28K

(a)

Note: segment length can vary

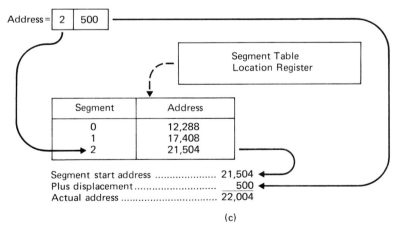

Address = | 2 | 500 |

Segment Table
Location Register

Segment	Address
0	12,288
1	17,408
2	21,504

Segment start address 21,504
Plus displacement............................   500
Actual address 22,004

(c)

Fig. 15.4 Program segmentation, an example: (a) Program loading; (b) Program A's segment table; (c) Address translation.

The first program in core is, as you might expect, the operating system. This software has been broken into three segments (Fig. 15.4a) holding, respectively; a core resident portion, some tables and pointers, and a region to hold transient modules which will be read in from a disk when needed. Each segment is a full 4096 memory locations long; hence, the segment table for this "program" has a rather unusual property. Consider the following table:

ADDRESS SEG. DISP.	ABSOLUTE ADDRESS	BINARY ADDRESS SEG. DISP.	ABSOLUTE BINARY ADDRESS
0 000	0	0000 000000000000	0000000000000000
1 000	4096	0001 000000000000	0001000000000000
2 000	8192	0010 000000000000	0010000000000000

The address as expressed in segment terms and the address as expressed in absolute terms are identical! This only happens, except by pure chance, in the operating system. It makes sense when you think about it; the operating system is the one place where machine-dependent programs must be written and the only place where absolute addressing must be used. When the operating system is running, no address translation is needed, but all addresses in all other programs must be "translated" through the program's segment table.

Let's assume that a program consisting of three segments has been loaded into core as described in Fig. 15.4(a). The segment table holds the start address of each segment in the program (Fig. 15.4b); the segment table is located in the table region of the operating system and is found through a special register called, predictably, the segment table location register.

At some point in the program, the address shown in Fig. 15.4(c) is referenced by the program. Using the high-order four bits of this address, the program's segment table, located through the segment table location register, is searched, yielding the address of the start of this segment. The contents of the last twelve bits in the address are added to this base address, giving the actual address in core.

In a multiprogramming system, each program will have its own segment table. Several different approaches might be used for linking to this table through the segment table location register. The use of stacks or queues of segment table addresses might be an excellent choice, with a hardware or software pointer indicating the location of the register pointing to the "active" program's segmentation table. Since dynamic address translation is not essential in the operating system, the contents of this special register might be loaded by a master scheduler or initiator program much as IBM loads the current PSW under MFT or MVT. This "register" need not even be a register; any known and consistent location would suffice.

Once again, please note that our sixteen-bit address example is only an example and not an industry standard; address sizes vary from manufacturer to manufacturer, and the exact rule for breaking an address into segment and displacement portions can vary even among the installations of a single manufacturer.

Core allocation is a little tougher under this kind of system than under MFT or MVT. The operating system must keep track of all free spaces no matter how small. A table something like the one pictured in Fig. 15.5 is probably maintained by such an operating system; the table simply lists regions of core which are in use and regions which are free. This table has nothing to do with programs which are in core and executing; it exists only for the convenience of the operating system's master scheduler and initiator programs (or their equivalents).

Start Address	Length *	Status
O	16K	In Use
16K	8K	Free
24K	16K	In Use
40K	4K	Free
44K	12K	In Use
66K	10K	Free

* Lengths, of course, would be in actual binary form rather than in the shorthand form shown above. The status would probably be represented by a simple bit flag.

Fig. 15.5 Core allocation table—segmentation system

The use of segments does allow for fairly efficient program loading simply because segments are smaller than complete programs and will therefore fit into smaller chunks of core. Segmentation is somewhat programmer oriented in that it allows for variable-length segments attuned to actual program logic; using a twenty-four bit address, for example, the high-order eight bits might be assigned to the segment number while the low-order sixteen hold the displacement, yielding a total of 256 segments ranging in size from a few to as many as 64K storage locations.

Paging

Segmentation breaks a program into pieces in a manner related to the logic of the program—individual segments can vary significantly in length. The number of bits in the displacement portion of the address does set an upper limit on segment size, but the "convenience of the program's logic" is the key factor involved in breaking down the program. Some fragmentation is still possible; if no segment is small enough to fit into an available piece of core, that core will be wasted.

Paging breaks a program into fixed-sized pieces called pages; page length is usually determined by hardware and other system factors. IBM, for example, uses two different page sizes in their paging systems: 2K and 4K. If you remember our discussion of core protection under IBM's MFT operating system, you may recall that core is allocated to programs in 2K portions; thus the 2K page. Assembly language programmers will certainly recognize the significance of the number 4K—this is the addressing limit of a single base register. Given such small pages with lengths so closely attuned to actual core allocation schemes, the risk of unusable regions of core is significantly reduced.

Beyond the fixed-size page approach, the implementation of a paging system is almost identical to that of a segmentation system. Programs are loaded into core in noncontiguous pages (Fig. 15.6). An address is broken into two parts (Fig. 15.7), a page number in the high-order positions and a displace-

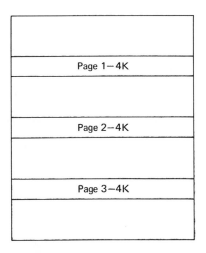

Fig. 15.6 Program loading under a paging system

Page Number	Displacement

Fig. 15.7 Addressing under a paging system

ment within the page in the low-order bits; addresses are dynamically translated as the program is executing through a program page table (Fig. 15.8). What was called a segment table location register will now be called a page table location register.

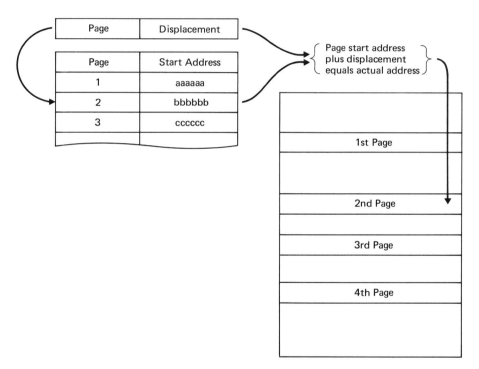

Fig. 15.8 Dynamic address translation under paging

Core allocation is a little easier to track under a paging system; core is simply divided into a series of fixed-length pages (Fig. 15.9), with a page frame table (Fig. 15.10) indicating the status (free or in use) of each page via a simple one-bit flag. In trying to locate a free spot in core, the master scheduler or

1	2	3	4	5	6	7	8	9
10	11	12	13	14	15	16	17	18
19	20	21	22	23	24	25	26	27
28	29	30	31	32	33	34	35	36

Fig. 15.9 Core divided into pages

Page frame number	Program ID	Page number	Status
1	Operating System	1	1
2	Operating System	2	1
3	Operating System	3	1
4	Operating System	4	1
5	Program A	1	1
6	Program B	1	1
7	Program A	2	1
8	Program C	1	1
9			0
10			0
11	Program A	3	1
12	Program C	2	1
			0

Fig. 15.10 The page frame table

initiator program (or their equivalents) need only search the page frame table for a "0" bit, assign that page to the program, and change the bit to a "1." It should be noted that there is a significant difference between this page frame table and the program page table described above. The page frame table is for the use of the operating system in allocating core, while the program page table supports dynamic address translation for executing programs which are already in core.

As we've seen, some wasted core is inevitable with any core allocation scheme; paging, even with its fixed size modules, shares the same problem, though not quite in the same way. To state the paging problem as simply as possible, *any* fixed size page is bound to be the wrong length. Perhaps a bit of additional explanation is in order. Programmers just do not write their programs in fixed-length increments; almost every program will have at least one page which is only partially used. Even if this averages only 1K per program, a multiprogramming system working with ten programs in core will waste a full 10K!

Segmentation and Paging

Both segmentation and paging allow the system to utilize noncontiguous, small pieces of core storage for active programs. We've considered the possibility of occasional waste due to the existence of a region smaller than the smallest segment or the fact that program length and page length may not be perfectly matched. Segmentation tends to be program oriented, dividing a program into pieces which complement actual program logic. Paging is a more hardware-oriented technique, with page sizes being geared to a system's core allocation scheme.

Combining segmentation *and* paging on the same system might be expected to give us the best of both worlds. Under such a system, a program could be broken into logical segments and the segments then subdivided into fixed length pages—the programmer could plan a segment structure while the system loads pages. How is this an improvement on a standard segmentation system? If a program need not occupy contiguous core, why must a segment? Under segmentation *and* paging, it doesn't, meaning that chunks of core smaller than the smallest segment can now be utilized.

Segment number	Page number	Displacement

Fig. 15.11 Segmentation and paging addresses

Of course, this technique is not without its cost. Dynamic address translation now involves two tables, with an address being divided into three pieces—the segment number, page number, and displacement (Fig. 15.11). First, the program's segment table must be found via the segment table location register (Fig. 15.12) and searched for the proper segment number. This table, in turn, gives the address of the segment's page table which can be searched for the base address of the page. This series of memory cycles is bound to have a negative impact on system overhead.

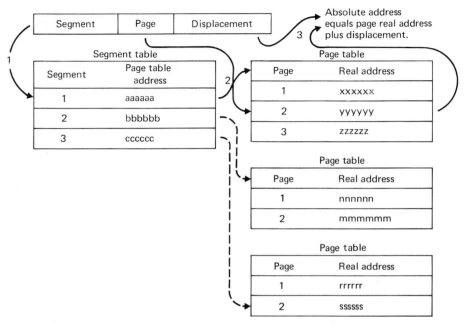

Fig. 15.12 Dynamic address translation under a segmentation and paging system

To help minimize this cost, many systems using the segmentation and paging approach provide a hardware boost to dynamic address translation through a series of special registers called associative array registers. Before delving into a discussion of the implementation of this feature, it might be instructive to digress for a paragraph or two and look into the underlying logic. Back in the late 1800s, an Italian economist named Vilfredo Pareto, following a study of the distribution of wealth in his native land, came to the conclusion that something in excess of 90% of the wealth was in the hands of something less than 10% of the population. A generalization of this idea became known as Pareto's Law. We see examples of this basic concept every day—a very large percentage of the earth's people live on a very small portion of the available land; a small percentage of the world's population uses a very large percentage of the world's energy; 80% of a company's patents are filed by 20% of the firm's employees.

Applying this law to a segmentation and paging system, it might be reasonable to state that a significant percentage of the system's address translation requests are associated with a relatively few pages. This makes sense when you think about it. Programs normally execute in fixed sequence, with numerous instructions lying between branches (deviations from this fixed sequence); once one instruction is executed within a given page, the chances are very good that the next instruction to be executed by the same program will be found on the same page.

Which brings us back to the associative array registers. As instructions are executed by the system, the base address of the "last several pages accessed" can be placed in these special registers. Before going through the table look-up process of normal dynamic address translation, these registers can be checked for the desired base address; if it's there, no additional address translation is needed. To save time, these registers are usually searched in parallel.

If the desired address is not in the associative array registers, of course, normal address translation through the segment and page tables takes place. In order to avoid clogging these registers with "obsolete" addresses, this actual address translation step is often the point at which these registers are modified, with the newly translated address replacing the contents of the register which has been "least currently" accessed. Consider, for example, a typical page. The first time a program branches to this page, dynamic address translation through the tables is necessary; following this step, the address of the new page is placed in the associative array registers. As additional instructions are executed within the page, the base address is in the registers and address translation is taken care of very quickly by hardware. Eventually, a branch to another page is encountered, and dynamic address translation must once again take place, with this new base address replacing the contents of one of the registers. If the program does not return to the original page, eventually all other entries in the associative array registers will be more current than the entry for "this" page, meaning that the reference to "this" page will be the next one to be dropped from the array to make room for a new page address.

The actual implementation of this technique will, of course, vary from manufacturer to manufacturer. Some use purely hardware stacks and queues. Others use core storage locations instead of separate registers and provide a special instruction for searching these "registers." Some use algorithms and rules to limit the number of references a single program can keep current. The basic concept of hardware-aided address translation for the "most commonly used" pages is, however, common.

Core allocation is implemented much as in a pure paging system, with the operating system maintaining a page frame table. Once again, remember that the page frame table is for the use of the operating system for the purpose of core allocation, and it has nothing to do with the actual execution of loaded programs.

Segmentation Systems and Paging Systems—Conclusions

The whole point of segmentation and paging, either singularly or in combination, is to divide a program into relatively small pieces so that random segments of noncontiguous core can be utilized. Some form of dynamic address translation is essential because of the noncontiguous nature of programs on such systems—programmers cannot be expected to forsee the exact location of their pages or segments. The end result is more programs on line within the same amount of core; this improves system efficiency.

Some languages—notably, PL/I and Assembly level language—include features which allow the programmer to define his own segment break points, and other languages will probably contain something analogous to PL/I's BEGIN block in the future, but, if a segmentation and/or paging system is to be implemented in such a way as to have a positive impact on system costs, the actual functions of subdividing a program should be system responsibilities pretty much transparent to the programmer; otherwise, any gains in system efficiency might easily be offset by increased programming and debug time.

We've already considered the possibility of wasted space due to chunks of core too small for even the smallest segment or logic which does not quite fill a complete fixed-length page. Another source of potential waste arises from the belief that every instruction in a program must be in core before that program can begin executing. A 10K block of core might be more than enough to hold a few extra pages or a complete segment, but if no *complete* program needs 10K or less, it makes no sense to load only a portion since, if the entire program must be in core before execution is possible, it couldn't run anyway. As we'll see in the next few pages, this belief is a myth.

Virtual Memory

We've already seen that programs do not have to be loaded into contiguous core in order to execute properly. We also know that the CPU is capable of executing only one instruction at a time. In this section, we'll be attempting to deal with the following question: Why is it necessary for *every* instruction in a program to be in core for that program to execute properly?

We've already seen cases where it was not necessary. Remember the overlay structures we discussed in our analysis of second-generation concepts? And what about subtasking—where complete modules of logic are rolled into core on an as-needed basis?

Segmentation and/or paging concepts provide an almost perfect framework for implementing a system in which only a part of a program is actually in core at any one time. Taking advantage of the roll-in and roll-out concepts we've already covered, why not load only a page or two of a program at a time, keeping the rest on some direct access device? This is the essence of a virtual memory system (Fig. 15.13).

It's not a new idea. Back in the early 1960s (prehistory as far as computers are concerned), Burroughs had a fully operational virtual system (they didn't call it "virtual") for their 5000 computer series. UNIVAC, CDC, and GE/Honeywell all had it during the 1960s. RCA was the first to use the term "virtual memory" in 1970. The key date in the development of the virtual memory

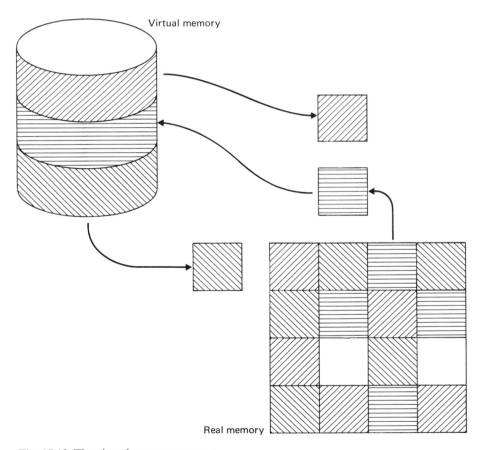

Virtual memory

Real memory

Fig. 15.13 The virtual memory concept

concept was, however, August 2, 1972, when **IBM** announced its System/370 series of computers; for the first time *the* major computer manufacturer had decided to make the virtual memory concept a key element in a full line of computers.

The word virtual means "not in actual fact"; virtual memory therefore means memory which does "not in actual fact" exist. Basically, the system works something like this. Programs are written as though there were an almost unlimited amount of space, and stored on disk or drum. Addresses on the direct access device are sequential just like core, so the disk or drum address of a given program or module is analogous to the address it might occupy if it were really in core. Storage on this "virtual memory" device is subdivided into segments or pages or both, and a few pages from each of several programs are moved into "real storage" for execution, with the dynamic address translation features we've already discussed handling the translation from a virtual address to a real address. As the instructions on a particular page are executed and, eventually, completed, this page can be rolled-out to virtual memory again and a new page rolled-in to replace it. In this way, only that portion of a program which is actually being executed need be in core, meaning that less real core must sit passively waiting for something to happen to the instructions or the data it holds.

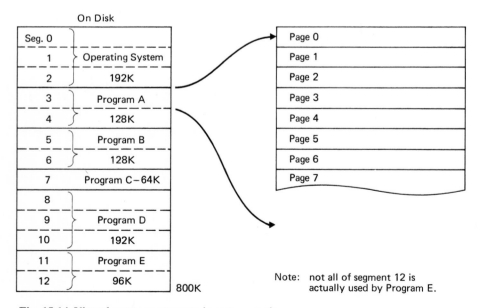

Fig. 15.14 Virtual memory contents in our example

Let's assume that our virtual system holds the programs shown in Fig. 15.14—an operating system and five application programs. This system is stored, in exactly the given sequence, on disk. Note the addressing scheme used in this virtual memory Fig. 15.15—it's very much like the addressing we studied in the segmentation *and* paging system of a few pages ago. Our disk-based virtual memory holds some 800K memory units; program D, to cite one example, actually needs only 160K but has been assigned to a 192K region to simplify segment addressing—after all, it's only virtual memory.

Segment number	Page number	Displacement

Fig. 15.15 An address in virtual memory

Page	Program	Program segment and page		Status
0	OS	0	0	1
1	OS	0	1	1
2	OS	0	2	1
3	OS	0	3	1
4	OS	0	4	1
5	OS	0	5	1
6	OS	0	6	1
7	A	3	5	1
8	B	2	9	0 ← Free page
9	X	1	1	1
10	B	2	1	0
11	D	5	12	1

Fig. 15.16 Real core—the page frame table

Over in real core (Fig. 15.16) the operating system has at its disposal a *real core* page frame table and a series of segment and page tables describing all of the pages *available* in *virtual* memory (Fig. 15.17). As the system begins the operation of bringing a page from virtual memory into real memory, it first searches the page frame table to locate an available page; once located, this page is changed to a "busy" status in the frame table and the actual page-in operation begins. When the operation is completed, the program page occupies the selected page frame, and the address of this page frame is entered into the segment and page tables.

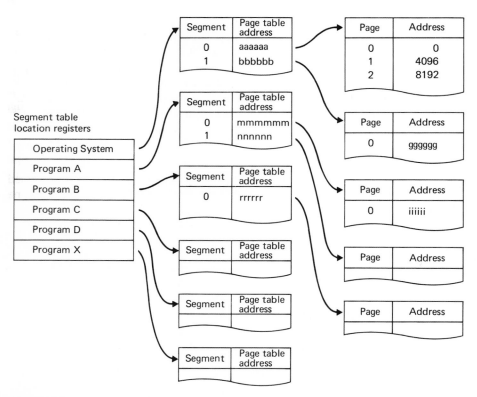

Fig. 15.17 Real core—segment and page tables

As a page is executing, addresses, which are expressed in virtual terms, are converted into real addresses by:

1. accessing the segment table using the high-order bits of the address as a key,
2. using the pointer in this table to locate the proper page table,
3. accessing this page table using the middle bits as a key, and, finally,
4. adding the displacement found in the low-order bits of the virtual address to the base address found in the page table.

On most systems, this rather tedious translation process is streamlined through the use of associative array registers.

What happens when a virtual address points to a page which is not in real storage? How does the system "know" if a given page is in real or virtual storage? In the segment and page tables, there is a one-bit flag called (by IBM at least) the "invalid" bit. If it's "off" (a 0 bit) the page is in real storage; if it's "on" (a 1 bit) the page is in virtual storage. When the dynamic address translation feature of our computer encounters a 1 bit at the end of the translation process, a "page fault" is recognized and an interrupt (perhaps a special SVC, perhaps a separate variety) is issued, causing a link to the operating system module responsible for the page-in operation.

What if a survey of the page frame table shows that there is no real core available for the new page? This means that some page must be paged-out. Many different schemes and algorithms for choosing the page to be paged-out (in prior chapters, we would have used the term "rolled-out," it's the same concept) have been implemented, ranging from simple LIFO and FIFO rules to more complex techniques designed to identify the least often used pages.

Bringing pages into core only when a page already in core refers to an address in a virtual-resident page is known as demand paging. An alternative technique attempts to predict the demand for a new page and bring it into core before it is actually needed; this is known as prepaging—it's an ideal, and obviously fairly difficult to implement. Strict programming standards, perhaps implemented through a special compiler might help. If segments really do hold logically related elements of a program, the page-in supervisor might be designed to always keep a few pages ahead of the currently executing page within the same segment.

One feature which is often available on a virtual system allows the programmer to designate certain pages or routines (which are translated into pages by the system) as key routines which are to remain resident for the life of the job step. If the routine really is a key one, any "least often used" page-out rule would probably achieve the same objective, but knowledgeable programmers should have the opportunity to "make sure."

You may note that the operating system as pictured in Figs. 15.14, 15.16, and 15.17 occupies the same locations in both real and virtual memory. Operating system routines perform such tasks as dynamically modifying channel programs and often refer to an absolute address (the pointer to the CVT is found in core location 16, for example); because of the unique requirements of operating system modules, it is highly desirable that the operating system be loaded into contiguous core. Most virtual storage systems have a "virtual equals real" feature in which selected modules or pages are loaded into real core in such a way that the virtual and real addresses are in fact identical. You may note that we never said that this operating system *must* begin at core address *zero*—it usually does, but it doesn't have to. This distinction will become important when we begin our discussion of multiple levels of virtual memory.

Multiple Virtual Memories

Remember, from Chapter 14, the remote time-sharing systems in which a program in the foreground partition was responsible for keeping track of the status of the numerous user programs active in the partition; we described this type of system as being somewhat analogous to an operating system running under the control of another operating system. This is basically what happens, on a larger scale, when a system supports multiple virtual memories; it involves multiprogramming at the operating system level.

Let's assume that the system pictured in Fig. 15.18 has been divided into three partitions. Partition 0 holds the master operating system responsible, ultimately, for everything. Partition 1 supports a complete virtual memory of its own under control of something like an MFT level virtual operating system; as far as this virtual operating system is concerned, it controls everything that happens within its real memory which, from its point of view, begins (core location 0) at the start of partition 1. In partition 2, another complete virtual memory system is supported, under control of still another operating system. Two complete sets of segment and page tables and page frame tables exist;

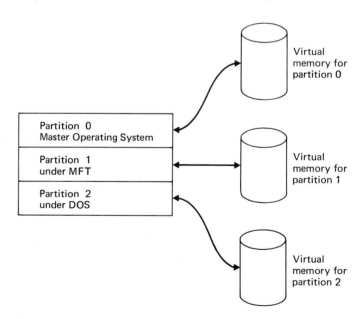

Fig. 15.18 Multiple virtual memories

one primary function of the master, overall operating system is to make sure that the various location registers point to the proper tables. Beyond this slightly more complex address translation, handling multiple virtual memories is not too much more difficult than handling one.

There is, however, one new problem—I/O. Each individual operating system existing in anything other than the core assigned to the primary control program contains a list of *virtual* input and output devices; in our example of Fig. 15.18, both virtual operating systems might well wish to refer to device 01 on channel 00 at the same time. The main control program is the final arbitrator in these cases, converting the "virtual" channel and device addresses of the secondary operating systems to real channel and device addresses.

There is one very big advantage to the multiple virtual memory approach. Try to imagine how many different programs can be handled concurrently!

Multiple Levels of Real Memory

Virtual memory systems involve at least two levels of memory—good, old-fashioned core and some direct access device like drum or disk. As electronic technology continues to make rapid advances, a new kind of memory based on solid logic and monolithic circuitry is beginning to come into use. This memory is super fast—much faster than standard core. Its speed is quite well matched to that of newer CPUs which use the same type of electronic components.

In order to improve the speed and efficiency of some of the newer and larger computers available today, three levels of memory are used. At one extreme is the virtual memory maintained on a direct access device—often disk, but the speed of drum storage makes it very attractive for this application. Next comes standard core—faster than drum but considerably slower than the newer memories. Finally, the CPU deals with high-speed memory. In terms of system implementation, a page starts on slow-speed virtual memory. The page-in monitor causes this page to be read into core. Once in core, the page is transferred into high-speed memory just prior to execution.

At present, monolithic memories are a bit more expensive than core—were this not the case, core would not be used at all. The use of memory hierarchies allows the system to enjoy the speed of monolithics at a reasonable cost—by going to standard core first, valuable high-speed memory space is not tied up waiting for a "slow" drum to complete an I/O operation. The trend in mono-lithic cost is, however, down; a good example of this trend can be found in the prices of pocket calculators which use the same kind of electronics. Eventually, assuming a continuation of this trend, monolithic memory will completely replace core.

Virtual Storage Access Methods

Paging calls for unusual direct access. For example, assuming that the virtual memory physically resides on disk, a segment/page address must be translated, via table look-up or some randomizing technique, into a relative address which can be used to compute an absolute disk address; a page is subsequently transferred from the direct access device into core as a fixed-size record. Similar problems of translating a segment/page address into a physical device address would exist no matter what direct access device was used to physically hold the pages. And yet, no matter what the physical device, the programmer can visualize simple sequential virtual addresses which look very much like good old-fashioned real-core addresses.

A standard access method, the basic direct access method for example, could handle this problem, but we're dealing with the transfer of program instructions. And, even though paging is nothing more than an I/O operation, it's a crucial I/O operation, with maximum efficiency being very important. Slow I/O in providing data to a single program will impact that program, but slow I/O on the operation (paging) that provides the application program instructions themselves impacts the entire computer system. So, it's not surprising that, on most virtual memory systems, the supplier has seen fit to provide a special-purpose access method to make the job of paging as efficient as possible. Often, such access methods are given special hardware boosts; it's even possible to implement such a special access method largely through hardware. These virtual access methods (like VSAM) are available today and are being used to support typical information storage and retrieval applications as well as paging.

Examine a virtual access method for a minute. It's designed to handle data in fixed size increments—pages. This does limit the flexibility of a virtual access method, but it is not a fatal defect.

On a more positive note, a virtual access method is designed to convert virtual addresses to whatever type of direct access address is needed to find a page on the virtual memory's physical device—maybe disk, maybe drum, maybe some other direct access device which isn't even in existence yet. In other words, the virtual access method is *device independent*. This is very important! A programmer, using VSAM, can, in effect, pretend that his or her data is stored in a sort of virtual memory and simply address a given record by its relative byte number, just as core is addressed. VSAM will take care of the actual conversion to a physical address. Let's say that the cost of solid logic memory continues to drop, finally reaching the point where it's cheaper than disk or drum storage. No problem for VSAM, we simply use the old "virtual" data addresses as real data addresses on the new device and keep running.

What about ISAM? Why continue to use cylinder and track addresses when we no longer have cylinders or tracks? Given the history of rapid technological change in the computer field, a device-independent access method makes a great deal of sense.

One final point on VSAM. On a virtual memory machine, it's almost essential that the manufacturer take steps to make paging more efficient. This would seem to imply that additional hardware boosts to the paging function will be developed—either new CPU features, new firmware, or new I/O devices. An access method like VSAM can utilize any such hardware boosts to make *data* I/O more efficient.

VSAM is available to support application program I/O today. Its use is growing as more and more users discover its advantages. If it makes sense to address computer memory as a sequentially numbered series of bytes or characters and to break programs into pages which can be stored on a virtual memory device and transferred (read) into real core on an as-needed basis, and if this type of main memory continues to support the most efficient possible functioning of the computer, doesn't it also make sense to handle data in exactly the same way? Just as virtual memory is not for everyone, VSAM is not for everyone, but the development of virtual access methods does hold promise of significantly improving the efficiency of I/O programming for many applications.

Segmentation, Paging, and Virtual Memory—Advantages

The biggest, practical, economic advantage of segmentation, paging, and virtual memory is better utilization of available real memory, meaning that, potentially, more programs can be placed on line yielding greater CPU utilization. This is particularly obvious in the multiple virtual memory systems we discussed above, and this factor will continue to grow in importance as advances in electronic technology lead to faster and faster processors.

One question that may arise in your mind is one of protection. We saw, in prior chapters, that the protection key in the PSW on an IBM computer is only four bits long; how can core protection for more than sixteen programs possibly be implemented on an IBM machine? Simple. All address translations involve a series of segment and page tables; an extra level of core protection—perhaps a few more core protection bits—can be added here.

Other advantages accrue to the programmer. In a virtual memory system, there is, for all practical purposes, no limit on program size. The programmer is relieved of the burden of planning overlay structures and fitting a program into a partition of limited size; the system assumes these responsibilities. The computer system itself receives some of the benefit—programs occupy only as much core as they actually require.

The big benefit, though, is economic. More programs on-line means that core, the major limiting factor on multiprogramming capability, can be eliminated as a limiting factor. With virtual memory, core is functionally limitless.

Segmentation, Paging, and Virtual Memory—Problems

Once again, what you get for nothing is nothing; there are costs and problems associated with these techniques. Probably the most obvious new cost is increased system overhead—it takes time to do all that paging and it requires space to hold all those segmentation and paging tables. Dynamic address translation isn't instantaneous either; the associative array registers help but do not eliminate the overhead loss. The size of these new operating systems with their increased functions creates still another overhead cost; virtual memory operating systems are big.

Of course, central processing units are getting faster all the time. As memory speeds begin to keep pace and cycle times begin to drop into the nanosecond range and below, the time loss for execution of an operating system module will become negligible, approaching the speed of hardware with considerably greater flexibility. This doesn't mean that the overhead cost will disappear; it will just become a bit more difficult to pin down.

A brand new problem on a virtual memory system is "thrashing." When real core is full (or close to it), a demand for a new page means that another page must be paged-out before the new one can be paged-in. If during a given period of time this happens frequently, the system finds itself spending so much time paging-in and paging-out that little time is left for useful work. This is called thrashing. Some systems have the ability to recognize this problem when it occurs and take corrective action, perhaps removing one or more programs from real core until things are running more smoothly, but thrashing can still have a negative impact on system performance.

Program design can also have a negative impact on performance. Consider, for example, the following simple FORTRAN program segment:

```
10    X = X + 1

15    ACCUM = ACCUM + Y

20    IF (X - 25) 10,10,30

30    AVG = ACCUM/X
```

and assume that, by pure chance, page 0 ends with statement number 15 and page 1 begins with statement 20. The program will obviously bounce from page to page, which is no problem if both pages are in core, but what if they're not. Expand a bit on this basic idea and try to picture a program which branches madly from routine to routine, often skipping over thousands of storage locations in the process; such a poorly planned program would be a disaster on a virtual memory system. Do such programs exist? Ask any programmer.

How can this be avoided? Special compilers can help, but they don't solve the whole problem—no systems programmer could possibly forsee every dumb move a programmer might make. The answer, instead, would seem to lie in good programming standards, a solution which tends to offset many of the "programmer flexibility" benefits touted by virtual memory marketeers. Top-down- or structured-programming concepts could prove to be most helpful here.

Conclusions

If core limitations make efficient utilization of a third-generation computer almost impossible in a given installation, then virtual memory may be the perfect answer. If another installation finds itself constantly seeking more core, then virtual memory may be the answer. If a faster central processor is what is needed, then one of the newer computers which support virtual storage may be the answer—but without the virtual feature.

Virtual memory does *not* make a computer faster, it simply increases its multiprogramming capability by making better use of available real core. A user may move from IBM's 360 series to a 370 and experience an obvious improvement in turnaround time, but he should—the 370 is a faster machine not because of virtual memory but because of electronic technology. Is virtual memory worth what it costs? For many users, yes it is, but not for everyone.

Summary

In this chapter, we've covered many of the basic concepts of segmentation, paging, and virtual memory systems. In segmentation, a program is broken into variable size segments which can be loaded into core in noncontiguous fashion, thus allowing fragmented pieces of free core to be utilized. Dynamic address translation is implemented through a series of segment tables. Paging is similar to segmentation except that pages are fixed in length and the length is chosen more for the convenience of the machine than for program logic considerations. Core allocation is a bit more complex in segmentation systems and paging systems; under paging, it's implemented through something called a page frame table.

A segmentation *and* paging system attempts to have the best features of both. Programs are broken into logical segments, but are loaded in page form, meaning that smaller regions of core can be utilized.

The underlying concept behind virtual memory can best be stated in question form—Why load the entire program into core when the CPU can only execute one instruction at a time? Under this system, a program is kept, in segment and/or page form, on a direct access device (the virtual memory unit) and individual pages are paged-in to core as they are needed. Multiple virtual memories can be supported on the same real machine.

The big advantage of these techniques lies in better utilization of core, meaning more programs on-line which in turn means better CPU utilization. The big disadvantage is increased overhead cost.

Exercises

1. What is meant by core fragmentation?
2. Explain dynamic address translation under a segmentation system.
3. Explain dynamic address translation under paging.
4. Explain the difference between a program page table and the page frame table. Relate these two concepts to job and task management.
5. Explain the function of associative array registers.
6. Relate roll-in/roll-out concepts to virtual memory.
7. What is the difference between demand paging and prepaging?
8. What is thrashing?

PART V

Special Purpose Systems and Applications

Overview of Part V

In the past few chapters, we've been discussing a number of general-purpose operating systems supplied by the computer manufacturer and designed to handle a wide range of applications. The reason for the general-purpose nature of these operating systems is not hard to fathom—such software packages are expensive to develop, the only way to recover these development costs is to sell many copies, and the only way to sell many copies is to be general. Within certain limits, these operating systems can be customized—core resident and transient modules can be selected, priorities reset, core reallocated, and so on—but the fact that the package is designed to cover a wide range of applications and job mixes means that a given user will often find that certain portions of the operating system are seldom used.

Some applications don't fit the "typical" mold expected by a standard operating system. In Chapter 16, we'll study such an application—manufacturing production control. Here, the cost of manufacturing downtime should the computer fail to function far outweighs the cost of the computer itself, and thus reliability, response time, and availability become far more important than the usual general-purpose measures of effectiveness: throughput and turnaround time. In a manufacturing process-control application, there are few long, compute-bound jobs and few "typical" batch jobs to contend with; thus not all of the facilities of a general-purpose operating system are needed. In fact, in systems running such a limited job mix, many operating system features become excess baggage—pure overhead. What is needed is a stripped-down version containing only those features which are absolutely necessary.

297

Management information systems are discussed in Chapter 17. In these systems, a need for greater data security and accuracy, coupled with requirements for flexible but controlled access to a data base, create operating system problems which go beyond the resources of a general-purpose system. We'll be discussing two software solutions which have gained increasing popularity over the past few years—data base management and data communications management.

In Chapter 18, we'll take a look at a very different class of computer applications, multicomputer applications, using computerized supermarket checkout as our primary source. No new operating system concepts will be introduced in this chapter, but the material does serve to illustrate that many of the functions handled by operating systems can be handled in other ways as well.

The final chapter, Chapter 19, is a summary of the entire text.

The theme of this section is simple. The function of an operating system is to maximize the utilization of a system's hardware, software, and data resources. To maximize means "to make the best possible use of," but "best" is a relative term. If the measures of effectiveness accepted by a given computer center match those of a general-purpose operating system, namely throughput and turnaround, fine—the installation should use a general-purpose operating system as supplied by the manufacturer of their computer. If not, the operating system, and *not* the requirements of the installation, must change. This means additions or modifications to an existing operating system or original software development. An operating system is a support software package and not a dictator. The examples of operating systems and computers presented in this section illustrate software which has been designed to fit the needs of the application.

CHAPTER 16

A Manufacturing Process
Control System

Overview

In this chapter, we'll be discussing the special requirements of a typical manufacturing process control system. In the general-purpose operating systems
covered in the last section, the cost of the computer itself was an important
consideration, and many operating system concepts were developed with the
idea of getting more work through a given hardware system. Multiprogramming, dynamic core allocation, and virtual storage, to cite a few examples,
represented attempts to maximize utilization of the CPU by placing more programs in core where the CPU's attention could be switched from program to
program, thus utilizing otherwise unproductive time. Production control or
manufacturing control is different. Here, the cost of downtime on a production
line dwarfs the cost of the computer; reliability, availability, and response time
are the key measures of computer effectiveness.

The production of computer printed-circuit boards will be used as an
example of a typical computer-controlled manufacturing operation (fitting in a
computer text). We won't dig into the details of the actual manufacturing
operation. Our objective is to discuss several types of computer applications;
thus the manufacturing operation will be simplified (apologies to production
people reading this text). Application areas will include: direct control of an
operation, data supply and numerical control, testing and quality control, and
labor data collection.

The Manufacturing Operation—Computer Circuit Boards

There are four major steps involved in the building of printed-circuit boards (Fig. 16.1). First, strips of copper foil and strips of a cloth-like fiberglass/epoxy material are bonded together to form the board (Fig. 16.2). In the next step (actually a series of related steps), one or more printed circuits are etched into the board, holes are drilled, and pins are inserted to provide a base for adding electronic components to the assembly or for connecting subassemblies (Fig. 16.3). Next, individual components—the AND, OR, and NOT logic blocks—are soldered onto this base (Fig. 16.4). Finally, the completed assembly is tested. This production flow ignores many details, of course, but it serves our purpose.

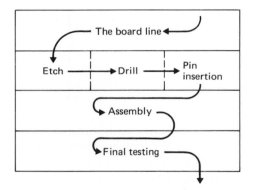

Fig. 16.1 Key steps in the manufacture of computer circuit boards

Before looking into how the computer helps to control each of these major process steps, it would be helpful to examine, for a moment, the nature of the business. Unlike automobiles, toys, and ready-to-wear clothing, large computers are rarely manufactured for inventory on the assumption that someone will eventually buy them. Instead, computers are made to order, with manufacturing building only what marketing has already sold (a fact which is reflected in the 6-month or longer lead time between order and delivery on many machines). An additional complication at the manufacturing level stems from the fact that a computer is often customized, with core size being variable and such hardware features as timers, integrated communications adapters, integrated file adapters, floating-point logic, and other modules being optional.

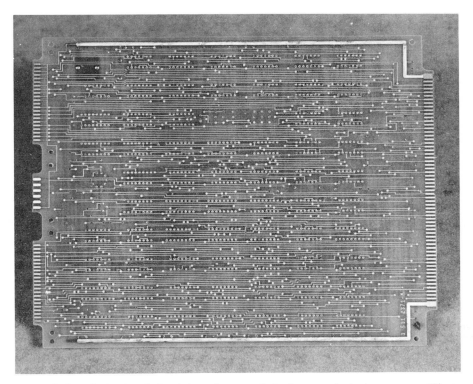

Fig. 16.2 A typical printed circuit board very early in the manufacturing process. (Photo courtesy of Cincinnati Milacron)

As a consequence of this made-to-order, customized approach, computer manufacturing is a "job shop" operation. In a job shop, an order (in our case an order is one or more computers) is broken into a number of identifiable pieces (sixteen units of circuit pattern 1234, ten of pattern 7612, fifty of pattern 9982, etc.) called jobs or job lots. These job lots are scheduled through the necessary manufacturing steps, with the job lot number providing a convenient mechanism for tracking jobs and checking progress.

Generally speaking, all the pieces in a given job lot are identical. This is not, however, true *between* job lots; the printed-circuit pattern needed for job lot #548 may be very different from the pattern etched on the pieces in job lot #349. These differences must be clearly communicated to manufacturing personnel if the work is to be done correctly. The problem of job-lot differentiation is, as we shall see, a key factor in the production control system we'll be discussing.

Fig. 16.3(a) A technician inspecting a glass master used to expose a printed circuit pattern on a circuit board (Reprinted by permission from International Business Machines Corporation)

Fig. 16.3(b) Tiny pins are inserted into drilled holes to provide a base for attaching electronic components (Reprinted by permission from International Business Machines Corporation)

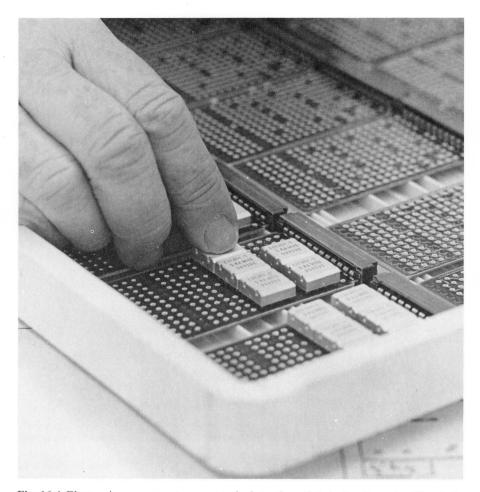

Fig. 16.4 Electronic components are attached to the printed circuit cards. The dark, pluglike connector at the base of each of these cards allows them to be connected to a larger assembly, the board, by simply "plugging them into" the pins described in Fig. 16.3(b). (Reprinted by permission from International Business Machines Corporation)

The First Step—the Board Line

The first step in this manufacturing process is, as you may recall, making boards. The operation is pretty simple on the surface. Rolls of fiberglass cloth are passed through "impregnation" machines which apply very tightly controlled amounts of epoxy resin to the cloth (Fig. 16.5a). At the other end of this process, the impregnated cloth is rewound and moved to a slitting operation where it is cut to board size. In some cases, these fiberglass/epoxy sheets are combined with sheets of copper foil in a sandwich-like arrangement.

Now for the complications. Epoxy is a very powerful glue. It must be wet when actually applied to the fiberglass cloth—dried epoxy has the consistency of a soft plastic and won't penetrate cloth very well. To make sure the epoxy is wet upon application, the epoxy resin is added in a heated chamber (Fig. 16.5b). At the other end of the machine, the epoxy impregnated cloth must be rewound. What if the epoxy resin is still tacky, still sticky, as we begin to rewind it? Obviously, since epoxy is a very powerful glue, the layers of impregnated cloth would stick together—result, expensive scrap. To insure against this potential loss, the cloth is allowed to pass through a cooling tower before it is rewound (Fig. 16.5b again).

The heating temperature, the cooling temperature, and the time spent in both phases of the operation must be closely monitored. Devices to measure temperature and the speed of the material are, of course, available, but just knowing that the heater is running twelve degrees high isn't enough. There must be a mechanism for adjusting key parameters in much the same way a thermostat continually adjusts the temperature of a building (Fig. 16.6). This type of control is called a feedback loop.

This function is often handled by a "dedicated" mini computer which constantly monitors temperature, speeds, and any other key parameters, tests actual values against control limits, and adjusts, automatically, for out-of-control conditions by increasing heat or speeding up the system or starting additional air conditioning units. On our system, let's assume that instead of using a dedicated mini we have assigned this continuous monitoring task to a partition of our centralized computer (Fig. 16.7). Obviously, response time is crucial—we just can't afford to make the board line wait thirty seconds while we process a few dozen paychecks, because a few seconds of out-of-control operation may be enough to relegate a $1000 roll of board material to the scrap heap. If the operating system keeps the computer from responding immediately to an interrupt from this source, then the operating system must go.

This kind of feedback-loop control is quite common in industry, with steel rolling mills and chemical plants representing perhaps the most widely known examples. The dedicated mini is the most popular solution for fairly obvious

Fig. 16.5(a) Fiberglass cloth is impregnated with epoxy resin in the first step of the board manufacturing process. (Reprinted by permission from International Business Machines Corporation)

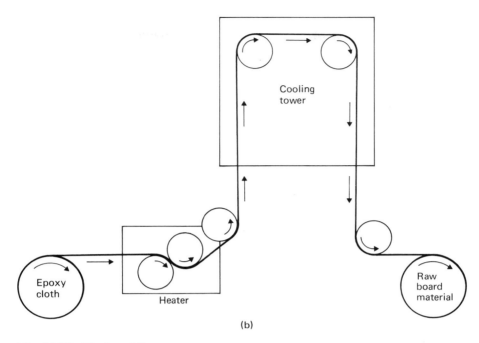

(b)

Fig. 16.5(b) The board line

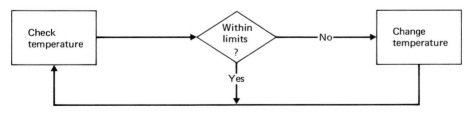

Fig. 16.6 The way a thermostat controls temperature is a good example of a feedback loop.

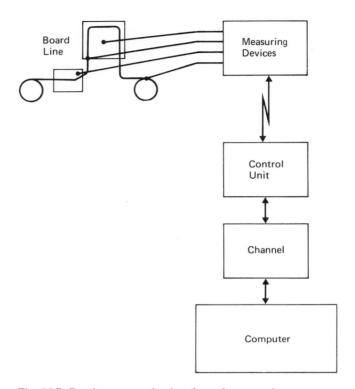

Fig. 16.7 Continuous monitoring through a central computer

reasons—a dedicated machine will never be busy doing something else. The use of a centralized facility, as in our example, has the advantages of centralized control and centralized expertise, and it has its advocates.

Step Two—Printed Circuit Etching and Drilling

The board line is pretty much a continuous operation, with one raw board looking just like any other raw board. It's in the second major manufacturing step where product differentiation begins. Here, raw boards are converted to printed-circuit boards through a photo-etch process, and there may be thousands of different printed-circuit patterns. Job lot #346 may call for 7 pieces of part number 812945 which is based on printed circuit pattern 4110, while job lot #347 represents 45 pieces of part number 877352 which uses printed circuit pattern 2250 as its base; hence, product differentiation.

The printed-circuit pattern, alone, is just the base of the computer circuit board; components must be added. To provide a mechanism for attaching these components, holes are drilled and pins are inserted. The pins serve three functions: they allow for simple component insertion through soldering or force fits, they simplify the connection of subassemblies, and they serve as part of the electrical circuit. Hole locations must be precisely controlled, exactly matching the printed-circuit pattern.

Rather than leave such a precise drilling operation to human control, our production process uses a numerically controlled drill press to turn out a hole pattern. At its simplest level, numerical control is implemented through a tape. The operator reads a part number or pattern number and selects and mounts a tape with a matching number; this tape contains, essentially, sets of points on an X-Y coordinate axis showing where holes are to be drilled. The N/C control mechanism reads the first set of coordinates, positions the drill at this location, and starts the drill. When the first hole is completed, the equipment reads the second set of coordinates, repositions the drill, and drills the second set of points. Assuming that the printed circuit board has been properly positioned on the drill press and that the correct tape has been selected, the holes *will be* in the right places.

There are two problems with this approach on our production line. The first is setup time—while the operator is mounting a new N/C (numerical control) tape, the drill press is idle. If we make several thousand copies of a single part, this is no problem, but a job shop might make 20 copies of part "A" followed by 7 of part "B" followed by a dozen of part "C", and each tape change means a few minutes of lost production. The second problem is the risk of human error—the operator will occasionally select the wrong tape, thus, instructing the drill press to drill the wrong hole pattern—result, scrap.

A solution to both problems is centralized data supply. In using this technique, each N/C controller contains enough memory (core, floppy disk, magnetic tape loop) to hold a complete drill pattern. Back in the photo-etch operation where product differentiation started, a card identifying the part number and circuit pattern was attached to the job lot. The drill press operator simply takes this card and inserts it into a card reader attached to the controller; as a result, the contents of the card are transmitted to the central computer (Fig. 16.8) which selects the proper N/C program from disk and transmits it to the N/C controller's memory. Now, the operation can go on as before, with N/C data coming from the memory unit rather than from a tape.

Once again, the computer must respond quickly to a request of this type; slow response means an idle machine which is exactly the problem we were trying to avoid. It's probably reasonable to assume that a drill-press operator can be instructed to insert the job-lot card first and then position the first

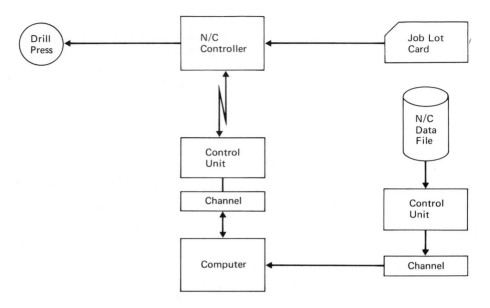

Fig. 16.8 Centralized data supply

circuit board on the press, making a response of a few seconds more than adequate, but rapid response to each and every transaction is still the key to this application.

The final operation in this major production step is pin insertion, essentially a manual operation.

The Third Step—Component Assembly

Once a board is prepared, components—AND, OR, and NOT logic gates, flip-flop memory circuits, etc.—can be attached to the pins; the printed circuits connect these components electrically. Although certain components may appear on several different parts, each job lot will probably call for a different mix of components. Because of a need for flexibility, this is largely a manual function; thus, there is no direct computer control of this process.

This is not to say, however, that there are no controls. Or that the computer is not indirectly involved. How, for example, does a worker in the assembly area know which components are to be added to a given circuit board? This information is normally transmitted through two documents: a bill-of-materials and a router. A bill-of-materials is a list of components or parts which go into an assembly; a router is an ordered list of the steps or individual operations needed to build the product. We have previously mentioned the job-lot card which was used in the drilling operation. A fairly standard procedure in a job shop is to create a job package containing this card, a copy of the router, perhaps a bill-of-material and a set of engineering drawings, and other critical information as the job is released to the manufacturing department. This package accompanies the job lot as it progresses through the shop. In our shop, the bulk of this package is printed (and the supporting data maintained) on the computer.

This is a batch application. It's completely different from on-line monitoring and centralized data supply.

Labor and Material Controls

Having just discussed the manual portion of our manufacturing system, let's begin consideration of the labor and material controls which are essential to any production operation. On our system, the raw data for implementing labor and material controls is collected on-line through a number of data entry terminals. As an employee completes one step on the router, the job-lot card and his or her own badge are entered into a terminal, sending a great deal of information to the computer. First, the system "knows" what this employee has just done and, by comparing the elapsed time between this and the last transaction to the standard time for the operation, we get the "actual versus standard time" statistic so often used in labor measurement and control. Beyond this labor control, the system also "knows" that job-lot #xxx has just finished an operation in the assembly process, and knowing the location of a job lot provides a great deal of material control.

Along with the card and badge input the worker is expected to enter the number of the operation just completed through a manual entry keyboard. Each operation has a standard cost. Knowing that a given operation has just been completed means that the value added by the operation can be added to the cost of the job lot, yielding a continuous tracking of work-in-process inventory value.

Labor and material data collection is not, of course, restricted to the manual assembly steps; every employee does it. The result is a data base which gives a very complete and accurate picture of the status of each and every job on the manufacturing floor, along with equally useful information on the activity of each and every employee. The data base is, itself, a valuable resource;

in the next chapter, we'll consider the use of such data in a management information system.

This is another response time application, with perhaps five or ten seconds being adequate. The big problem is peak loads—manufacturing people (like anyone, really) have a habit of waiting until quitting time before reporting their activity, leading to a concentration of transactions in the fifteen or twenty minutes just before shift end. During this period of time, on-line data collection is a very different kind of application than during the rest of the workday, when an occasional transaction arrives every so often. Our computer must be able to handle the peak-load condition.

The Fourth Step—Final Test

Computer circuits are tested electronically; a known binary pattern is fed into the circuit and the resulting output compared against what it should be. If they match, the circuit is good. This application is much like the data-supply function discussed above, except for the fact that test data instead of N/C data is supplied to the memory of a tester's controller in response to the input of the job-lot card.

Process Control System Requirements

Our manufacturing system is totally dependent upon the computer; if the computer goes down, the line goes down. Let's assume that our plant employs 1000 people. A full day of downtime means that 1000 people must be paid for a full day's work even though they did nothing. The cost could easily hit $50,000! Add the cost of overtime needed to catch up, the cost of missed production schedules (lost business), the opportunity losses associated with a stagnant inventory, and other costs too numerous to mention, and you get a picture of the true cost of computer downtime in such a production environment. Reliability is the most important measure of system effectiveness, and money spent to improve reliability is money well spent.

Throughout our discussion of individual production control applications, response time was seen to be a key requirement; thus, response time becomes another important measure of system effectiveness.

Finally, we have availability, a measure of effectiveness which, to a large degree, is covered by the first two. Reliability and response time, however, say nothing about the ability of the computer system to handle such applications as the creation of job-lot packages in batch mode or programmer tests and assemblies. Such applications must be handled. In considering this measure of effectiveness, we'll look at operating system modules and approaches which allow such programs to be run while making sure that they do not dominate the computer.

What happened to throughput? Throughput is a measure of the amount of work going through a computer; a high throughput is an indication that the computer is being used efficiently. By efficiency, we usually mean that computer costs have been minimized; i.e., the objective is one of selecting the smallest or least expensive computer which will do the job. In a manufacturing environment, minimizing *computer* cost may have a disastrous effect on overall *system* cost. This application is different.

Reliability

Reliability is essential in a production control environment; how can it be achieved? The usual approach is to back up key hardware and software components of the system. The computer itself is the key hardware component, of course; in many production control systems, the computer is duplicated (Fig. 16.9), with a manual or program-controlled switch automatically shifting from one computer to the other in the event that one should fail. Often, as in Fig. 16.9, the entire computer hardware system is duplicated, with two sets of channels, two sets of I/O devices, two sets of control units, and two copies of the data base. This is known as *duality*; what it means is that before an entire system can go down, two computers or two channels or two control units must fail. The odds of two computers failing at the same time are much lower than the odds of just one failing.

It could happen, though. Even with a dual system it is possible to have full system downtime; the probability of such an occurrence can be computed using the reliability formulas which can be found in any good statistics or operations research text. To protect against this occurrence, a second level of protection can be, and often is, implemented. Human beings can monitor the temperature and speed indicators on the board line—true, scrap may occasionally be produced, but the cost of extra scrap is much lower than the cost of shutting down. Equipment for loading the memory of the drilling controller and the tester controller from paper tape or mylar tape can be provided as emergency backup—even with the inefficiencies introduced by long and frequent setups, tape loading beats doing nothing. The creation of job-lot packages, being a batch operation, is much less sensitive to downtime; no problem here. On-line data collection, however, must be backed up. Many on-line data collection systems handle this problem by batching transactions

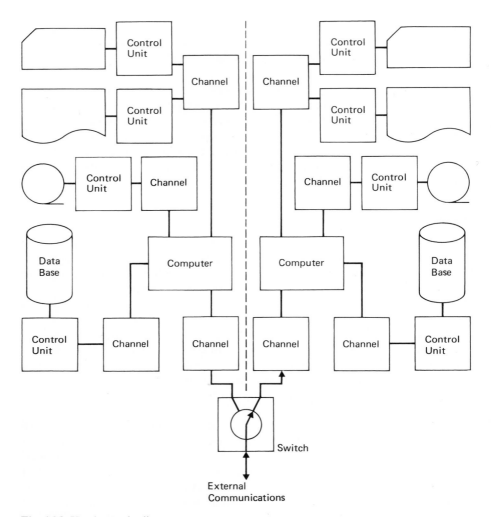

Fig. 16.9 Hardware duality

to a floppy disk built into the control unit (Fig. 16.10) in the event of computer downtime; it's not quite as good as real-time editing, but at least critical data is not lost. As a final level of backup, the designer of any on-line data collection system should include, in his system plan, a mechanism for manually recording information for later entry.

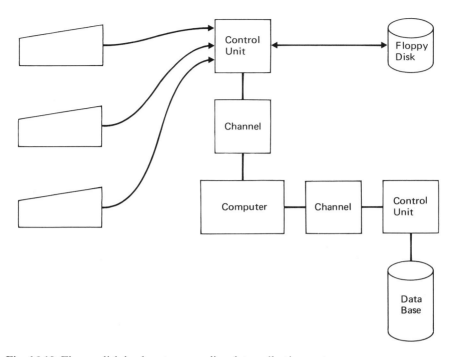

Fig. 16.10 Floppy disk backup to an on-line data collection system

Data base reliability is also crucial. Frequent checkpoints are a good idea, with, perhaps, the on-line files being dumped to tape on a daily basis. We'll be considering this problem in greater detail in Chapter 17.

Program failures can hurt too. Documentation is crucial—the responsible programmer might be on vacation when program failure occurs or, worse yet, he may have left the company. Very tight control must be exercised over the release of new programs, with heavy program testing standards and detailed program reviews. A backup copy of the program library is a good idea too.

Response Time

The best way to get the kind of response times needed by this process-control application is by using a computer which supports multiple levels of interrupts. On such a computer, an interrupt coming from the board line monitors could link directly to the program which interprets this information, and a direct hardware link is much faster than a software link—in an IBM System/360, by contrast, the interrupt would transfer control to an interrupt handling routine which would *subsequently* transfer control to the desired program.

In support of the board line or a similar application requiring extremely fast response, the responsible program can be made core resident. When response time needs are less extreme, a small core-resident module can load the desired program.

Good software can, of course, get around the inherent limitations of a computer using a few, generalized interrupt levels; an IBM System/360 can be used to control a process control application like the one we've been discussing in this chapter. The 360 series of computers was not, however, designed with this particular application in mind.

One other factor is crucial to any system with a rapid response time requirement—the system should be underloaded. If 70 or 75% of available CPU time is being utilized, there will be frequent intervals when all available core and CPU time is in use; this is bound to degrade response time. If, on the other hand, only 20 or 25% of available time is utilized, system resources will usually be available.

The on-line data collection application we discussed above included, as you may remember, the problem of peak loads. During the day, a load-and-execute mode is more than adequate for this routine, but, at the end of a shift the volume of transactions coupled with the overhead associated with a load-and-execute mode of operation (disk I/O on each transaction) could seriously degrade response time. During these peak periods, the program which handles transactions should be made core resident, eliminating much of the overhead. The operating system should support such status changes, perhaps through operator intervention, perhaps through automatic system action.

Availability

We've already discussed one aspect of system availability—the system should be underloaded. This means that the computer will cost more than it might under a throughput orientation, but computer costs are not the key costs in a computer-based process-control system.

What about the batch applications such as: preparing job-lot packages, testing new programs, adding or changing N/C or test data, and others? Some might be done on the backup computer, but this isn't the whole answer. Why not break the computer's core memory into foreground and background partitions? Programs requiring rapid response could run in the foreground partitions, while batch type jobs are relegated to the background. The background has low priority, meaning that an interrupt in any foreground partition automatically drops the batch job into a wait state until the interrupt is fully processed. By limiting the system to a single background partition, most of the computer would still be available for more time-critical applications; given intelligent scheduling, the background should provide all the batch support a system like this should ever need. If batch requirements become too heavy, the application really isn't a production-control application as discussed in this chapter.

One more feature is needed to guarantee system availability—time slicing. At its simplest level, a timer is started as soon as a program module gains control of the CPU. If the program has not issued either a request for I/O or a WAIT macro or reached normal program completion during an allotted slice of time, a timer interrupt terminates the program. This protects the system from program loops and other errors and keeps long running programs from dominating.

Why Won't a General-Purpose Operating System Do?

A general-purpose operating system, as the name implies, is designed to handle a very broad, "general" range of applications. Generalized software is, almost by definition, more complex and longer running than customized software. Manufacturing process control, as discussed in this chapter, is *not* a broad, general application, being instead rather closely interrelated with the manufacturing process. To put it as simply as possible, the overhead of a general-purpose operating system gets in the way in an environment like that described in this chapter. We need customized software.

Production Control—a Final Note

Not all manufacturing installations use process monitoring or centralized data supply or on-line data collection; in fact, the kind of installation envisioned in our example is by far the exception rather than the rule. Traditional production control involves order (job-lot) tracking, job-lot scheduling, cost and scrap reports, and actual-versus-standard-labor reports; most if not all these applications can be run under a standard general-purpose operating system. Our objective in this chapter was to present a special, unusual application which did not fit a standard mold, and not to develop a new definition of production control.

Even within manufacturing operations which use direct monitoring and numerical control, the use of a single, centralized computer is the exception. Mini computers and micro computers are an important force in this market.

Finally, a few words about on-line data collection. Response time requirements of on-line data collection systems are well within the limits of a standard computer running in a moderately loaded state under a general-purpose operating system. What was important in the application we've been discussing in this chapter was the *mix* of programs. This mix excluded compute-bound jobs and many other types which must be handled by a general-purpose system. Combined with the "cost of downtime" problem, this particular application in this particular plant called for a special-purpose, customized hardware/software package which might not be directly applicable anywhere else in the world. But, isn't that what we mean by "special purpose"?

Summary

In this chapter, we studied a special-purpose computer application—manufacturing process control. The system contained three basic types of applications: direct monitoring of a manufacturing operation, centralized data supply for numerical control and product testing, and on-line data collection. All three require rapid response time. In addition to these unusual applications, the system does some batch work which is handled in a background partition.

System reliability was a key factor because of the high cost of downtime. Reliability was achieved by duplicating key hardware components, providing local hardware backup (like paper-tape equipment to load N/C controllers in an emergency), taking frequent checkpoints of key files, and carefully controlling the release of new programs.

The most important cost component in this environment was downtime. Since the manufacturing process was dependent upon the computer, computer downtime meant idleness for the entire plant; thus the traditional measure of computer effectiveness—throughput—has no meaning. The computer (and its operating system) are still being used to minimize cost, but the definition of cost is different.

Response time was another key measure of computer system effectiveness. A computer capable of supporting multiple levels of interrupts will generally do better on response time than a computer with a limited number of interrupt levels.

The final measure of effectiveness was system availability; i.e., the computer must be ready when needed. Both reliability and response time contain a part of the availability consideration; additional factors included running the computer with a light load, making a low-priority background partition available to batch-type programs, and time slicing.

General-purpose operating systems are designed to handle a "general" range of applications. Because the application package in our example doesn't fit a general pattern, a general-purpose operating system will not do.

Exercises

1. What is the relationship between system loading and response time?
2. How can a system's reliability be improved?
3. Why wasn't a general-purpose operating system adequate for the application described in this chapter?
4. Do some reading on airline-reservation systems. Relate your research to the material covered in this chapter.
5. Do some research into our national air-defense system (SAGE) and relate it to this chapter.

CHAPTER 17

Data Base Management and Data Communications

Overview

In Chapter 16, we considered a class of computer applications for which the traditional third-generation operating system provided more support than was needed; as a consequence, operating systems for applications such as production control are often stripped down versions of a general-purpose package or complete new operating systems written to support a particular application or installation. In this chapter, we'll be covering another type of "special purpose" computer-based system for which the facilities of a general-purpose operating system are far *less* than adequate, necessitating additional software support.

The application we'll be looking at is a management information system. Primary considerations in this system wil! include: data collection, data verification, data storage and retrieval, and an ability to produce quick, often one-time-only, reports in response to management requests. The new software modules include a data base management package and a data communications controller.

Early Computer Applications—Cost Justification

Payroll was, for many firms, one of the very first computer applications. The reason for using a computer to do payroll is easy to pinpoint. The computations for a ten employee payroll might take an hour if done manually; a one hundred employee payroll might be expected to consume ten hours; a one thousand employee payroll gets us up to one hundred hours or two and one-half full-time people. As the firm grows, the manpower time (and thus cost) of processing payroll grows, and it doesn't take too much imagination to see that by automating this highly repetitious task and doing it on a computer, these costs can be brought under control. Payroll is easy to cost justify—if we don't get a computer, we'll need twenty-five full-time payroll clerks within two years. Add the advantages of speed and accuracy, and there's no way any large firm can avoid using a computer for payroll processing.

Other early computer applications—accounting, ledgers, accounts payable, accounts receivable, inventory, bill-of-material processing, report generation—are equally easy to cost justify on their own merits. A basic argument in each case is cost reduction—it's less expensive to do the job on a computer than to do it manually.

Most firms believe in cost justifying any new project; if the expected benefits do not outweigh the cost of achieving those benefits, no sense investing the money or manpower. These early computer applications fit beautifully into the cost justification mold, with each single computer application standing on its own. Programmers quickly learned that core minimization and CPU-time minimization were very important, measurable attributes of a good program and, given the relatively slow speeds and limited storage of early computers, these were important. This approach did, however, lead to a method of organizing data which, as we shall see, has come back to haunt many companies.

Essentially, data files were designed to match the application. An employee's home address, for example, might show up in several different files—the personnel file, a payroll file, and an education department file to cite a few examples. On the surface, this kind of data redundancy seems a bit inefficient, but consider the impact of, for example, requiring the payroll program to use the address in the personnel file. Each transaction handled by the payroll program would call for an extra I/O operation, and space to hold the personnel record would have to be provided in the payroll program; both factors tend to hurt the apparent efficiency of the payroll program under a system which insists that each program stand on its own.

Thus programmers wrote (and continue to write) programs with customized data files designed to improve the efficiency of "that" program with little or no consideration being given to the overall efficiency of the entire data-processing system. A systems analyst or management scientist would probably use the term "suboptimization" in describing such an approach.

The MIS Idea

Management first became aware of the problems being created by the "independent file" approach in the mid-1960s when articles on Management Information Systems (MIS) began appearing in technical and managerial journals. At its core, the MIS idea involves two key arguments: first, data or information is a key resource in any organization, essential to intelligent, informed decision-making, and, second, the computer is a veritable treasure-trove of information which should be readily available to management.

Under the "independent file" approach, this information is *not readily* available. Let's consider an example. Manufacturing has need for a new expediter, and management in all sincerity feels that this is a perfect opportunity for moving a woman into a position of some responsibility. Since, due to previous promotional policies, the qualifications of the female employees are less well known to management, data processing has been asked to aid in the search, and to provide, within the next two weeks, a compilation of information which is certainly available on the computer—namely, a list of all female employees who have at least five years of experience with the company, a college degree, some experience in a manufacturing department, and some managerial training. A reasonable request? Not so says the data-processing department—six months and thirty thousand dollars.

Why? How could a simple list of existing data possibly require six months of programming effort? Easy. A good part of the basic data is on the personnel file, but work history (some experience in a manufacturing department) is on a history file considered to be highly confidential by the personnel department. It will take at least three weeks to negotiate the release of this data. Further complications are expected to arise from the fact that the history file hasn't been very well maintained. If an employee was a college graduate when first hired, it's recorded on the personnel file, but if a degree were earned after initial employment this information would be found only on the education department's external education file. This wouldn't be so bad except that information in the personnel file is organized by social security number while the education department uses their own number key—there is no way to merge these two files except by matching names (which might work well if both files reflected name changes due to marriage, but they don't). Management training is even tougher. The firm has an internal program, with a simple list of attendees maintained in chronological order. Voluntary education is a second possible source of such training, but the voluntary education department uses its own (strange) course codes and maintains lists of attendees haphazardly, at best. Again, external training at a local college or university would show up on the education department's external education file.

The programming department sees a need for combining information from several different files into a single new file and writing a program to select records from this new file. Each source file must be read by a separate, new program which creates a new, partial record; these partial records must be merged into the new file format requiring another new program before the desired program can be executed. Thus, six months and thirty thousand dollars for a list of maybe fifty names. And accuracy cannot be guaranteed—due to name changes and poor file maintenance.

Good intentions thwarted, management decides to promote a young, male, production-control engineer who has frequently demonstrated his ability and is in line for promotion anyway; the morale of the female employees is again undermined; and a letter is sent to a technical magazine complaining about the publication of science fiction under the guise of MIS.

The Central Data Base Approach

The fact that data is on a computer does not necessarily mean that it's available for use; information is not really usable unless it is properly indexed, cataloged, and maintained. In other words, if you can't find it, you can't use it. The outcome of the little vignette presented above might have been far different had management, some years before, recognized this fact and begun to treat data as the essential corporate resource it really is.

This is the essence of the central data base approach. Rather than allow each individual application programmer to create files structured to fit the needs of a specific application, all data is gathered into a single, integrated, central "data base," and individual programmers select the pieces needed by their programs from this central source.

The central data base approach is most often implemented through a software module, the data base monitor or data base manager (Fig. 17.1) which resides in core and serves as an intermediary between the application program and the operating system. *All* requests for I/O involving the data base must pass through the data base manager. In many systems, the programmer codes a CALL macro or a special data base macro, passing control to the data base

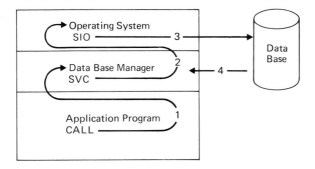

Fig. 17.1 The data base manager, a software module

manager which, subsequently, issues the necessary supervisor calls. Usually, the programmer is totally unaware of the file structure, organization, and physical location of the data he requests; the data base manager handles all these details.

Consider the following simple example. As part of the personnel data maintained on each employee in an organization, a data base will certainly contain the individual's name, address, and department number. Let's assume that we have two application programs, one to list all employees by department and another to produce a mailing list of employees for the company newsletter. The first program needs only the employee name and department number; the latter program has no use for department number. Under the traditional file approach, both programs would be required to provide space for all these fields; under the central data base approach, this is not necessary.

The first program might include the following statement

```
CALL DBMGR (NAME,DEPT)
```

which links to the data base manager (DBMGR). The data base manager, in turn, issues the necessary I/O instructions and builds a record containing only the employee name and the department number, passing this record to the application program. Later, the second program executes the instructions generated by a macro which reads

```
CALL DBMGR (NAME,STREET,CITY,STATE,ZIP).
```

In response, the data base manager accesses the necessary physical file or files, builds a record containing only the requested fields, and passes this record back to the application program. The data might all reside on a single physical file or several different files might be involved; the files might be organized sequentially or directly or using the indexed-sequential technique; the application programmer need not be aware of the details of file access.

The Advantages of the Central Data Base Approach

There are a number of advantages to centralizing data in this way. First, data redundancy is eliminated or at least brought under control. Why, for example, store an employee's home address in two or three different files? Store it once and allow each program needing the address to access this information from the same source.

Closely related to the data redundancy problem is the problem of file updating and file maintenance. At a university, a student's campus address is often found in several different files—the bursar's file for billing purposes, the registrar's file for grade reporting, the alumni file for future donation requests, a student-aid file, and others. If the student moves, as students often do, is it reasonable to assume that the address will be corrected in every file? With a central data base, this redundancy is eliminated; the address (or other piece of information) need be corrected only once, and every application program has the correct information.

Even more important than the elimination of data redundancy and improvements in data accuracy is the fact that individual application programs written under a central data base concept are independent of the actual data. Again, an example serves well in illustrating this idea. Several years ago, the post office decided (for good reasons) that a zip code was required on all addresses. In many computer centers, this seemingly minor change raised havoc. The addition of a five character field to an address meant that *every* program using the data in this record had to be revised to reflect the longer field length. This was especially tough in an assembly language shop where programmers were in the habit of using highly efficient (they thought) relative addressing. The fact that a program did not need the zip code to achieve its objectives was beside the point; if the new longer record was accessed by the program, the program was modified to allow for the extra room.

Under central data base management, all such changes are incorporated in the data base manager. Programs not needing the zip code don't have to be rewritten—they continue to get the data elements they have always requested. The change is invisible. Only programs needing the new data element must be modified.

Beyond the simplification of program modification, central data base management has a positive effect on the programmer as well. Freed of the need to pay attention to the details of physical I/O, he can devote more time to the application itself. After all, what's more important to a manufacturing-process-control programmer, a knowledge of manufacturing or a knowledge of computer I/O techniques?

Some Disadvantages and Costs

Once again, what you get for nothing is nothing. There are costs and disadvantages associated with the central data base approach.

The biggest and perhaps most obvious cost is creating the data base in the first place. Picture an installation with thousands of programs and thousands of files created without the aid of a central data base approach. All these existing programs must be rewritten before the data base can be implemented, and the cost can be enormous. A new company buying its first computer is in a much better position to go data base. Often, because of this cost factor, only a few "key" applications are converted to the data base concept, with many production programs continuing to run under the old "independent and redundant" file system. The big problem here is that there are few if any benefits which can be *directly* related to the creation of the central data base and the rewrite of existing programs; benefits accrue to new applications written against the data base. Given the old "each data processing activity must stand on its own merits" approach, this initial, crucial step is very difficult to justify.

From a purely technical point of view, here is little doubt that a good programmer creating his own customized file and using the optimal access method can write a program which is far more efficient in terms of CPU time and net core requirements than would be possible under even the best data base system. This is single program optimization to be sure, but these factors continue to be widely accepted as measures of program (and programmer) efficiency. A good, well-designed data base manager may outperform a poor or average programmer, but there is little doubt that a good programmer can do better with tight controls over his I/O operations and data structures than any generalized software package. What is more important though—individual program efficiency or the flexibility afforded by centralized data base management? No general answer is possible; each individual data-processing center must answer this question in light of its own needs and objectives.

Finally, we have the cost of the data base manager itself. Since all application programs must go through this module to access the data base, the manager must be an extremely well-written program. Put another way, the data base manager is a monster, very expensive to write and debug. Many firms using the central data base approach have chosen to purchase or lease a package from the computer supplier or an independent software house rather than write their own. There are many excellent packages on the market.

Data Base Implementation, a Typical Data Structure

Rather than continue with this general discussion, let's consider how an installation with a data base management system might have handled the "list of all female employees with . . ." problem. A convenient starting point for this discussion might be the actual structure of the data.

This application requires several different kinds of data. On one extreme, we have information such as name, address, social-security number, current department, and so on which is needed frequently—at least once a week for payroll purposes. On the other extreme, we have education data which is rarely if ever needed. The "single huge record holding everything" approach is obviously uneconomical, but the data elements must be tied together in some way.

The data base management system solves this problem by using pointers imbedded in the "key" record to link to secondary records (Fig. 17.2). Assume, for example, that the key personnel record for each employee holds social-security number, name, address, department, salary information, income-tax information, and other data elements used on a repetitive basis. A pointer containing the volume number and relative address (assuming a direct access device) of this employee's work history file is also found in this key record. Another pointer links the key record to each of the employee's education files; the simple fact that a centralized data base exists would point up the inefficiency of using unique "this department only" codes and filing systems, leading, let's assume, to education department use of social-security number as a key.

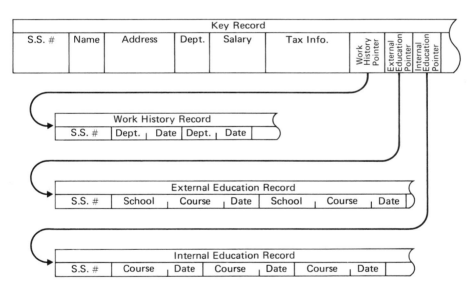

Fig. 17.2 The record structure of a typical data base

For normal, day-to-day data processing activities, the bulk of the personnel information would be found on a single physical file. Application programs wouldn't really care since the data base manager routine has full responsibility for all physical I/O, but the physical I/O must still be done, and the fact that the data base manager is able to fairly efficiently do one-seek/one-read I/O for most requests is an indication of a well-designed data base.

Management's request for a list of all employees meeting certain qualifications represents a special application. Given the data base described above and a data base manager routine entered through a CALL macro, the application programmer might write a simple, single-loop program designed to read the entire personnel file in sequence. At the start of the loop, the programmer codes a CALL macro requesting the employee name, address, sex, present department, a list of prior department assignments, the highest degree earned, and course work taken in any school which might possibly be interpreted as management training. The data base manager routine, having access to a complete set of file formats, discovers that pointers to much of the requested data can be found in the key personnel record; thus this record is retrieved, the desired fields are selected and moved into the record being built for the application program, and the pointers are used to find the secondary education and work history records for this employee. As these records come into core, the data base manager selects requested fields and continues to build a special, new, customized record for the application program. Finally, all relevant data has been selected, and the requested record is passed back to the program which begins a series of comparisons—is this employee female, does she have a college degree, is a manufacturing department found on the list of departments she has worked for—culminating in the listing of information for all employees who meet all criteria (or the rejection of those who don't) and a branch back to the CALL macro for another record. Inefficient? Perhaps, but don't forget that this is a special, one-time-only program. The important thing is the ability to respond to a reasonable request, not program efficiency.

Of course, not all data bases are organized in exactly this way; there are many approaches and a detailed discussion of alternative structures is beyond the scope of this book. A few key concepts have, however, been illustrated. First, secondary data elements can be located through pointers contained in a primary record (the key record in the above example). This pointer concept might well be used to tie all manner of data together, perhaps linking personnel data with payroll data, work history, educational data, a skills inventory, and other information about the same person. To allow for a multitide of starting points, secondary records and other primary records (like payroll data) might include a pointer back to the personnel record. Most commercial data base management systems differ in the technique used to implement the pointer and linkage concept, but almost invariably include some data linkage similar, in essence, to that described above.

Another key idea which, unfortunately, is often neglected by data base system salespersons is simply this: the structure of a data base should reflect the realities of a given data-processing installation. We saw an example of this above—the primary or key personnel record held, in a single physical record, the data elements most commonly used, allowing for fairly efficient input and output most of the time. The data base manager should consider I/O efficiency, and the fact that application programmers don't have to be concerned with the physical I/O operation is no excuse for inefficiency. A well-structured data base controlled by a well-written data base manager can be both flexible *and* efficient.

Queries

Not all management requests for special information involve such massive data processing; often, all the manager wants to know is the current stock status of a particular part in inventory, the latest cost estimate of a new product, personnel information on an individual being considered for promotion, or similar, limited information. Such "queries" are best handled through a terminal, with the manager entering a request in a special, limited, English-like language; it doesn't make sense to insist that such limited, one-time-only requests be handled by a professional programmer. Special software designed to accept and interpret management queries is commerically available.

The query approach does, however, create a few new problems. The first is security; with much of a company's key operating data available to a terminal user, what's to prevent an employee from retrieving data on his boss's salary or a competitor from accessing cost and production data from a remote terminal? Assuming a data base, part of this security problem can be dealt with by the data base manager; since all transactions against the data base must pass through this module, the data base manager is a perfect place to incorporate safeguards like special user-number or password checks designed to limit access to confidential data. Another common feature of a data base system is a logging facility—all transactions going through the data base manager are identified and recorded, which may be enough to keep all but the most determined away. A better approach, however, is to keep the unauthorized user off in the first place; thus something more is needed.

Another problem created by the query approach stems from the fact that multiple terminals are often involved. As we saw in our analysis of several operating systems back in part four of this text, handling a large number of independent terminals requesting service at unpredictable intervals is not one of the strong points of many third-generation computers. Once again, something more is needed.

Data Communications Management

The "something more" is often a software module designed to handle data communications. In a typical configuration, one partition of the computer is assigned to the communications monitor, and the operating system passes all

I/O involving associated terminals to this software routine. Within the partition, the data communications monitor handles such functions as: ascertaining the identity (passwords, etc.) of a user before permitting a transaction to start, keeping track of terminal/application program relationships, handling terminal I/O operations, allocating core, handling roll-in/roll-out problems, and others. If this sounds like a mini operating system, you're very perceptive.

Like data base software, a data communications monitor is a complex program, very expensive to develop. Commercial packages are available. Query languages are often a part of such packages. Other applications include on-line data entry and on-line file maintenance; in support of these functions, data communications monitors are often designed to be compatible with a specific data base management software package—IBM's CICS data communications package works well with their IMS data base package, and CINCOM's ENVIRON/1 data communications software is designed to work with TOTAL, to cite two examples.

Putting the Pieces Together—an MIS System

Rather than simply assume that everyone knows exactly what a management information system is (a dangerous assumption since it's hard to find many experts who agree on any single definition), let's take a few sentences to describe the applications and activities that our model firm considers to be part of their MIS system. First, we have a common data base. This data base is expected to reflect, as accurately as possible, the latest, up-to-the-minute information available; thus on-line data entry and on-line file maintenance (through CRT terminals) are key elements. The information on the data base is to be made available to selected management personnel through a series of terminals; a query language designed to allow management to bypass the programming department on short-term, one-time-only data requests is a second key component. The system must be able to handle more complex data requests on an overnight basis through the programming department or through semi-professional programming personnel associated with a nonprogramming department (an accountant who knows some RPG, for example); thus, facilities must be provided for unscheduled batch and RJE programs. The final system component consists of regular, scheduled, batch jobs—standard reports, payroll, and others.

A diagram of the software modules needed to support such a system is shown in Fig. 17.3. An operating system, a standard, vendor-supplied operating system, is found in low core. Next, comes a spooling package; we'll be doing a great deal of batch I/O on this system, so spooling is essential. A function

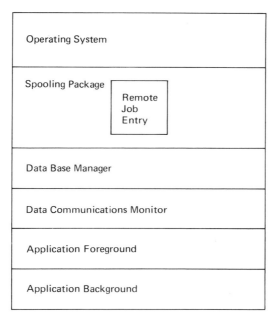

Fig. 17.3 The allocation of main memory partitions
for a typical management information system

performed by most spooling systems is job queueing—reading a job stream and
writing it to a direct-access device or tape for later execution. An added feature
of this particular spooling package is a remote job entry module which allows
jobs to be entered through a remote terminal and added to the spooled job
stream.

The next core partition contains the data base manager. Data base management software can be implemented in either of two ways: as the sole resident
of its own partition or as an access-method-like routine in the application
program's partition (Fig. 17.4). The major disadvantage of locating the data
base software in each application-program partition is the difficulty of inter-
partition communication; core communications regions common to all programs can help but are liable to programmer manipulation. With a single
master data base monitor residing in its own partition, all programs must
utilize the *same* set of software to access the data base, giving better control
over the simultaneous access problem; if, however, only one or two partitions
actually access the data base, this approach means that one less partition is
available to application programs.

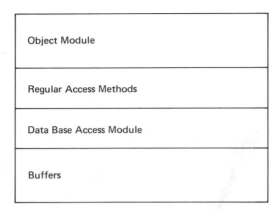

Fig. 17.4 Data base management in an application program's partition

The next partition (Fig. 17.3) houses the data communications monitor. This software package manages the partition, allocating space for small, terminal-oriented application programs and requesting the help of the operating system and the data base manager whenever necessary. All terminal applications are handled here.

The final two partitions handle batch jobs. The first of these is assigned primarily to short specials and programmer tests and assemblies; when there are no such jobs on the job queue (spooling), the partition is available for scheduled production runs. The final core partition is restricted to scheduled production runs.

Core priority matches the order in which the partitions were presented. The operating system, as usual, has top priority—it must handle interrupts for one thing. The heavy I/O load characteristic of a spooling operation makes spooling an excellent choice for second priority. A similar argument can be made for the data base manager; its only reason for being is to handle I/O. Terminal applications are usually very I/O oriented, but at times an occasional long-running program can be introduced (a statistical summary of some data, for example); this partition should have a fairly high priority, but not as high as the "safer" spooling and data base management routines. Two background partitions house batch-type jobs, with the generally shorter specials and tests having higher priority than production work. The priority scheme is not an attempt to recognize the relative importance of an application (production work is certainly more important than a programmer's compilation); instead, the priority scheme is a recognition of the impact of each application type on the computer system's operation. To cite one example, if a production job were given top priority, a CPU-bound program might lock all other users off the system for ten minutes; giving this job a lower priority and allowing other, less-important jobs to interrupt it might stretch the elapsed run time to eleven or even twelve minutes, but the availability of the system to other types of applications more than offsets the minor inconvenience to this schedulable job.

The Impact on the Applications Programmer

Let's, for a moment, consider this system from a slightly different perspective, that of a given application program. The program, let's imagine, is written in COBOL to run under control of the data communications monitor. Between the programmer and the outside world are a number of layers of systems software (Fig. 17.5). First, of course, we have the ever-present operating system, but our programmer, in this environment, can't even communicate directly with the operating system. All terminal I/O is filtered through the data communications monitor and all data file I/O is screened by the data base manager;

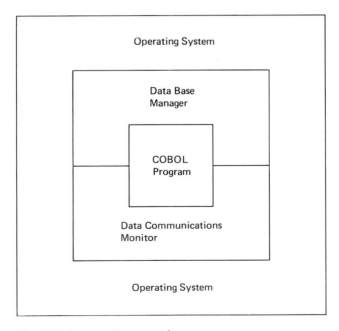

Fig. 17.5 Layers of system software

only if these software modules approve is the I/O request passed along to the operating system. There's very little a programmer can do, accidently or intentionally, to disrupt the system, particularly when a higher-level-language program is subjected to this on-line scrutiny. This happens to be another strong argument in favor of data base management and data communications, at least as far as corporate management is concerned.

Future Directions

Data base management systems and data communications monitors are among the hottest selling software packages on the market today. Look for these functions to be an integral part of any future computer system, either through vendor-supplied software, as a operating system option, or, even more likely, through a combination of hardware and software.

Summary

In this chapter, through the medium of a management information system application, we introduced the essential concepts of data base management and data communications management. These software packages grew from a need to make the information and processing resources of the computer available to a broader spectrum of the organization, particularly management. Flexibility and quick response were among the primary needs answered by these software packages.

Data can be made available to more members of an organization if it is treated like the valuable resource it is and properly managed and controlled. Historically, computer programmers have designed independent files for each application in an effort to make *that* application as efficient as possible. This approach often led to data redundancy and, subsequently, data inaccuracy due to difficulties inherent in maintaining and updating redundant data.

Using the centralized data base approach, data is carefully structured to avoid redundancy, with related records being linked through pointers. To access the information on a data base, the application programmer must first transfer control to a data base manager routine which performs the actual I/O; by routing all such transactions through a single software module, considerable control is gained. Often, the application program will ask (through a CALL macro or a special data base management macro) for specific data elements, with the data base manager doing the physical input or output operations and building the requested record; thus individual programs can be made independent of physical I/O considerations, an important factor in an area as subject to technological change as is data processing. As an added bonus, the application programmer, freed from the need to worry about I/O, should be able to concentrate more fully on the application.

Data communications software is needed to handle terminal applications. Essentially, a data communications monitor controls a partition in much the same way as an operating system controls a computer. A common feature of data communications software is a query language which allows unsophisticated computer users to access a data base and retrieve selected data.

One final benefit of data communications and data base management software is added security. Since all application programs must function within the constraints imposed by this software, another level of control is created. Logging facilities, another common feature of these modules, also helps to minimize security problems.

Exercises

1. Why do programmers plan independent files designed to fit a particular application?
2. Discuss the advantages of data base management.
3. Discuss the *dis*advantages of data base management.
4. Explain how pointers can be used to link related records.
5. What functions are performed by data communications software?
6. Data base management can be implemented in an independent partition or as a sort of quasi-access method.   Explain the difference.
7. Discuss the layers of system software separating the programmer from hardware, especially when a compiler language is used on a system with data base management, data communications management, and spooling.

CHAPTER 18

Multicomputer Applications

Overview

A "hot" topic in the computer related literature of the past few years has been the decentralized *mini*computer versus centralized *maxi*computer conflict. The minicomputer advocates say, in essence, that since the cost of minicomputers is coming down, it makes a great deal of sense to allow each major function of an organization to have its own computer and do its own programming. The advocates of the maxicomputer concept argue that, with modern operating systems, virtual memory, and terminals, all data processing activities can be centralized in one or more large computer centers, with the various functions of the organization using common data bases and common software. This is really the old question—"Shall we centralize or decentralize the management function?"—made current by technological developments. Both positions have their supporters.

Not all professionals consider the maxi vs. mini to be an "either/or" problem. Big computers and small computers have their advantages; why not take advantage of the best features of both? In this chapter, we'll study an application which does—computerized supermarket checkout. In this application, a minicomputer located in the supermarket controls daily operations, sending data to the chain's central computer where various management reports and other traditional data processing activities are handled. This involves CPU-to-CPU communication between the main computer and the supermarket's mini. No new software or operating system techniques are introduced in this chapter. Instead, the application utilizes almost all the techniques covered in prior chapters, a fitting wrap-up to the text.

Some Trends in Hardware Development

Anyone who has considered the purchase of a pocket calculator over the past few years certainly knows that the cost of these devices has been dropping rapidly, and, unlike many products where a drop in cost is accompanied by a drop in quality or capability, pocket calculators have actually improved in every conceivable way as the cost dropped. Why? Competition is part of the answer, but doesn't tell the whole story. The real reason lies in significant progress in the ability of industry to manufacture solid-state circuitry. Technological improvements in the manufacturing process have led to lower-cost circuits, and lower-cost circuits, in turn, mean that a lower selling price will still yield a profit.

The circuits which go into an electronic pocket calculator are much like the circuits which go into a modern computer; thus it's not surprising that the cost of computers is also dropping. This is especially true with minicomputers and microcomputers. Today, for not much more than the cost of a good remote batch entry terminal, a customer can buy a minicomputer and write his own programs; these small, modern machines are often as powerful as a good second-generation machine. Since they are so inexpensive (and becoming cheaper), why not simply give everyone who needs a computer his own mini? This would eliminate problems with computer access. Also, recent history has shown the large, centralized computer to be a very serious security and reliability problem; by decentralizing and dispersing data processing activities among a number of minis, the danger of "putting all the eggs in one basket" is eliminated.

Large computers have also benefited from the advances in electronic technology. On these larger machines, the "cost per unit of computation" is a commonly used measure of computer economics, with, perhaps, one "third-plus" generation computer replacing two third-generation machines at $1\frac{1}{4}$ the cost of one. Faster core plus a faster main processor and operating systems (including virtual memory) allow the user to take advantage of the power of these large machines. The ability to handle so much work on a single machine provides a strong push for centralizing computer operations, thus taking advantage of common software and common data.

Both approaches have their weaknesses. A large, centralized machine does offer a convenient target to the saboteur, and downtime, be it caused by human or hardware failure, can have a devastating impact when all organizational activities are dependent upon this single data processing center. A centralized computer implies that outlying activity centers will communicate with the machine over telephone lines or some other communications medium; teleprocessing media are outside the control of the organization and represent a common source of difficulty. Finally, a centralized data processing operation tends to create a core of specialists who, due to their effective control of access to the firm's data resources, are in a position of real (and often uncontrolled) power.

The major weakness of most minis is software. There are few well-tested, complete statistical packages available on most minis, to cite one example. Many machines, particularly on the small end of the scale, are restricted to a single compiler; in some cases, programs must be written in a very-low-level, very-limited assembler language. Core capacity is a problem, limiting the size of any program or requiring the programmer to use sophisticated overlay structures; the old problem of no one but the programmer having the slightest idea of what's going on tends to resurface. As if these software problems were not enough, the "decentralized mini" approach eliminates any possibility of data base centralization.

Why not take advantage of the best features of both? In this chapter, we'll be discussing an application which does exactly that—computerized supermarket checkout. In this application, each supermarket in the chain has its own minicomputer controlling the day-in-and-day-out activities of the store. On a daily basis, information is transfered from each mini to the chain's central computer, where traditional data processing functions and central data base controls are implemented. As we'll see, the minicomputer is restricted to a single application, while the large, central computer system handles "number crunching" and provides flexibility. Since essential supermarket operations are handled by the mini, downtime on the central computer has little impact; since these functions are local, the teleprocessing network does not present a problem.

Throughout the discussion which follows, we'll be assuming that computerized checkout has been installed and running for some time. Since the most interesting part of the application is in the supermarket, we'll start with the minicomputer side.

Within the Store—the Mini

Have you noticed the product codes which now appear on almost every packaged product found on supermarket shelves (Fig. 18.1)? These codes are an integral part of computerized checkout operations; they uniquely identify a product by size, type, flavor, and so on. Next time you go to the supermarket, check the codes on any popular brand of pudding or gelatin dessert; you'll find that each flavor and size has a different number.

In a supermarket with computerized checkout, the clerk, rather than reading the price of each item and keying it into a cash register, simply slides the product over a reader. The reader accepts the product code and passes it along to the minicomputer (Fig. 18.2), where the current price of the product is selected

Fig. 18.1 Product codes (Photo courtesy of Kroger Company)

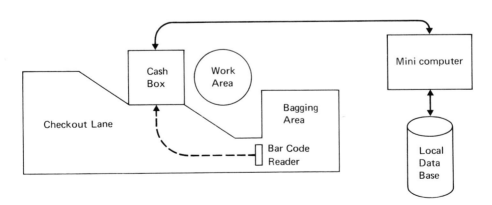

Fig. 18.2 A computerized checkout system

from a table or a file. Appropriate sales tax is computed and the price and tax are added to the customer's bill. For the customer's information, a list of all purchases is printed at the checkout station. While this is going on, the computer deducts "1" from the current inventory stock on the product, yielding up-to-the-second inventory information. As a final step, the total bill is compiled, the clerk enters the amount of the customer's payment, and the computer computes and prints the change due. Should a customer change his mind, the clerk depresses a cancel button and passes rejected or returned merchandise over the reader, adding the product back into inventory and subtracting the price (and tax, if appropriate) from the bill.

Why would a supermarket install a computerized checkout system? Starting with an advantage often claimed for the customer, the checkout operation should be faster, as anyone who has waited while a stock boy ran back to the produce department to check on the price of celery can certainly imagine. With price information stored on a computer, clerical read time and typing time disappear, along with the annoyance of unmarked products. From the store's point-of-view, this means that more customers can be pushed through fewer checkout lines, thus reducing personnel costs.

Another key advantage to computerized checkout is a reduction in pricing errors. If a clerk makes an error and overcharges you, chances are you'll call it to his attention as soon as you catch it, but what if the error is in your favor? Contrary to popular belief, most retail stores lose more than they gain through employee error. Computers make fewer mistakes than people.

Employee training is a problem in a noncomputerized supermarket—it takes time to train a checkout clerk. With computerized checkout, this training time is cut to a minimum.

These advantages seem trivial when compared to the impact of computerized checkout on product marking and inventory. How much does it cost a supermarket to stamp a price on each and every item for sale? Consider just the labor alone—hours and hours each week. With a computerized checkout system, the price must be entered once on the computer; from this point on, the correct price is simply retrieved from the computer in response to the reading of a product code.

The continuous inventory maintained by the computer is another tremendous advantage. Prior to computerization of the checkout function, the stock status of key products was manually compiled and hand-carried by courier to the supermarket chain's data processing center where inventory-analysis programs determined order quantities and planned shipments to make optimum use of a truck fleet. The process of compiling inventory information was lengthy, expensive, limited to a relatively few key products, and very prone to error. Now, stock status of every product is simply transmitted from the minicomputer to the central computer at the close of each business day. Spot checks and inventory samples are used as a check on the accuracy of the computerized system and as a source of data on the store's shoplifting loss.

The picture isn't, however, entirely rosy. The labor union, of course, takes a dim view of the loss and/or downgrading of a number of jobs in each super- market. They like to point to the lack of flexibility in a computerized system, using as their favorite example the time the computer "went down" in one store. With no prices marked on individual items and no trained checkout clerks, the store was forced to either close or trust customers to mark prices with a marking pen. (The store, incidentally, chose the latter option, and was happy to report a loss of less than five percent over normal business for the night.) Another big question still to be resolved is the impact of computerized checkout on customer buying habits. The jury is still out on this one.

The Central Computer

Like most large food chains, the firm we are studying takes advantage of large-lot buying power and efficient inventory and distribution systems to gain a cost advantage over smaller competitors. The inventory and distribution systems make heavy use of the computer. In addition to keeping track of what's available and where it's located, the computer calculates economic re- order quantities for each product stocked and prints order forms when the actual stock falls below this level. Inventory reports allow management to identify slow- and fast-moving products, important information to retailers.

Distribution is closely related to inventory; this function involves moving stock from central warehouses to the individual stores. Using a computer, an attempt is made to fill each truck and also to have each truck drive the shortest possible route between supermarkets. This problem is solved using linear programming techniques.

The company has centralized all its data processing in a single, large computer. In addition to the two key applications described above, this com- puter handles all the traditional data-processing applications like payroll and record keeping. Prior to centralization, each warehouse and branch office had its own computer; now, these installations use remote batch terminals and communicate with the central computer over telephone lines. A query language allows managers and branch personnel to obtain the status of various products via typewriter terminals.

The central computer has an operating system with what should be by now, predictable features. It's a virtual system with a spooling package, remote job entry, data base management, and data communications management. An addition to the RJE facility allows CPU-to-CPU communications between the main computer and the minicomputers located in each store. This communication takes place at planned intervals at the command of the central computer's operating system. The inventory data supplied by the store minis is used by the central computer in its inventory and distribution programs. Prices and shipments are passed to the store minis at the start of each business day, giving each store access to the most up-to-date, accurate information available.

Why Use the Mini?

We could, of course, simply attach the checkout terminals in each supermarket directly to the central computer via telephone lines. This approach might reduce the cost in each supermarket, but telephone-line charges could easily wipe out any savings, particularly if a new store were located a great distance from the center. To counterbalance this very limited potential for lowering cost, consider the risk of doing everything on a single, centralized computer—if the computer goes down for any reason, *every* store in the chain is temporarily out of business. With minicomputers in each store, downtime on the central computer affects no one and downtime on any single mini hurts only a single store. There is one more reason for not using straight teleprocessing to handle all stores—our telephone system may well be the best in the world, but in a computer/terminal operation, the telephone line tends to be the least reliable component when extremely long connect times must be maintained.

The supermarket application is a natural for a minicomputer. The equipment is relatively inexpensive, a critical point when a large number of units must be purchased. The equipment is very reliable; most hardware problems on a solid-logic computer show up in the first few hours of use and, once these are corrected, the equipment usually functions with minimal breakdowns. The application itself is relatively simple—accept data from a central computer, store it on disk, read data from a code reader, look up matching part numbers, accumulate a bill, add or subtract inventory data, and send information to the central computer on request.

Why Not Do It All on the Mini?

If the minicomputer is so good, why bother with the central machine? The main reason is that a minicomputer is not at its best when attempting to handle the kind of programs required to support the sophisticated inventory and distribution systems used by this firm. In short, a small machine can't handle big programs as well as a big computer can.

There's another reason for rejecting any attempt to do more with the minicomputers. Once these machines are removed from a single-application mode, a need for local expertise is created. If programmers and operators are needed for each supermarket, much of the economic benefit of computerized checkout will be lost. Closely related to this problem is a question of reliability—most computer errors today are program or data errors and not hardware errors; by restricting the minicomputer to a single, well-tested application program which is in use in many other installations, the variable of programming change is eliminated. Supermarket personnel *should* view the mini as a magic box and keep their hands off it. Programmers may not like this approach, but by, in essence, sealing the computer, reliability can be vastly improved.

Summary

In this chapter, we've considered a specific application of computers—automated, computerized checkout in a supermarket. A minicomputer located in the supermarket itself is responsible for reading product codes from a package, locating the price on a price list, accumulating the customer's bill, computing change, and maintaining inventory information. On demand, information is sent to a centralized computer which maintains a corporate data base and uses this data to solve complex inventory and distribution problems. The central computer also handles traditional data processing activities, RJE operations from branch locations, and a query system through conversational terminals. It incorporates most of the operating system concepts we've discussed in the preceding seventeen chapters, including virtual memory, spooling, remote job entry, data base management, and data communications management.

The important concept presented in this chapter arises from the dual nature of this application—a small-scale single-purpose application requiring high reliability and quick response as opposed to large, number-crunching, linear programming applications. The solution was to use two very different computers, a maxi and a mini, and attempt to marry their best talents. This application once again shows that there is no general answer to the question: What's the best solution? Before this question can even be intelligently asked, it is essential that the application be fully understood and that the measures of effectiveness be identified. If accuracy on a 500-variable linear programming problem is a criterion, don't use a mini. If high reliability and full availability for long periods of time every day are considered to be crucial, don't rely on terminals and telephone lines. Rules of thumb and pet theories are no substitute for knowledge of a system.

In the next few pages, we'll deviate from our usual practice of terminating a chapter with a summary and discuss, in brief, a few similar multicomputer applications.

The Twenty-Four Hour Teller

The latest news in the banking industry is the automated, twenty-four hour teller (Fig. 18.3), a device which allows card holders to make banking transactions at any time of day without the aid of a teller. The customer sees a solid, steel door which opens as the proper card is inserted, revealing a bank of pushbuttons and, usually, a small display screen. As a means of verifying identification, the customer is required to enter a four or five digit check number before proceeding with any banking transactions; after entering the proper identification code, he or she may use the terminal to cash a check, make a deposit, make a withdrawal, obtain a cash advance on a charge card, and handle a number of other banking transactions.

Inside the automatic teller is a safe, the mechanical and electrical components needed to read the card, support the display, and dispense money, and

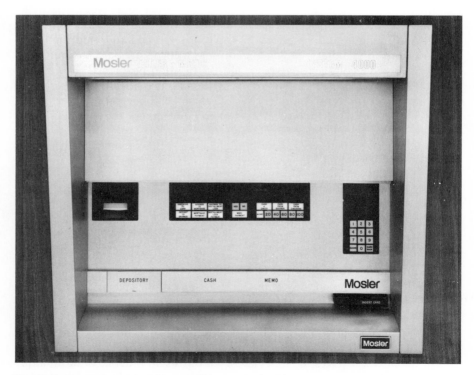

Fig. 18.3 An automated, 24-hour-teller terminal. (Photo courtesy of the Mosler Safe Company, a Division of American Standard Corporation)

a minicomputer. The minicomputer controls all banking transactions. Depending on the model, the minicomputer maintains a list of all transactions on paper tape, magnetic tape, or disk; at regular intervals, this information is sent, via courier or teleprocessing line, to the bank's central computer, where reports, file updates, and other traditional banking data processing activities are carried out.

The immediate advantage to using automatic tellers is customer convenience—banking services, at least a limited subset of banking services, can be made available to the customer on a twenty-four hour basis without need for a human teller (who represents both a cost and a security risk). As banks compete for a share of a limited local banking market, marginal differences in customer convenience can often make a major difference in market share, with customers switching from one bank to another to take advantage of what they see as better service.

The real potential for automated teller systems, however, lies in the area of branch banks. Every time a new shopping center opens, a new branch bank opens, often at a cost of hundreds of thousands of dollars. The reason for this is a developing trend in the banking industry to make banking as convenient as possible—hopefully, increased convenience will lead to an increased market share.

An automatic teller can handled many of the functions of a branch bank at a fraction of the cost. Why not simply install a twenty-four hour teller in a corner of the supermarket? The advantage to the bank is obvious—a new branch (or its rough equivalent) for under fifty thousand dollars. The supermarket likes this arrangement too—the presence of banking services allows the supermarket to get out of the check-cashing business.

In many states, there are legal questions surrounding this approach which have yet to be resolved. As with computerized checkout systems, there remain nagging doubts as to the degree of customer acceptance of an automated solution to what has been, traditionally, a business transaction involving human interaction. From a technical and economic point of view, however, automated teller systems using a local minicomputer to handle simple transactions and a centralized, large computer to take care of a data base and large-report generation makes a great deal of sense.

Source Data Automation

In any manufacturing operation, the collection of labor and production control data is a problem which must be dealt with. Traditional time cards and hand-written labor sheets are prone to error and cheating. In many firms, the answer has been to install a series of data collection terminals, with employees using a combination of cards, badges, and simple keyboard entries to report activities (clock-on, clock-off, the completion of an operation, etc.) as they occur.

Often, these terminals are connected directly to a minicomputer which checks incoming transactions for accuracy, requests corrections from a manufacturing manager or timekeeping when necessary, and stores the data. At regular intervals, this data is transferred to a central computer which maintains a data base and runs the programs which analyze the data.

Intelligent Terminals

An intelligent terminal is one which is capable of performing some logical functions. In a typical configuration, the intelligent terminal is used as a remote job entry station, sending programs and job streams to a central computer where they enter the spooled job queues to be executed at a later time; output is sent back to the terminal.

A common application for such terminals is data compression. Typically, these terminals support a card reader, a printer, and, perhaps, a console-like typewriter and a card punch; these devices frequently handle records containing a considerable number of blank spaces. The printer must often be formatted and column headers must be printed. The intelligent terminal allows raw data to be sent between the terminal and the central computer, stripping blanks from input data and adding blanks, column headers, and page controls to the printed output. This means that a minimum amount of data must be transmitted over teleprocessing lines, and the line is often a major bottleneck.

Is it reasonable to call a teleprocessing terminal a minicomputer? The dividing line between a terminal and a minicomputer is fuzzy at best. With full terminal intelligence, the remote user can do his simple, day-in-and-day-out data processing without bothering the central computer and without using expensive teleprocessing lines; whenever an application requires the facilities of a larger machine, the remote mini can simply "change hats" and become a remote job entry terminal. Mini/maxi computer configurations have a future in general-purpose data processing too.

Summary

Not all computer applications require the services of a big computer, but there are applications which are beyond the capacity of a mini. A combination of both types of computers, allowing the user to take advantage of the best features of both, is being used to solve a number of data processing problems.

Exercises

1. Hardware costs are dropping, but personnel costs are not. Programming is largely a manual operation. What impact might these few, simple facts be expected to have on the future of programming?

2. In the supermarket application, why is a minicomputer used within the individual supermarkets?

3. Why can't a minicomputer do the entire supermarket job?

4. Can you see any possible relationship between a supermarket's mini and the 24-hour, automatic teller which might someday be located in the supermarket?

5. One of the problems cited in the discussion of using local minicomputers to handle an entire data-processing operation was the increased need for local expertise. What's wrong with local expertise?

6. Visit or read about a computerized checkout system or a 24-hour teller system in your area, and prepare a short paper describing the hardware and the system.

CHAPTER 19

A Summary of
Operating System Development

Overview

This chapter is a summary of the operating system concepts covered in this text. To give the material a sense of continuity, the development of operating systems has been tied to a loosely drawn history of computers; precise chronology is not crucial, but the reader should have (or gain) a sense of the evolutionary development of key software concepts. Should any of the information in this chapter prove to be unfamiliar, you've missed something. Go back and review.

Early Development—the First Generation

During the computer's first generation, there was little need for operating system software. Computers were new and unfamiliar; their use was pretty much restricted to highly mathematical scientific and military applications and research activities, with "hands-on," "at-the-console" programming being common if not standard. Assemblers and compilers, or at least the essential concepts of this type of software, were developed during the first generation. Other support software developments included the use of macros, library programs, standard subroutines, and utility programs like sort/merge routines.

The Second Generation

The computer's second generation was ushered in when transistors came to replace electronic tubes as the key computer component. With transistors came reduced size, higher speed, and improved reliability. More important (at least for our purposes), the second generation marked the beginning of significant business use of the computer. With the businessman came strong consideration of the economic factors of computer use; since the computer was so expensive relative to other office equipment, maximum utilization of hardware became a key and the idea of throughput as a measure of computer effectiveness was born.

Job scheduling was, very early in the game, recognized as a means of increasing throughput. By grouping jobs with similar equipment requirements, a computing center could take advantage of common setups. Even noncommon setups could be minimized by scheduling and planning with, to cite one example, tapes being mounted during the execution of a job not using tapes. To implement scheduling, the operator needed a means for grouping jobs; the most common solution to this problem was the JOB card, often with some form of JOB CLASS parameter.

During the second generation, "production" programs were generally stored on a core image library and read directly into core for execution, thus saving card read and compilation time. Libraries and library maintenance programs became important.

Compilers were developed to support many different source languages. During the compilation operation, precoded source statements could be added to the source module from a source statement library through the use of a COPY statement or through macro generation. Once a job was compiled, additional object-level code could be added to the module by the linkage editor or loader program from an object library. The resulting load module became a candidate for addition to a core image library.

Special software was needed to implement these functions. We've already mentioned the need for library maintenance software; various compilers and a linkage editor or loader program were also essential. Many of the features of a job control language were developed to allow the programmer to communicate with these special support-software modules.

As computers became faster, the speed disparity between the CPU and its I/O devices became more and more obvious. During the second generation, this speed disparity forced throughput-conscious data processing operations to use higher speed I/O devices like tape, disk, and drum. Because of the nature of these devices, individual physical records must be separated by inter-record gaps; blocking is used to improve the effectiveness of these devices. Blocking means that the programmer must deal with physical records consisting of several logical records—on input, logical records must be deblocked, while on output, physical blocks must be built from individual logical records. To aid the programmer in these blocking and deblocking functions, access methods were developed. Access method logic was, and still is, added to an object module by the linkage editor.

Multiple buffering was another technique designed to improve throughput. Rather than simply reading (or writing) one record at a time, several physical records can be read into core buffers. Logical records are handled, one at a time until a complete physical record (buffer) has been exhausted; logical records are then processed from another buffer while the first buffer is replenished in parallel, another function of an access method.

Data management began to develop during the second generation, with software modules designed to create and maintain data files, create and maintain indexes, take care of libraries, create and check labels, and randomize direct-access addresses. Sequential, indexed-sequential, and direct file organizations were fully supported through OPEN and CLOSE macros and the various access methods.

Other key operating systems concepts were also developed during the second generation. In some installations, the slow card-reading, punching, and printing operations were moved off-line, an early form of spooling. Checkpoint/restart logic was included in many programs. Timer interrupts were implemented to protect against endless program loops. A few good programmers even used overlay structures, an early form of virtual memory.

One final note on the second generation—most data processing installations ran programs in a serial batch mode, one program at a time.

Early Third Generation

Solid logic circuits replaced transistors as the third generation was ushered in. Computers became even faster, and the speed disparity between the computer and its I/O devices became even more pronounced. Increased speed is useless unless customers can take advantage of it; why build a 150-mile-per-hour train when tracks can support only 30-mile-per-hour traffic? The solution was multiprogramming.

Under multiprogramming, a number of programs reside in core, sharing the CPU. Much like a chess master playing a number of concurrent opponents, the CPU switches its attention from program to program, servicing each in its turn. The most common mechanism for implementing multiprogramming is the interrupt concept, with the CPU being notified of occurrences needing the services of the operating system. Typically, all I/O operations must pass through the operating system which, by switching or chaining program status words, transfers control to another program. Channels help too, relieving the CPU of the need to actually control I/O; upon completion of the I/O operation, the channel simply interrupts the CPU.

This kind of multiprogramming is basically passive in nature, with the operating system waiting until a program issues a request for I/O or until an external channel completes an operation before transferring control to another program. On some systems, a timer is used to restrict each program to a preset slice of time; should the program request I/O before expiration of the time slice, fine, but if the program is still executing at the end of its allotted period, a timer interrupt returns control to the operating system where multiprogramming logic can be implemented. Time slicing is common on time-shared systems.

There is, of course, a cost associated with multiprogramming—overhead. A resident operating system is needed to implement a multiprogramming system, and this operating system uses both core and CPU time as well as secondary storage space.

Since a number of programs share core storage, core allocation is an obvious problem which must be handled by the operating system. Many operating systems, like IBM's DOS and OS/MFT systems, divide core into a number of fixed-size partitions. Others, like IBM's OS/MVT, assign core in variable-length blocks as a program is loaded. Some systems include a facility for increasing and decreasing the amount of core allocated to a program after the program starts running—multitasking, GETMAIN, and FREEMAIN.

Core fragmentation is often a problem, with chunks of core becoming unusable because of their location and size; a 96K compile followed by a 90K link edit might leave 6K of unused space in between two programs, space which is too small for any complete program. One solution to the problem is dynamic core relocation, a shifting and realignment of programs to bring all the small, unutilized chunks of core together producing, hopefully, a single partition big enough for a complete program.

Another solution is program segmentation. Why must an entire program be loaded into *contiguous* core before the program can be executed? Program segmentation is a technique for breaking a program into logical segments each of which is addressed relative to the beginning of the segment; given segmentation, contiguous program loading is not necessary and small chunks of core can be utilized without a need for dynamic relocation. Simple paging achieves the same result by breaking a program into a number of fixed-length, relatively addressed pages.

Scheduling programs was important back in the second generation; it's just as important in the third generation, but the fact that core is occupied by multiple programs complicates the problem. Often, the problem is handled by spooling jobs to a number of work queues (on disk, usually) by job class (the JOB card again); the operating system has the responsibility for reading and enqueueing the job and, later, for loading the job into core. An individual partition might be assigned to each job class, with the operating system loading the next job on the queue when the partition becomes available. Priority within job class is often supported, with a high-priority job moving to the front of its class queue.

At this point, it might be a good idea to differentiate between a job and a job step. A job might consist of a number of different programs—compilers, the linkage editor, sorts, utilities, application programs—to be run in a fixed sequence; each individual program is a job step. The programmer submits a job; job steps are loaded and executed by the computer.

Under IBM's operating systems, the functions of reading, enqueueing, and loading job steps are handled by a set of operating system modules known collectively as job management. Normally, if sufficient core is available each of the steps in a job is executed before a partition is turned over to a different job. Not all operating systems use this approach. In some cases, a high-priority program can cause other programs to be rolled-out of core, thus making room; the original program resumes processing when the high-priority job is finished.

A key component of any operating system is a series of tables allowing the operating system software to keep track of core assignments. Such tables are essential if destructive overlays are to be avoided.

Once a job step has been loaded and is ready to begin executing, it becomes, at least on an IBM machine, the responsibility of task management. The main function handled by the operating system in support of active programs is interrupt processing. Interrupt processing implies that the executing program can be "interrupted" and control of the CPU turned over to the resident operating system. On an IBM machine, this transfer of control is implemented by switching program status words, with a new and an old PSW field for each of the five types of interrupts recognized by the System/360 and System/370 lines of computers. Other manufacturers use approaches involving the stacking or queueing of interrupts.

Another key function performed by task management (or its equivalent on a nonIBM machine) is resolving conflicts resulting from two or more programs being ready to use the CPU at the same time. At its simplest level, the fixed- and even variable-length partitions created for core-allocation purposes are chained together in a set sequence—foreground before background, for example—and this sequence determines internal priority. Under IBM's OS/MFT operating system, partitions are chained together via a series of task control blocks; when attempting to transfer control of the CPU to a new program, the operating system simply follows this chain, passing control to the first ready program encountered.

Not all operating systems use such fixed priorities, however. In some cases, the programmer is allowed to indicate the program's priority through a control card, and the operating system is designed to always pass control to the highest priority job step in core, reverting to a fixed sequence in the event of ties. Other systems are designed to work on a first-in/first-out rule or a last-in/first-out rule or a biggest-program/first-out rule or a smallest-program/first-out rule; any programmable decision rule can be, and probably has been used some- where. There are good priority schemes and bad priority schemes, and the "best" rule depends upon the actual job mix of an installation; however, on a modern, high-speed computer, *any* programmed rule is better than operator intervention.

In addition to scheduling jobs, loading jobs, handling interrupts, and resolving internal priority conflicts, an operating system must be capable of resolving I/O device conflicts on a system with more than one program core resident. What happens when two or more programs want the same tape drive at the same time? Chaos, unless the operating system intervenes.

Job management is partly responsible for resolving this problem, post- poning the loading of a job step until all required I/O devices are available— better to force a job step to wait on queue than to allow it to occupy core while waiting for a tape drive to become free, thus freezing out other jobs. If job management is to perform this function, a full set of information on I/O device requirements must be made available; this is the function of DD cards in IBM's Job Control Language. As its final contribution to the solution of this problem, job management builds a series of tables linking the I/O assignments for each active job step to a set of master system tables, thus allowing task management to keep track of all system I/O assignments.

Once job management has loaded a job step, it becomes a task and thus the responsibility of task management. Again using the IBM system as an example, control of the multiprogramming I/O problem is achieved by forcing all I/O operations to pass through the supervisor or resident operating system. The instructions which actually control an I/O operation are privileged (i.e., can be executed only by the operating system); the programmer must transfer control to the operating system via a supervisor call interrupt in order to start any I/O. Once the supervisor has control, the tables created by job management can be checked and flags set, providing a mechanism for controlling access to data.

What if a program requests an I/O operation but, because of interference, the operating system is unable to start it immediately? And, what if a channel has just completed an operation but another I/O interrupt is being processed? In both cases, the interrupt must be queued or in some way kept pending. On computers using interrupt queueing or stacking, this does not present a problem, but on the IBM machines with their PSW switching approach, it does. Within an IBM computer, a separate table must be maintained to hold "requested but not yet started" I/O operations; the latter problem, finished but not yet ac- knowledged interrupts, is handled by hardware and kept pending within the channel.

A feature we haven't mentioned yet, mainly because it's a part of the solution to all the problems discussed above, is core protection. On the IBM line of computers, core protection is implemented through a four-bit field in the program status word. All core assigned to the operating system is assigned protect key $(0000)_2$, and the core assigned to each other program partition is given its own unique four-bit key. During the execution of a program, any instruction which would result in the destruction (and in some cases, the simple accessing) of core outside the program's own protect key region results in a protection interrupt and, usually, program termination. This protection idea is also the key to the implementation of the privileged instruction concept so crucial to I/O control; a privileged instruction can be executed only when the protect key is $(0000)_2$.

On-line spooling is common on many third-generation machines, with the slower card and print operations being handled when the CPU has no other work to do—i.e., when all application programs resident in the computer are in a wait state. Special spooling routines, often incorporating accounting functions, are one of the more common add-ons to a standard, vendor supplied operating system.

In the area of data management, this period has shown few major advances. Access methods and library functions are still pretty much as they were back in the late second generation, with the only really new function being the system residence library needed to support the operating system. As we shall see shortly, however, data management has become one of the hot topics of the 1970s.

Physically, an operating system of the third generation consists of both core-resident and transient modules. Often, the customer has a number of options, and an operating system can be somewhat customized with key modules being made core resident and less-used modules being left on disk and brought in on an as-needed basis. In addition to this executable software, most operating systems contain a number of control blocks and tables which help the system keep track of computer activities.

Not all manufacturers have used the IBM approach of course. Some, like Xerox, have chosen a multiple interrupt approach, with each program being associated with its own interrupt; others, like Control Data Corporation, have gone with multiple processors, handling operating system functions and application-program functions with different sets of hardware. The functions are the same, but the means of implementing these functions can be quite different. Another complicating factor arises from the very nature of operating system functions. Essentially, this software serves to "bridge the gap" between hardware and the application program. Many of these functions can be performed by either hardware or software, and different manufacturers have chosen different routes for implementation. Software is a human-related function—people write it; the obvious trend in people costs is up. Meanwhile, the trend in the cost of electronic hardware is down. As these cost trends continue, it will become economically attractive to implement more and more operating system functions through hardware.

Into the 1970s

As electronic technology advanced, computers became even faster, further aggravating the speed disparity between the computer and its I/O devices; even with ten or fifteen application programs in core, many users were discovering that CPU utilization was still unacceptably low. If multiprogramming was the answer before, more multiprogramming seemed to be the obvious solution, but core capacity (or monolithic memory capacity) set a limit on the number of concurrent programs and main memory was too expensive to be expanded without limit.

Virtual memory provided a solution. Since the CPU can only execute one instruction at a time, why must an *entire* program be resident in main memory before any execution can begin? On a system with virtual memory, a program is broken into segments or pages and stored on a direct access device; only active pieces need be present in core or main memory, with inactive pages or segments staying on the virtual memory to await roll-in. The logic is not new—roll-in/roll-out and program overlay structures have been around since early in the second generation. What is new is the fact that increasing computer speeds have made paging logic and virtual memory concepts so attractive.

Another major trend of the 1970s has resulted from a growing awareness of the importance of data resources; strong sales of data base management software has been the result. Under the data base management approach, data is organized in an integrated manner rather than in the old "customized to fit the application" way so popular in the past. Thus data redundancy is minimized, file updating is simplified, and data access is made easier.

Closely associated with many data base management packages are a number of query systems allowing managers and other nonprogrammers to access the data base. Since these queries are most conveniently entered through a terminal, the demand for terminal support and, with it, the demand for data communications software has grown. The combination of data base management and data communications also supports on-line data updating through terminals.

Perhaps a bit less obvious is the impact such support software is beginning to have on the programmer. The operating system, of course, prevents him from directly controlling I/O operations; with virtual memory, he loses control over addressing. With an additional level of system software—data base and data communications management—he has even less control over the destiny of a program. If a higher-level language is used, the programmer is reduced to doing little more than coding a solution to an application problem—the once very challenging computer-related problems have been absorbed by the operating system, the compiler, and the data base and data communications software.

From the standpoint of management, these trends are very positive. Too many companies have gotten themselves into trouble by becoming overly dependent upon a few programmers. By shifting many of the more esoteric problems of programming onto support software, much of this over-dependence is eliminated, and application programmers are allowed to concentrate on the application rather than on the idiosyncrasies of I/O control or the internal timings of a particular machine; these problems are interesting, and the programmer who dealt with them effectively has long been among the more highly respected practitioners of his craft, but programs written to maximize internal computer efficiency all too often have proven to be poorly documented and difficult to debug and maintain. Reducing the programmer to a coder through the use of advanced systems software may have a negative impact on programmer job interest but, when all the factors of program cost are considered, the net impact on the entire corporation is often very positive. There is, of course, a cost, less "tight" programs, but as computers become faster and faster, the benefit derived from shaving an instruction or two becomes less important.

Another apparent trend of the 1970s, also arising from the downward trend in electronic-component costs, has been the emergence of a minicomputer and microcomputer market. In addition to support of dispersed data processing, these small, inexpensive machines are gaining increasing popularity in multicomputer applications, with a local mini handling the second-by-second problems of a given single application, passing collected data to a larger machine for more traditional data processing.

Toward the Future

Electronic technology continues to advance and, with it, the cost/performance ratio of computer components gets better and better; the most obvious example of this trend is the ever-decreasing cost of pocket calculators. There is a limit to this improvement, of course; electricity is limited to the speed of light, light travels roughly one foot in one nanosecond, and computer logic circuitry has at least a minimum density. More improvement is due before this limit is reached, however.

On minicomputers, the impact of this trend is obvious—declining cost coupled with increasing power and reliability. The use of minis will grow, particularly among smaller users and in multicomputer applications.

The impact on larger computers is a bit less obvious. Operating systems have developed along software lines largely because of the cost of hardware; many of the functions performed by an operating system could have been performed by hardware, but the cost of making *flexible* hardware has been much higher than the cost of coding flexible software. As hardware costs continue to drop and labor costs continue to rise, the breakeven point is shifting. Hardware flexibility is also improving, with logical functions being built on easily replaceable cards. Look for more and more operating system functions to be performed by hardware, including, perhaps, much of data base management and data communications.

With the growth of systems software (be it in software or hardware form), there will be less emphasis on what we now call "good" programming. Shaving ten instructions from a program used to mean saving several milliseconds on each iteration; as computer speeds increase, the ten instructions represent perhaps ten nanoseconds. Given the fact that less than fifty percent of available CPU time can actually be utilized anyway, such "effective" programming leads to little or no measurable savings.

In addition to an ability to write "tight" code, the most respected programmers of the past possessed an intimate knowledge of I/O and were able to write very efficient I/O routines. With data base management, data communications, and operating systems functions in the way, such direct control of I/O becomes impossible. The job of the programmer will change as a result of these trends. A few "super programmers" will be responsible for the development of operating systems and other support software (or hardware or hardware/software hybrid), with application programs being written primarily in higher-level languages by less skilled coders or application experts who just happen to write programs. So much of what we now call programming will be done by systems software that a knowledge of this software (or at least the functions performed by this software) will be imperative to any future data processing professional. This is why a knowledge of operating systems is so important.

Summary

The entire chapter represents a summary of operating system developments and a brief investigation of probable future trends in the data processing field. If you understood all the topics in this chapter, you have a pretty good grasp of the contents of this book; if you did not recognize some of this material, go back and review.

APPENDIX A

A Summary of
DOS Job Control Statements

Primary Reference

IBM Publication # GC24-5036, *DOS System Control and Service*. Certain statement formats in this appendix are reproduced, with permission, from that publication.

Portions of several of the generalized job control statements are taken directly from this publication. The excerpts are reprinted by permission from International Business Machines Corporation.

Statements:

ASSGN assigns logical I/O unit to a physical device:

$$// \quad \text{ASSGN} \quad \text{SYSxxx,address} \quad \left[\begin{Bmatrix} ,\text{X'ss'} \\ ,\text{ALT} \end{Bmatrix} \right]$$

where   **SYSxxx** is the symbolic unit name;

address is the physical device address expressed as:

X'cuu' where c = channel and uu = device, or
UA which indicates that unit is unassigned, or
IGN which indicates that the device is to be ignored (i.e., disabled);

X'ss' is an optional parameter used to specify mode settings for magnetic tape;

ALT indicates that this is an alternate magnetic-tape drive assignment.

358

CLOSE closes a logical unit:

$$
//\quad\text{CLOSE}\quad\text{SYSxxx}\quad
\left[
\begin{cases}
,\text{X'cuu'}[,\text{X'ss'}] \\
,\text{UA} \\
,\text{IGN} \\
,\text{ALT}
\end{cases}
\right]
$$

where parameters have the same meaning as in ASSGN.

DATE places a date in the communication region:

    //   DATE   mm/dd/yy

or

    //   DATE   dd/mm/yy

DLAB contains file label information for direct access file creation and label checking:

    //   DLAB   'label fields 1-3'   C

          xxxx,yyddd,yyddd,'systemcode'[,type]

where   **'label fields 1–3'** is a 51-byte character string containing:

         a 44-byte alphameric file name,
         a 1-byte numeric format identifier,
         a 6-byte alphameric file serial number;

         C is any nonblank character in column 72;

         xxxx is the volume sequence number;

         yyddd is the file-creation date;
         the second yyddd is the expiration date;

         'systemcode' is a 13-character string within apostrophes (recommended contents, blanks);

         type = SD for sequential, DA for direct access, ISC for Indexed Sequential using load Create, or ISE for other Indexed Sequential.

DLBL replaces DLAB and VOL statements in current versions of DOS:

    //   DLBL   filename,['file-ID'],

          [date],[codes],[data security]

where   **filename** is a 1–7 character (alphameric) file name—first character must be alphabetic;

'file-ID' is the 1–44 alphanumeric file name field as described under the DLAB statement (It's optional; filename is the default.);

date is either the retention period or the expiration date;

codes is identical to the DLAB type parameter;

data security = DSF for a date secured file.

EXEC indicates end of control information for a job step and identifies the core-image library program (phase) which is to be loaded and executed:

    //   EXEC   [programname]

where   **programname** is the name of the program to be loaded and executed. If blank, the load module just produced by the linkage editor is assumed.

EXTENT defines an area or extent of a direct access file:

    //   EXTENT   [symbolic-unit],

              [serial-number],[type],

              [sequence-number],

              [relative-track],

              [number-of-tracks],

              [split-cylinder-track],

              [B=bins]

where   **symbolic unit** is the SYSxxx form symbolic = unit name of the desired volume (If omitted, the unit from the last EXTENT is used. If this is the first or only EXTENT, the unit from the DTF is used.);

serial number is the volume's serial number (If omitted, the serial number from the last EXTENT is used. If this is the first or only EXTENT and no serial number is coded, the serial number is not checked.).

type is 1 for a data area, 2 for an overflow area, 4 for an index area, and 8 for a split cylinder data area;

sequence number is the relative location of this extent within a multiextent file;

relative track is relative track address of the track where the data extent (indexed sequential file) is to begin;

number of tracks indicates the number of tracks to be assigned to this file;

split-cylinder track indicates the upper track number for split-cylinder sequential files;

bins identifies the 2321 data cell bin.

JOB indicates start of a job:

```
//    JOB    jobname [accounting information]
```

where   **jobname** is the 1–8 alphanumeric character name of the job;

accounting information is optional with the installation (If specified, separate from the jobname by a blank.).

LBLTYP defines the amount of main storage to be reserved at link-edit time or at execution time for label processing.

```
//    LBLTYP    ⎰TAPE[(nn)]⎱
                ⎱NSD(nn)   ⎰
```

where   **TAPE(nn)** is used to indicate that only tape labels and no non-sequential DASD file labels are to be processed;

NSD(nn) indicates that nonsequential disk file labels are to be processed. (This also allows for other types as well. The nn indicates the largest number of extents to be processed for a single file.)

OPTION specifies job control options:

```
//    OPTION    option1[,option2,...]
```

where   typical **options** include: LOG or NOLOG, DUMP or NODUMP, LINK or NOLINK, DECK or NODECK, LIST or NOLIST, LISTX or NOLISTX, SYM or NOSYM, XREF or NOXREF, ERRS or NOERRS, CATAL, STDLABEL, USRLABEL, PARSTD, 48C, 60C (60-character set), and SYSPARM.

RESET resets certain I/O assignments to the standard assignment, within the partition:

$$
// \quad \text{RESET} \quad \left\{ \begin{array}{l} \text{SYS} \\ \text{PROG} \\ \text{ALL} \\ \text{SYSxxx} \end{array} \right\}
$$

where   **SYS** resets all system logical units;

PROG resets programmer logical units;

ALL resets all logical units;

SYSxxx resets the specified unit.

RSTRT allows programmer to restart a checkpointed program.

```
//    RSTRT    SYSxxx,nnnn[,filename]
```

where   **SYSxxx** is the symbolic name of the device on which checkpoint records are stored;

nnnn identifies the checkpoint record to be used for restarting;

filename is the symbolic name of a disk file used for checkpoint (disk volumes hold multiple files).

TLBL contains file label information for tape label checking and writing. Replaces TPLAB and VOL commands.

```
//    TLBL    filename,['file-id'],[date],
```

$$
\left[\left\{ \begin{array}{l} \text{file-serial-number} \\ \text{set-identifier} \end{array} \right\} \right]
$$

$$\left[\left\{ \begin{array}{l} \texttt{volume-sequence-number} \\ \texttt{file-section-number} \end{array} \right\} \right]$$

[file-sequence-number],

[generation-number],

[version-number],

where   **filename** is a 1–7 alphanumeric character file name which must match the symbolic name of the program DTF;

'**file-ID**' is the 1–17 alphanumeric name associated with the file on the volume (If omitted on output, the filename is used; if omitted on input, the file-ID is not checked.);

date is a retention period;

file serial number is the volume serial number of the first volume of the file (The set-identifier is the ASCII file version.);

volume sequence number is the relative number of the volume in a multivolume file (The file section number is for ASCII files.);

file sequence number is the relative position of the file on a multifile volume;

generation number is used on generation data sets to modify the file ID;

version number is used to modify the generation number.

TPLAB provides file label information for tape label creation and checking. Used in conjunction with a VOL statement; replaced by TLBL:

```
//    TPLAB     {'label-fields 3-10'
                 'label-fields 3-13'}
```

where   the operands field contains either a 49-byte or a 69-byte character string, enclosed in apostrophes, which holds the exact contents of either positions 5–53 or 5–73 of the actual tape label.

UPSI allows the programmer to set program switches in the communications region:

```
//    UPSI     nnnnnnnn
```

where   nnnnnnnn represents the desired settings of the eight program switch bits—a 0 sets the associated switch to 0, a 1 sets the switch to a 1, and an X leaves the switch setting unchanged.

VOL is used in conjunction with DLAB or TLAB statements in support of label checking.

```
//    VOL    SYSxxx,filename
```

where   **SYSxxx** is the symbolic device name;

filename is a 1–7 alphameric character file name which must match the symbolic name assigned in the program DTF identifying the file.

XTENT defines an area or extent on a DASD file. Largely replaced by the EXTENT statement.

```
//    XTENT    type,sequence,lower,upper,

              'serial no.',SYSxxx[B₂]
```

where   **type** identifies the area type with 1 indicating a data area, 2 indicating an overflow area, 4 indicating an index area, and 8 indicating a split-cylinder data area;

sequence is the relative position of this extent within a multiextent file;

lower is the lowest DASD address in the extent;

upper is the highest DASD address in the extent;

'serial no.' is the volume serial number;

SYSxxx is the symbolic device address;

B₂ is the currently assigned cell number if a data-cell device is used.

Linkage-Editor Control Statements

PHASE assigns a phase name and gives main storage load address for the phase.

INCLUDE indicates that an object module is to be included. If the operands field is blank, the module is on SYSIPT; i.e., it's in object deck form.

ENTRY provides for an optional phase entry point.

ACTION specifies linkage-editor options.

APPENDIX B

Summary of Job Control Language for the IBM System / 360 and System / 370 Operating System

Primary References

Brown, G. D., *System/360 Job Control Language*, Wiley, 1970.
IBM #GC28-6703, *Job Control Language User's Guide*.
IBM #GC28-6704, *Job Control Language Reference*.
The format for describing the individual JCL statements was taken directly from IBM #GC28-6539, *Job Control Language*, as were Figs. B.1, B.2, and B.3.

General JCL Rules

JCL Card Format:

> //name   operation   operands   comments
> fields are separated by one or more blanks.

Valid Names: a job name, step name, or DD name may consist of from one to eight alphanumeric characters, the first of which must be alphabetic.

Continuation of a JCL Card:
1. Break after any comma, including the comma on the original card.
2. Code "//" in the first two columns of the continuation card.
3. Resume the coding of parameters anywhere between columns four and sixteen of the continuation card.

Rules for Using Parentheses: when the first subparameter is the only one coded, parentheses are not needed. When more than one subparameter or a positional subparameter other than the first one is coded, parentheses are needed.

The JOB Card

Function: job separation. Secondary functions allow the programmer to pass accounting information and other parameters to the system. (See Fig. B.1.)

Parameters:

`accounting information.`

This is an installation-dependent positional parameter, normally containing an account number followed by other accounting information. It's optional but can, at the installation's request, be made a required parameter.

`programmer's name`

This second positional parameter consists of a one- to twenty-character name which may be composed of letters, numbers, and a period. If the field contains any other characters (like a blank, for example) it must be enclosed in a set of apostrophes.

`MSGLEVEL=(jcl, allocations)`

//Name	Operation	Operand	P/K
//jobname	JOB	[([acct'] [,acctg information])]	P
		[programmer's name]	P
		$\left[\text{MSGLEVEL} = (\begin{bmatrix} 0 \\ 1 \\ 2 \end{bmatrix} \begin{bmatrix} ,0 \\ ,1 \end{bmatrix})\right]$	K
		[COND = ((condition), . . .)]	K
		[RD = request]	K
		$\left[\text{RESTART} = (\left\{\begin{array}{l}* \\ \text{stepname} \\ \text{stepname.procstep}\end{array}\right\}[,\text{checkid}])\right]$	K
		[PRTY = nn]	K
		[MSGCLASS = x]	K
		[TYPRUN = HOLD]	K
		[TIME = (minutes,seconds,)]	K
		[CLASS = jobclass)	K
		$\left[\text{REGION} = (\left\{\begin{array}{l}\text{nnnnnK} \\ \text{value}_0\text{K}\end{array}\right\}[,\text{value}_1\text{K}])\right]$	K
		[ROLL = (x,y)]	K

Legend:
P   Positional parameter.
K   Keyword parameter
{ }   Choose one.
[ ]   Optional; if more than one line is enclosed, choose one or none.

Fig. B.1 The JOB statement—general form

Specifies the printing of job control statements and device allocation messages. The two positional subparameters are interpreted as follows:

JCL	MEANING
0	Print JOB Card only.
1	Print all JCL including that generated by cataloged procedures.
2	Print only JCL in job stream.

ALLOCATIONS	MEANING
0	Print messages only if job abnormally terminates.
1	Print all messages.

    COND=(condition,...)

This parameter is normally coded on an EXEC card. If coded on the JOB card, condition parameters on subsequent EXEC cards are cancelled.

    RD=request

Allows for automatic restart and suppression of checkpoints.

    RESTART=stepname

Requests step restart.

    PRTY=nn

Priority within job class—low is zero; high is 13.

    MSGCLASS=x

Allows the programmer to specify the device to which job scheduler messages are to be spooled.

    TYPRUN=HOLD

Holds the job in the input queue until the operator issues a RELEASE command.

    TIME=(minutes, seconds)

The TIME parameter is normally coded on an EXEC card. If coded on the JOB card, it sets a time limit for the entire job.

```
CLASS=jobclass
```

Specifies the job's class.

```
REGION=nnnnnK
```

This is another parameter which is more commonly coded on an EXEC card. If coded on the JOB card, the parameter sets an upper limit for the entire job; therefore you must allow enough space for the biggest job step.

```
ROLL=(x,y)
```

Allows the roll-in/roll-out feature to be implemented. The first subparameter indicates if this program can be rolled-out; respond with "YES" or "NO." The second subparameter indicates if this program can cause another program to be rolled-out; once again, respond "YES" or "NO."

The EXEC Card

Function: identifies the specific program (directly or through a cataloged procedure) to be executed. (See Fig. B.2.)

Parameters:

```
PGM=program name or PROC=procedure name or just plain
procedure name
```

This is the first positional parameter, and it fulfills the function of the EXEC card. If no keyword is coded, PROC is assumed.

```
COND=(condition1,condition2,...)
```

Allows the programmer to specify conditions for bypassing the job step.

```
PARM=value
```

Allows the programmer to pass parameters to a program.

```
ACCT=(accounting information)
```

//Name	Operation	Operand	P/K
//[stepname]	EXEC	PGM = program name PGM = *.stepname.ddname PGM = *.stepname.procstepname.ddname [PROC =] procedure name	P
		COND = ({ (condition) / EVEN / ONLY } [,(condition), . . .])	
		COND.procstep = ({ (condition) / EVEN / ONLY } [, (condition), . . .])	
		PARM = value PARM.procstepname = value	K
		ACCT = (acctg information) ACCT.procstepname = (acctg info)	K
		RD = request RD.procstepname = request	K
		DPRTY = (value 1, value 2) DPRTY.procstepname = (value 1, value 2)]	K
		TIME = (minutes,seconds) TIME.procstepname = (min,sec)	K
		REGION = ({ nnnnnK / $value_0$ K } [,$value_1$ K]) REGION.procstepname = ({ nnnnnK / $value_0$ K } [,$value_1$ K])	
		ROLL = (x,y) ROLL.procstepname = (x,y)	K

Legend:
P   Positional parameter
K   Keyword parameter.
{ }   Choose one.
[ ]   Optional; if more than one line is enclosed, choose one or none.

Fig. B.2 The EXEC statement—general form

This is a rarely used parameter which allows the programmer to provide job-step accounting information. Accounting information is usually passed through the JOB card.

        RD=request

As on the JOB card, this parameter allows for automatic restart and suppression of checkpoints.

        DPRTY=(value1,value2)

The dispatching priority determines which of the several programs concurrently resident in core on a multiprogramming system gets first access to the CPU in the event of conflicts.

TIME=(minutes,seconds)

Sets a time limit for the job step.

REGION=nnnnnK

Sets a limit on the amount of main storage available to the job step.

ROLL=(x,y)

//Name	Operation	Operand
// ⌈ddname │procstepname. ⌊ ddname ⌉	DD	⌈ DSNAME = identification ⌉ ⌊ DSN = identification ⌋ [UNIT = (unit information)] [UCS = (UCS information)] ⌈ VOLUME = (volume information) ⌉ ⌊ VOL= (volume information) ⌋ ⌈ DCB = (attributes) │ ⌈dsname │ DCB = ⟨ *.stepname.ddname ⟩ [,attributes]) │ ⌊ *.stepname.procstep.ddname⌋ [LABEL = (label information)] ⌈ DISP = ([status] [,disposition]) │ SYSOUT = x │ SYSOUT = (x ⌈ ,progname ⌉ [, form#]) │ ⌊ , ⌋ ⌈ SPACE = (direct access space) ⌉ │ SPLIT = (direct access space) │ ⌊ SUBALLOC = (direct access space) ⌋ ⌈ SEP = (ddnames) ⌉ ⌊ AFF = ddname ⌋
		⟨ * ⟩ [,DCB = ([BLKSIZE = block] [,BUFNO = number])] ⟨ DATA ⟩
		DUMMY, . . .
		DDNAME = ddname [,DCB =([BLKSIZE = block] [, BUFNO = number])]

Legend:
{ }   Choose one.
[ ]   Optional; if more than one line is enclosed, choose one or none.

Fig. B.3 The DD statement—general form

As with the JOB card ROLL parameter, this parameter allows the programmer to specify if this job step can be rolled-in and rolled-out (x) and if this job step can cause another to be rolled-in and rolled-out (y).

The DD Card

Function: specifies details—physical location, logical configuration—of data sets. (See Fig. B.3.)

Parameters: DSNAME or DSN
Identifies a data set by name:

$$
\text{DSNAME=}
\begin{cases}
\texttt{name} \\
\texttt{name (area name)} \\
\texttt{name (member name)} \\
\texttt{name (generation \#)} \\
\texttt{\&\&name} \\
\texttt{\&\&name (member name)} \\
\texttt{\&\&name (area name)} \\
\texttt{*.ddname} \\
\texttt{*.stepname.ddname} \\
\texttt{*.stepname.procstep.ddname}
\end{cases}
$$

UNIT
Requests a particular type of physical I/O device:

$$
\text{UNIT=}
\left(
\begin{bmatrix} \texttt{address} \\ \texttt{type} \\ \texttt{group} \end{bmatrix}
\begin{bmatrix} \texttt{,P} \\ \texttt{,n} \\ \texttt{,} \end{bmatrix}
\texttt{[,DEFER][,SEP=(list of ddnames)])}
\right.
$$

Units can be requested by actual channel/device address (address), by IBM model number (2400 is a particular model of tape drive—this is the "type" option), or by a general group name as defined by the installation. The second form:

    UNIT=AFF=ddname

allows the data set to be mounted on the same physical device used by a previous data set (referenced by DDNAME) in the job.

Getting back to the first form of this parameter, the second positional subparameter allows the programmer to specify parallel mounting of all the volumes in a multivolume file by indicating the actual number of volumes; if the number of volumes is specified in the VOL subparameter, the programmer simply codes "P." The DEFER subparameter, the third positional subparameter, postpones issuance of a volume mount message until the actual OPEN macro is executed. The SEP subparameter is a keyword subparameter which indicates to the system that data sets listed as part of the subparameter are to be placed on physically separate devices—if, for example, a program were to access both input and output disk data sets, the SEP subparameter could cause these data sets to be maintained on separate disk volumes, thus minimizing head movement.

UCS
This parameter allows for the mounting of a special print chain or print train for a nonstandard character set on a 1403 printer.

    UCS=(character set code [,FOLD] [,VERIFY])
                            [,   ]

VOLUME or VOL
Allows for the specification of volumes; i.e., specific tape volumes or disk volumes.

    VOLUME=([PRIVATE] [,RETAIN] [,volseq#] [,volcount] [,] [SER=(list of serial #s)])
            [   ] [,   ] [,   ] [,   ]   [REF=dsname   ]
                                                            [REF=*.ddname   ]
                                                            [REF=*.stepname.ddname   ]
                                                            [REF=*.stepname.procstep.ddname]

The primary option is the SER or REF subparameter which allows the programmer to specify either a specific volume or a group of volumes directly, by serial number, or indirectly by referring back to a prior job step. The PRIVATE subparameter gives exclusive use of the data set to the requesting program. The RETAIN subparameter keeps the volume mounted between job steps. The third positional subparameter allows the programmer to indicate that processing is to begin with a volume other than the first one on a multivolume file. The fourth positional subparameter allows the programmer to specify the number of volumes in a multivolume file.

DCB
Specifies details about actual data format.

LABEL
Specifies the label type as well as the relative file number on a multifile tape volume and indicates whether the file is to be accessed for input or output.

```
LABEL=([data set seq#] [,SL        ] [,PASSWORD] [,IN ] [,] [EXPDT=yyddd])
                        [,SUL ] [,  ]           [,OUT]     [RETPD=nnnn ]
                        [,NSL ]
                        [,NL  ]
                        [,BLP ]
                        [,    ]
```

The first subparameter, which is positional, indicates the relative file number on a multifile volume; if blank, relative file #1 is assumed. The second positional subparameter identifies the label type. Specifying "IN" or "OUT" as the third positional subparameter allows the programmer to override a program specification of INOUT access in the OPEN macro for BSAM files; it's of primary importance to FORTRAN programmers. The final subparameter allows for the specification of an expiration date or retention period.

DISP
Specifies the status and disposition of a data set. The first positional subparameter indicates the status of the data set at the beginning of the job step. The second subparameter indicates what is to be done with the data set at the conclusion of the job step, while the third subparameter indicates the disposition in the event of abnormal job-step termination.

$$
\mathtt{DISP=(}\ \begin{bmatrix}\mathtt{SHR}\\ \mathtt{NEW}\\ \mathtt{OLD}\\ \mathtt{MOD}\end{bmatrix}\ \begin{bmatrix}\mathtt{,DELETE}\\ \mathtt{,KEEP}\\ \mathtt{,PASS}\\ \mathtt{,CATLG}\\ \mathtt{,UNCATLG}\\ \mathtt{,}\end{bmatrix}\ \begin{bmatrix}\mathtt{,UNCATLG}\\ \mathtt{,CATLG}\\ \mathtt{,DELETE}\\ \mathtt{,KEEP}\end{bmatrix}\ \mathtt{)}
$$

SYSOUT

Specifies the use of a system output device. Since the disposition of the system output devices is specified by the system, the DISP parameter is not coded.

SPACE

Specifies the amount of direct access space to be allocated to a data set. The first form

        SPACE=(ABSTR,(quantity,address[,directory]))

allows the programmer to specify actual, absolute track addresses for his data set; the second and third positional subparameters indicate the number of tracks and the absolute address of the first track to be assigned. The final subparameter allows for the assignment of directory space for an indexed sequential or partitioned data set.

   The specification of absolute tracks is a rare option under OS; more commonly, the second form of the SPACE parameter is used:

$$
\mathtt{SPACE=(}\ \begin{Bmatrix}\mathtt{TRK}\\ \mathtt{CYL}\\ \mathtt{blocksize}\end{Bmatrix}\ \mathtt{,(quantity}\ \begin{bmatrix}\mathtt{,increment}\\ \mathtt{,}\end{bmatrix}\begin{bmatrix}\mathtt{,directory}\\ \mathtt{,index}\end{bmatrix}\mathtt{)}\ \begin{bmatrix}\mathtt{,RLSE}\\ \mathtt{,}\end{bmatrix}\begin{bmatrix}\mathtt{,CONTIG}\\ \mathtt{,MXIG}\\ \mathtt{,ALX}\\ \mathtt{,}\end{bmatrix}\mathtt{[,ROUND])}
$$

Using this form, the programmer can request tracks (TRK), cylinders (CYL), or blocks of a given size. Following specification of the type of space allocation required, the programmer requests an amount of space, asking first, through a series of positional subparameters, for a primary allocation, next, for a secondary allocation in the event that the primary allocation proves to be insufficient, and finally for directory or index space. Note that, in terms of punctuation, the entire "quantity" request is treated as a single positional subparameter, with the quantity, increment, and index sub-subparameters being enclosed in a set of parentheses.

The RLSE subparameter allows the programmer to return all unused space to the system at the conclusion of the job step. CONTIG allows the programmer to request contiguous space, MXIG allows for the allocation of the largest contiguous free area on the volume (as long as it's larger than the request), and ALX provides the five largest contiguous free areas on the volume (again, with a "larger than the request" restriction). ROUND causes space allocated by blocks to be aligned on cylinder boundaries.

SPLIT
Allows a space allocation to be split among several different physical volumes, thus minimizing head movement in the processing of a data set.

$$\text{SPLIT=} \begin{cases} n \\ (n,\text{CYL},(\text{quantity}[,\text{increment}])) \\ \% \\ (\%,\text{blocksize},(\text{quantity}[,\text{increment}])) \end{cases}$$

Space can be split in terms of the number of tracks per cylinder to be assigned or the percentage of tracks per cylinder to be assigned to a given data set. Normally, a number of SPLIT parameters are coded on a series of separate DD cards indicating, in essence, how an initial space request is to be subdivided.

SUBALLOC
Allows space on the same physical volume to be suballocated among a number of data sets.

$$\text{SUBALLOC=}(\begin{Bmatrix} \text{TRK} \\ \text{CYL} \\ \text{blocksize} \end{Bmatrix} ,(\text{quantity} \begin{bmatrix} ,\text{increment} \\ , \end{bmatrix} [,\text{directory}]) \begin{Bmatrix} ,\text{ddname} \\ ,\text{stepname.ddname} \\ ,\text{stepname.procstepname.ddname} \end{Bmatrix})$$

SEP and AFF
The SEP parameter allows the programmer to specify channel separation between two data sets. The AFF parameter allows the programmer to copy a SEP parameter from another DD card.

DUMMY
Causes the I/O operations specified on the DD card to be bypassed.

* or DATA:
The asterisk or (*) character in the operands portion of the DD card indicates that data follows in the job stream; this parameter is generally used to indicate that punched card data is to be read through the system input device. DATA implies the same thing, but allows for the inclusion of cards with // punched in the first two columns.

DDNAME:
Postpones definition of data set parameters until a subsequent DD card with the specified DDNAME is encountered.

Special DD Cards

The JOBLIB Card:

```
//JOBLIB    DD    DSN=library-name,DISP=SHR
```

allows programs in a private library to be loaded and executed. The JOBLIB card follows the JOB card and makes the library available to all subsequent job steps; the JOBLIB card and the SYSCHK card are the only DD cards which can legally precede the first EXEC card.

The STEPLIB Card:

```
//STEPLIB    DD    DSN=library-name,DISP=SHR
```

like the JOBLIB card, allows programs in a private library to be loaded and executed. The STEPLIB card follows the EXEC card and is effective for a single job step only.

The SYSABEND Card:

```
//SYSABEND    DD    SYSOUT=class
```

provides an abnormal termination dump of the system nucleus.

The SYSCHK Card:

```
//SYSCHK    DD    DISP=OLD,DSN=checkpoint-library
```

describes a checkpoint library data set. Follows the JOB card and the JOBLIB card if present.

The SYSUDUMP Card:

```
//SYSUDUMP   DD   SYSOUT=class
```

provides an abnormal termination dump of the user's program area including registers, data set allocations, and traces.

The PROC Card:

```
//procedure   PROC   keyword parameters
```

assigns default values to symbolic parameters in a cataloged procedure.

The Delimeter Card:

```
/*
```

is used to mark the end of a card file.

The Command Card:

```
//   command   operands
```

allows operator commands to be entered through the job stream.

The Null Card:

```
//
```

is the end-of-job marker in some systems.

The Comments Card:

```
//*   comments.
```

is used to add comments to the JCL job stream.

INDEX

INDEX

abnormal termination, 140, 141

absolute address, 44–46, 169, 276, 289, 292

access method, 42, 51, 65, 66, 68, 69, 88, 127, 128, 130, 131, 172, 181, 211, 212, 216, 229, 236, 246, 248, 249, 292, 331, 349, 350, 354

accounting field (DOS), 96

accounting information parameter, 116–119, 366

ACCT parameter (EXEC card), 368

ACTION statement (DOS linkage editor), 364

activity, file, 52

address, 27–31, 165–169, 170, 172, 176, 191, 276, 286

address constant, 211

address translation, 276, 291, 293

addressing, 165, 166, 169, 259, 272–275, 287, 355

AFF parameter (DD card), 375

AND logic, 24, 25

ASCII-8 code, 15, 16, 30, 31, 33, 40, 189

assemble (or assembler), 18, 19, 21, 166, 167, 255, 256, 348

assembler level programming, 18, 19, 21

ASSGN card (DOS), 106, 107, 204, 215, 358

associative array registers, 282, 283, 288, 294

ATTACH, 232, 262

automatic teller, 344, 345

availability, 160–162, 312, 316, 317

background, 203, 206, 210, 214, 215, 265, 269, 316, 317, 352

background partition, 203, 206, 210, 214, 215, 265, 269

backup, 313–316

backward reference, 122

bar code reader, 338

base (of a number system), 8

base address, 274, 276, 278, 281, 283, 288

base plus displacement addressing, 45, 52, 169, 170; see also relative addressing

base register, 169, 170, 272

BASIC, 20

batch (or batch processing), 59, 265, 267–269, 311–313, 316, 317, 330, 332

Batch Time-sharing Monitor (BTM), operating system for Xerox 5/7, 269

Baud, 38

BCD code, 14, 15, 33

bill-of-materials, 311

binary coded decimal; see BCD code

binary data, 11–13

binary-level programming; see machine-level programming

binary numbers, 7–10, 18; see also computational data

bit, 11, 13, 165, 166, 170, 171, 187, 189

BLKSIZE subparameter (DD card, DCB parameter), 139, 140, 145

block, 34, 41, 42, 51, 65, 146

block key, 42

block size (or blocksize), 104, 128, 139, 210

blocking, 34, 41, 65, 68, 127, 134, 140, 212, 349

board, circuit, 300, 305, 310

book (DOS source statement library member), 216

Boolean algebra, 24

bottleneck, 346

branch, 166, 168, 171

branch table, 181

broadband line, 38

buffering (or buffer), 30, 31, 37, 65, 66, 68, 69, 104, 128, 172, 212, 249, 350

bulk storage, 36

Burroughs Corporation, 267, 285